WRITE UP
THE CORPORATE LADDER

Successful Writers Reveal the
Techniques That Help You
Write with Ease
and Get Ahead

Kevin Ryan

AMACOM

American Management Association

New York • Atlanta • Brussels • Chicago • Mexico City • San Francisco
Shanghai • Tokyo • Toronto • Washington, D.C.

This publication is designed to provide accurate and authoritative
information in regard to the subject matter covered. It is sold with
the understanding that the publisher is not engaged in rendering
legal, accounting, or other professional service. If legal advice or
other expert assistance is required, the services of a competent
professional person should be sought.

Library of Congress Cataloging-in-Publication Data

Ryan, Kevin, 1951–
    Write up the corporate ladder : successful writers reveal the
techniques that help you write with ease and get ahead / Kevin Ryan.
      p. cm.
    Includes bibliographical references and index.
    ISBN 0-8144-7150-1 (pbk.)
    1. Business writing. I. Title.

    HF5718.3.R9 2003
    808'.066658—dc21

2003002552

10 9 8 7 6 5 4 3 2 1

CONTENTS

PREFACE

Write Up the Corporate Ladder shows businesspeople the rules-free, intuitive writing process professional writers use to clearly and concisely convey their ideas to others. It's a practical, commonsense approach to writing that anyone can master. More important, this method will help you write with ease, improve your critical-thinking and problem-solving skills, and save your company time and money on every project you write.

While this book is about writing, it's also about clear thinking because in one sense writing is simply the physical representation of our thoughts on paper. Writing and speaking are the two primary ways we share our ideas and conduct business. Of the two, writing is not only the dominant form of business communication in the world, it's also a fundamental part of everyone's thinking process, which is why learning to write well also helps us become better thinkers.

Your value as a business professional is measured, in great part, by your ability to think up and implement innovative ideas, whether it's a solution to the employee parking crisis or a breakthrough product that will put your company on the Fortune 500 list. The goal of this book is to help you learn how to effectively and persuasively communicate your good ideas and advance your career.

> "I met [a venture capitalist] at a conference. We were talking about how hard it is to find good employees. He said when he's looking to either hire a new person or invest in a training program for a current employee, the two skills he looks for are the ability to think critically and to write clearly. That's more important than anything else. And I just thought, 'How interesting. Here's a high-finance person who is oriented to making millions and millions of dollars and these are the two skills he values most; and they have nothing to do with finance.' Regardless of all the computers and televisions in our culture, we're still a very verbal society. Words are really important."

Rhonda Abrams, author of
The Successful Business Plan: Secrets & Strategies
(from her interview in Part II)

Acknowledgments

To Jan, James, and Kelley. (I owe you 728.5 hours.)

A heartfelt thanks goes to authors Rhonda Abrams, Ken Blanchard, Richard Bolles, Marcus Buckingham, Humberto Cruz, Gail Evans, Greg Farrell, Michael Lewis, Suze Orman, and Roy Williams, and to executives Nick Balamaci, Mitch Bardwell, Jere Brooks King, Ed Burghard, Paul Carlucci, Roger Conner, Shelagh Lester-Smith, Victor Nau, Bill Oliver, and Ken Sternad for giving so generously of their time and opinions.

I'd also like to thank Kevin Cantwell, Richard Capullo, Bill Cutting, Kim Davidson, Allen and Annie DiGioia, James Finn III, Kathleen Fox, Jamie Grant, Barry Huddleston, Colleen Ivins, Maria Jones, Joe Lake, Brian Levi, William Licatovich, Sharon Mack, Dave Malone, Jerry Manley, Linda Melgoza, Carol Mitchell, Sam Morgan, Theresa Odom, Gary Peattie, Mike and Bea Pike-Locke, Sean Reily, Gen Ryan, John Ryan, Pat and Karen Ryan, and Maureen Snider for their valuable feedback and unstinting support.

PART

I

THE "PLAN THEN WRITE" METHOD

For more than forty years, I have studied the documents that public companies file. Too often, I've been unable to decipher just what is being said or, worse yet, had to conclude that nothing was being said. . . . There are several possible explanations as to why I and others sometimes stumble over an accounting note or indenture description. . . . Perhaps the most common problem, however, is that a well-intentioned and informed writer simply fails to get the message across to an intelligent, interested reader. In that case, stilted jargon and complex constructions are usually the villain.

Warren E. Buffet, chairman of the board, Berkshire Hathaway, Inc., from his Preface to *A Plain English Handbook: How to Create Clear SEC Disclosure Documents* (Office of Investor Education and Assistance, U.S. Securities and Exchange Commission, 450 5th Street, NW, Washington, D.C. 20549, August 1998), p. 1.

ESTABLISHING STANDARDS

What Does Good Writing Look Like?

Many businesspeople are pretty good at spotting a major spelling, grammar, or punctuation error—in other people's writing, if not always their own. That's because after twelve or sixteen years of writing in school, they've looked through enough dictionaries, grammar books, and punctuation guides to be familiar with the standards of correct usage. Yet many people still find it difficult to tell the difference between good, mediocre, and poor business writing because no fixed standard exists. There are as many implied standards as there are writing courses and writing books, which is part of the problem.

The handful of rules and tips one instructor chooses to teach—and I say "chooses" because there are hundreds of writing rules, far too many to present in a single book, seminar, or semester—can vary radically from those taught by another instructor. For instance, some teachers say it's okay to use contractions in business writing, others say it's not. If you were taught contractions are wrong and read "they're" instead of "they are" in a letter, you think, "That's bad writing."

Standard Problems

Lack of standards can cause hard feelings and even chaos among groups working, for instance, on a collaborative report. Worse yet, the problem can turn good writers into unconfident writers with a terrible case of writer's block. Case in point: A bright and gifted manager I know who is also an excellent writer was told long ago by a boss (with no explanation) that she was a bad writer. From that point on, writing was a nerve-racking chore, and it was years before she turned her attitude around.

I'm guessing her boss saw a typo or two or maybe even a passive construction in one of the manager's sentences and, based on what he remembered from a high school English class, was quick to pronounce his employee a lousy writer. How many other people has he rattled with his misguided, though undoubtedly well-meaning, writing standards?

How to Judge Business Writing

Business writing should be measured by these two yardsticks and in this order: clarity of message and then mechanics (e.g., grammar, spelling, and punctuation), with the most weight going to clarity of message (see Figure 1-1). Unfortunately, over the years, this order has become reversed. In many businesspeople's eyes, not just mechanics but perfect mechanics became the criterion for judging writing. It's easy to see why. Compared to errors regarding clarity, mechanical errors are easy to teach, and catching them is rewarding detective work that makes us feel smart.

Figure 1-1. Message and Mechanics.

MESSAGE	MECHANICS
No fixed standards. Many implied, and therefore confusing, standards.	Established standards (dictionaries, grammar, and punctuation guides).
Producing a clear message is not an inexperienced writer's first concern. If the mechanics are correct, the writer assumes the message is clear.	Main concern of writers while writing.
Quality writing is not easy to teach, test, identify, and measure.	Easy to teach, test, identify, and measure.

"I was recently offered an honorary doctorate and a teaching position at Wesleyan College in Georgia. I wanted to write a personal letter to the president of the college, declining its wonderful offer, because I was fully committed for the year. Rather than worrying about whether what I was writing was letter-perfect, I focused on choosing the words that would convey my heartfelt regret at having to decline what I knew was an honor. Now, did I spell check the letter and try my best to make sure that the commas and periods were in the right places? Yes. Did I obsess about it? No."

Suze Orman, author of
The 9 Steps to Financial Freedom
(from her interview in Part II)

The Mechanics of Shakespeare

Writing mechanics did not always have the same priority they do today. For example, up to the eighteenth century, the word *which* had been spelled in a variety of ways, from *weche* and *wich* to *wyche* and *whych*. Of the six existing signatures by Shakespeare, each one is spelled differently. However, no one then, or now, considered the man unintelligent because he spelled his name phonetically and, apparently, by whim.

English spelling wasn't standardized until Samuel Johnson wrote the first comprehensive English dictionary, published in London in 1755. Even so, some people do not think standardizing the language was an improvement. Anthony Burgess—author, semanticist, translator, and critic, but probably best known for writing *A Clockwork Orange*—describes the English language of Shakespeare's day as a "melting pot—not fixed and elegant and controlled by academics, but coarsely rich and ready for any adventures that would make it richer."[1]

Frosting on the Cake

In Chapter 6 on the science of writing, I explain more about the importance and role of mechanics. They're very important, but business writers should not even think about proofreading for mechanical errors until they have a clearly written draft in hand. Like frosting on a cake, mechanics should be applied last. Now I'd like to address the idea of perfection. Perfect mechanics are impossible to achieve 100 percent of the time for paid professional proofreaders, much less your average business writer.

Writers—even published authors—are their own worst proofreaders. Mistakes can slip through no matter how good you are at proofreading. After working on a draft, your mind tends to skip over errors and read what you think you wrote instead of what you actually did write. It's human nature. Your draft says "it it albe" but when you proof it, your mind reads "it is able," and you hand in the document with this glaring mistake. It happens.

That's why professional writers pay professional proofreaders to check their work. Even then, mistakes can show up in the printed piece. Also, it's a known fact that you cannot put two professional proofreaders in a room and have them agree on every application of the rules. One will insist that *Web site* is the correct spelling and that you must put a comma before the word *and* in a series of items, while the other is equally sure that *website* is correct and the comma is optional. Also, companies in the business of writing (e.g., magazines, publishers, ad agencies) print articles, books, and brochures with errors even though computer spell checkers, professional writers, editors, and proofreaders have checked the copy many times.

> **"When people get too focused on the mechanical process of writing, anything from sentence structure to punctuation usage, it's apparent they're looking for a formula or a set of rules to abide by. That's a trap. And any time that you think you're going to write everything according to some formula, you're setting yourself up to be incredibly average at best, a failed writer at worst."**
>
> Roy Williams, author of
> *The Wizard of Ads*
> (from his interview in Part II)

What's a Business Writer to Do?

In short, the deck is stacked against business writers when it comes to proofreading their own work for errors. We expect businesspeople to turn in perfectly edited reports, memos, and letters even though it's a known fact that 1) even experienced writers are not the best proofreaders of their own work, and 2) businesspeople do not have the time or budget to send every e-mail and report they write to a professional editor.

Here are two solutions.

1. ***Improve your proofreading skills slowly over time.*** You don't have a choice anyway. Becoming a good proofreader takes time. You can start by keeping a list of the errors you typically make, so you can refer to it when proofreading everything you write. You can also change your attitude from, "I can't make a mistake while I write," to "It's okay to make mistakes, as long as I learn from them." Knowing that you are free to make errors while creating a draft and that you can fix them later will reduce much of the anxiety associated with writing.

2. ***Apply the 3P Principle: private, public, promotional.*** If what you write is for private eyes—for example, an e-mail to colleagues, a letter to human resources requesting benefits information—and you don't

have time to let someone proofread it, do the best proofreading job you can based on the tips in Chapter 6. If the proposal you write is for public eyes, clients or potential clients, or someone who can promote you or otherwise influence your career—for example, your CEO—make sure the piece is read by a very good proofreader, a professional if possible.

Not Now!

Here's a story that illustrates several of my points about proofreading. A friend of mine, a published poet, received a glowing letter from the director of a prestigious national literary competition announcing that he was one of the finalists. The director was inviting him to the poetry festival, and while complimenting him on his work wrote, "Of course, you will not be eligible for the prize."

My friend couldn't believe it. Here the director is congratulating him on his fine work, but no prize? The problem: *not* should have been *now*. "Of course, you are now eligible for the prize."

A simple mistake, but it should have been caught. My friend is down-to-earth and has a good sense of humor, so he laughed it off. But in the wrong hands, the typo could have caused hard feelings. This example also highlights two of the 3P Principles: public and promotional. Though written to one person, the letter could have ended up in the public forum—an interview with the poet, a letter to the editor—and it could have resulted in bad publicity for the literary competition and festival. That's a worst-case scenario, but a real possibility nonetheless.

Standards: How Do I Know Good Writing When I See It?

The remainder of Part I goes into more detail on the message and mechanics of writing. Before going further, however, we need to define good business writing so we have a starting point for the discussions in the rest of this book.

Not everyone will agree with the standards I list here. That's okay. I want companies to use them as a starting point to establish standards their employees can use to judge the quality of what they write and read every day at work. These two definitions are the foundation for the five Business Writing Standards.

Definition 1: Quality Business Writing. Writing that communicates a business message the first time and makes the writer look polished and professional on paper. It's simple, straightforward communication.

Definition 2: Unacceptable Business Writing. Writing that does not communicate a business message and requires a second communication to clarify meaning or, even worse, causes a business problem. Poor writing wastes time and money. It also makes the writer look unprofessional, which can affect his career and the company's image.

Five Business Writing Standards

1. ***Excellent Business Writing.*** Clearly conveys your message and makes you look smart.

Example

Dear Bob Kelly,

It has been brought to my attention that your account is now 90 days past due. The amount you currently owe is $10,985.46. If you have any questions regarding the bill, please contact Ann Smith at 555-5555, and she'll be happy to explain any details. I'm sorry to say that unless I receive payment in full by May 15, company policy requires me to send your account to collections. I hope we can resolve this to our mutual benefit.

Sincerely,
Mary Jones

Explanation

- ✎ **Message:** Clear. The reader knows exactly what he has to do, and the tone is pleasant but firm. There are many reasons why a company pays its bills late. You don't want to lose a long-term relationship with a client because of one unfriendly memo. The tone pushes this example into the excellent category.

- ✎ **Mechanics:** No mistakes. This is the standard that all private business writing should strive for, and all public and promotional writing should achieve.

2. ***Good Business Writing.*** Clearly conveys your message with a few minor mistakes.

Example

Dear Bob Kelly,

Our records indicated that your account is now 90 days past due. You currently owe $10,985.46, so if you have any questions about your account, please contact Ann Smith immediately at 555-5555. Unless I receive payment in full by May 15, your account will be turned over to a collection urgency.

Sincerely,
Mary Jones

Explanation

- ✎ **Message:** Clear. The tone is firm and while not unpleasant it certainly isn't friendly. However, the reader will probably not feel offended. After all, he is late paying his bill.

- ✎ **Mechanics:** The verb *indicated* should be present tense, *indicates*. The word *urgency* is a typo and should be *agency*. This is acceptable writing by writers who have no proofreaders available to proof their work. In other words, a boss should not label an employee a "bad" writer for turning this letter in. He should praise the person for writing a clearly worded message and then, as an afterthought, point out the two mechanical errors that slipped by.

> "Writing is weighted very heavily across the board, especially in annual reviews and promotions. For our annual reviews, we ask employees to write a list of the contributions they've made to the firm that year. The list must be succinct, just two- or three-sentence statements that highlight their accomplishments at Deloitte Consulting. When it comes to promotions, we dig a lot deeper into their communications skills. We not only look into what they've done for the firm, but how well they communicate with colleagues and clients. We're a consulting firm, so communication is our business. If our employees write and speak well, we will be successful. Compensation increases are based on the annual reviews and promotion reviews, so good communication skills factor into both."
>
> Victor Nau, partner,
> Deloitte Consulting
> (from his interview in Part III)

3. Borderline Business Writing. Conveys your message, but makes you look unprofessional.

Example

Attn: Bob Kelly

Our record indicated that your account is way overdo almost 90 days. You owe $10,985.46 if you have any questions contact Ann Smith at 555-5555. Unless I received payment by May 15, you're account will be tuned over to a collection agency.

Sincerely,
Mary Jones

Explanation

✎ **Message:** I understand the message and do not have to write or call the sender to clarify any points, but the mechanical errors draw so much attention to themselves that they cause me to stop and reread certain words and phrases. The many errors also make me think this person is not very sharp.

✎ **Mechanics:** *Indicated* should be present tense, *indicates. Overdo* should be spelled *overdue.* The phrase "way overdo almost 90 days" is too wordy and informal. The second sentence is a run-on; there should be a period after $10,985.46. *Received* should be *receive. Tuned* is a typo and should be spelled *turned.* Is this acceptable business writing? For a bank manager or human resources representative, the answer is probably no. If everything they write looks like this, I would expect it to be an issue at their next annual review. However, a dispatcher's or technician's promotion may not be in jeopardy for writing at this level. Companies should determine what qualifies as borderline business writing and publish the standard.

4. Bad Business Writing. Does not communicate the intended business message, wastes the time of both parties by requiring a second communication to clarify the first, could create a business problem, and makes the writer look unsophisticated.

Example 1

Attn: Bob Kelly

According to our records, you are past due 90 days on your account of $10,985.46. We will be calling a collection agency if you do not contact Ann Smith immediately at 555-5555. We must receive payment in full by May 15.

Sincerely,
Mary Jones

Explanation 1

- ✎ **Message:** Clear communication did not take place. Bob Kelly will have to call and ask for clarification: Does he have to call Ann Smith immediately to keep from going into collections or send a payment by May 15?

- ✎ **Mechanics:** Example 1 has no mechanical errors. This is an example of communication that is bad even though it has no grammar, spelling, or punctuation problems.

Example 2

Attn: Bob Kelly

After looking through our records of the passed 6 months regarding your several accounts receivables and digital ledger entries, according to those records of $10,985.46, you are due 90 days in delinquency. We will be left little choice but to take such action as we deem legalistically allowable as to calling a collection agency if you do not communicate with Ann Smith immediately at 555-5555 concerning your lack of payments to our established accounts payable. As much as we dislike taking the actions implied, payment must be receipted to us in full by May 15 of the coming month or such measures will be duly considered and acted upon.

Sincerely,
Mary Jones

Explanation 2

- ✎ **Message:** Clear communication did not take place. The memo is wordy; full of jargon and muddy thinking. Bob Kelly will have to call and ask for clarification: Does he have to call Ann Smith immediately to keep from going into collections or send in a payment by May 15?

- ✎ **Mechanics:** *Passed* is a typo and should be spelled *past*. The noun *receipt* is used as a verb, *receipted*.

5. Bottom-Line Bad Writing. The message is not clear and mechanical errors add to the confusion. The company could lose money because of this memo.

Example

Attn: Bob Kelly

According to your records of $1098.546, you are past do 90 day we will be calling a collection agency. If you do not contact Ann Smith immediately at 555-5555, we must recieve payment in full by May 15.

Sincerely,
Mary Jones

Explanation

✎ **Message:** It's not clear when the money is due or when it will go to the collection agency. Worst of all, Bob Kelly might send a check for $1,098.55 and claim he's paid his bill in full, and use this memo as proof.

✎ **Mechanics:** The first sentence should read *our* records, not *your*. *Do* should be spelled *due*. *Day* should be *days*. The first sentence is a run-on. It should be divided into two separate sentences by adding a period after the word *days* and capitalizing the word *We*. The word *receive* is misspelled. However, as originally written, a reader could assume the first sentence ends after the word *do*, and that the word *In* was left out to begin the second sentence—"In 90 days we will be calling a collection agency"—which further muddies the question as to what action the reader must take and when.

Why Business Writing Matters

Good standards promote good business writing. And good writing is necessary to maintain a positive image of your company and conduct business (e.g., generate sales, improve products, streamline supply chains, speed product to market, etc.). In short, quality writing will help move your company forward and ensure its success.

On the flip side, the goal of business writing is not to entertain, tell a story, or have multiple hidden meanings. That's the job of screenplays, novels, and poetry.

In addition, in the business world time is money, so you need to make your point and move on. Computers, personal digital assistants (PDAs), the Internet, and other high-tech tools are funneling more and more information to everyone's desktop. This data needs to be processed, which usually means it must be converted into something written: a report, presentation, letter, or e-mail. It's more important than ever that messages are communicated clearly, concisely, and quickly.

Evaluation Tool

Businesses frown on throwing money at a problem without first determining what is wrong and then estimating the price to fix it. Business writing should be no different. A company can't evaluate the quality of its writing without a yardstick to measure good, bad, and bottom-line bad writing. The five Business Writing Standards are a starting point. Companies can customize them to meet their particular business writing needs.

Memo: How Napoleon Lost Waterloo

Most poorly written memos don't ruin a company overnight, but here's one that caused even more dramatic results. It cost the lives of thousands of people and helped Britain win one of the most important wars in Western history.

During a decisive moment in the Battle of Waterloo in 1815, Napoleon dictated a memo to his chief of staff. The memo ordered one of his commanding generals, Grouchy, to turn his 33,000-man army away from the Belgian village of Wavre where the Prussian army (Britain's ally) was holding the eastern end of General Wellington's battle line. Grouchy was to immediately march back to Waterloo and provide the crushing blow needed to defeat Wellington's British forces at the center of the battlefield. Here's how Wellington biographer Elizabeth Long-

The Dilbert Quote Contest

This collection of absurd business writing has been floating around the Internet a long time. Whether the contest is real or another example of Internet lore, the following "winning" entry is an excellent example of bad business writing:

"As of tomorrow, employees will only be able to access the building using individual security cards. Pictures will be taken next Wednesday and employees will receive their cards in two weeks."

While it has no mechanical errors, the garbled message requires anyone who receives it to contact the sender and ask for clarification.

ford describes what happened in her book *Wellington: The Years of the Sword.*

> This was Napoleon's chance urgently to redirect Grouchy away from Wavre and towards Waterloo. Instead, the opening sentence of his reply perfectly illustrated the looseness of his thinking: "His Majesty desires you will head for Wavre in order to draw near to us." In the circumstances [this sentence is] a plain contradiction, since Wavre lay north of Grouchy and Napoleon ("us") to the west. Grouchy was also to "push before him" the Prussians who were marching in "this direction"—an operation which, taken literally, would mean Grouchy pushing the Prussians towards Wellington—and reach Waterloo "as soon as possible." In this verbal fog Grouchy was to discover only three luminous words: "Head for Wavre." They were to prove fatal.[2]

Grouchy marched on Wavre and the Duke of Wellington defeated Napoleon, which changed the course of European politics for the next 100 years. One lousy memo played a key role in ending the reign of Napoleon and making Britain a superpower. The mechanics were good, but the message was hidden behind a "verbal fog" of "loose thinking."

As a side note, Wellington clearly understood the value of good writing and that it truly was mightier than the sword. During battles he kept a pen, not a pistol, in his holster.

CHAPTER 2

THE PROCESS

How Professional Writers Write

This chapter introduces the Plan Then Write method, a process that will show you how to achieve the highest standard of excellent business writing, as defined in Chapter 1. Plan Then Write is a four-step process (see Figure 2-1). It is based on the approach that experienced and professional writers (professionals are experienced writers who get paid for their work) discover after years of writing. While working on future business assignments, use this page as a cheat sheet until the process becomes second nature.

Figure 2-1. Plan Then Write.

PLAN THEN WRITE

1. Plan

2. Write and Rewrite

3. Edit 1

4. Edit 2

Step 1. *Plan.*
- ❑ Choose a format.
- ❑ Define your subject by making a bullet list of your main point and supporting points.
- ❑ Determine your audience (who are the readers and what do they know and not know about your subject?).
- ❑ State your purpose (what is your reason for writing?) and state your call to action (what do you want your audience to do?).

Step 2. *Write (and keep writing and rewriting until you have a final draft).* Keep these guidelines in mind: Start with the easy parts.

Focus on "thinking clearly on paper," not writing rules. Writing is the act of problem solving using your writer's intuition as a guide. Change your plan as you discover new ideas, and make liberal use of bullet lists and subheads.

Step 3. *Edit 1.* Proofread your final draft for your known art and science problems.

Step 4. *Edit 2.* Give your draft to an experienced or professional proofreader.

This is the foundational process that experienced writers use. Obviously, there are as many variations of this method as there are writers. For example, some writers start and end at step 2. They plan as they go and incorporate the Edit 1 step in the last revision of their draft. I know of an experienced writer who spends the majority of his writing process in the planning stage, writing a detailed outline that makes step 2 almost a fill-in-the-blank exercise. Regardless of how writers choose to use this four-step process, it's an easy to follow, proven approach to writing well.

Chapters 3 through 6 will discuss the details of the Plan Then Write process and explain further the steps I've just outlined. But first, here's a brief overview of why process-based writing instruction is more effective than rules-based writing instruction, and a comparison of the art and the science of writing.

Writing Trouble

When I first started my training and consulting company, I met many businesspeople who had trouble writing letters, memos, and reports. Most were college graduates and many kept a small library of writing reference guides on their desks, so I knew they were concerned about writing well. Yet for all their academic and on-the-job writing experience, they lacked confidence and did not know how to consistently produce clear, quality writing.

That's when I took a close look at my own writing process. Basically, I planned what I was going to say (sometimes I planned a lot, sometimes a little, and sometimes not at all), then started writing and rewriting and did not stop until I had a complete final draft. That's it. I followed a simple process and rarely if ever thought about writing rules.

The method wasn't new. My writer friends approached writing the same way. Not the exact same way—people develop habits that work for them—but just about. I had also read articles about professional writers who followed the same simplified, rules-free approach. While this process was well known to experienced writers, others had never heard of it. When asked about their writing process, businesspeople talked about following rules and the need to learn more rules in order to improve.

Rules-Based vs. Process-Based

The process-based approach to writing is much less complex than the one taught in schools, which is centered on "correctness" and teaching one rule after another. The problem with rules-based writing is that students think you learn to write by following a rigid set of laws, and that if someone writes poorly the solution is to memorize yet more rules. But when students study seemingly endless lists of rules and still don't see a big difference in their writing, frustration sets in and so does dejection: "I'll never be a good writer."

Writing by the rules makes you live in constant fear of breaking rules you've never learned or heard about, but are sure exist out there somewhere. It also gives the wrong impression that writing follows a neat, formulaic procedure that, once learned, will ensure a perfect outcome each time—like mastering a recipe for bouillabaisse.

Experienced vs. Inexperienced

I did some research to see if anyone had studied the difference between how experienced and inexperienced writers write. I found lots of material. But first let me explain the difference between these two terms. By "inexperienced," I mean a writer who is not confident of his writing skills and doesn't understand how to consistently produce good writing. He will write an excellent report one day, a poor one the next, and not be able to explain why each turned out the way it did. Inexperienced writers are not necessarily bad writers. You can be a fair to average writer and fall in this category. Experienced writers are confident of their abilities and know how to recognize and produce good writing time after time.

The research I found on these two types of writers, and the rules-based vs. process-based approach to writing each one takes, has been around for decades. For instance, in his book *Writing—Research, Theory, and Applications,* Stephen Krashen, professor emeritus at the University of Southern California (USC), writes: "Studies show that good writers differ from poor writers in their composing processes, that is, they have better and more sound procedures for getting their ideas down on paper. Specifically, good writers differ in three ways: in planning, rescanning, and revising."[1]

By rescanning, Krashen means nothing more than stopping while writing your draft to reread sentences and paragraphs to see where you're heading and if what you wrote needs revising. If you consider rescanning part of the rewriting stage—you can't rewrite what you don't reread—then "planning, rescanning, and revising" is another way of saying Plan Then Write.

"I wrote a book with Norman Vincent Peale called *The Power of Ethical Management.* I invited Norman and his wife, Ruth, to attend a feedback dinner I organized at the Skaneateles Country Club near our summer cottage in upstate New York. Since Norman had begun his ministry in nearby Syracuse, 300 people attended. We got into some heated discussions about what worked and didn't work in the draft of the book. After we finished this process, I asked Norman to speak to the group. He was about eighty-eight at the time. He stood up and said, 'I've never been to a free-for-all like this in my life. I've written thirty books and when I finish one, Ruth and I pray. But Ken doesn't trust that process.'"

Ken Blanchard, author of
The One Minute Manager
(from his interview in Part II)

Research Proves It

Krashen doesn't stop there. "The research strongly suggests that grammar instruction is not effective in helping students to write."[2] He goes on to cite a wide variety of studies on good vs. poor writers, including a study by Nancy Sommers who compares student writers to professional writers. "Sommers reports that for the student writers, revision was basically rewording and adherence to school-learned rules. Student writers assumed that their desired meaning was present in their first draft; revision was simply a matter of finding the best words to express it. Sommers' experienced writers viewed revision differently; for them, revision was an effort to 'find the line of their argument.' The first draft may just be an attempt to 'define their territory,' while subsequent revisions help experienced writers continue to create meaning."[3]

That statement is echoed in the opening line of another research paper, "Revising Writer-Based Prose," by Linda Flower, professor of rhetoric at Carnegie Mellon University and one of the leaders in the field of writing theory. "Experienced writers rework their papers again and again. Novice writers correct the spelling."[4]

And finally, Karen Gocsik, Ph.D., director of composition at Dartmouth College, puts the process-based method in a historical perspective:

Perhaps the most influential development in composition theory and practice in this century took place in the late sixties and early seventies with the emergence of process pedagogy. Up until the late sixties, composition classes, influenced by the principles of New Criticism, were largely text-based. . . . In these writing classrooms, professors rarely discussed the process of composing. Rather, they emphasized text: its clarity, authority, and correctness.

Process pedagogy aims to shift attention away from the text and towards the processes that created it—processes that should be understood as fluid, complex, and, above all, highly individual. . . . These [processes] include invention (brainstorming, freewriting, etc.), organization (nutshelling, outlining, etc.), drafting, and revision.[5]

In short, plenty of research exists that proves a process-based approach to writing is more effective than a rules-based approach.

The Outlaw and the Writer: A Parable

Experienced writers "forget" about the rules while writing, the same way Tiger Woods forgets about the rules of putting while putting. Thinking too much about free throws is one reason why Shaquille O'Neal has trouble making them. Overthinking anything usually leads to trouble.

A scene in the classic movie *Butch Cassidy and the Sundance Kid* illustrates why businesspeople should only concentrate on one idea—

writing a clear, concise message—instead of concentrating on many ideas or rules. After escaping to Bolivia, the two train robbers decide to go straight and apply for jobs as payroll guards at a mining company. During their job interview the supervisor asks Sundance if he can shoot. Sundance pushes his coat back from his holster and starts to get in his gunslinger's stance when the old man, not understanding what Sundance is about to do, stops him and says, "No . . . can you shoot?" He takes the pistol out of Sundance's holster and puts it in the outlaw's hand.

Sundance holds the six-shooter at arm's length, closes one eye, and aims down the barrel at a plug of tobacco some twenty yards away. He shoots and misses. As the supervisor shakes his head, Sundance puts the pistol back in his holster and says, "Can I move?"

When the old man asks what he means, Sundance whirls, draws, and hits the plug of tobacco once, then again a split second later as it flies through the air.

Experienced writers "move"; inexperienced writers "aim." Experienced writers write without consciously thinking about rules or anything else that might stop the flow of ideas from their brain to the paper or computer screen. Inexperienced writers allow rules to stop them dead in their tracks.

> **"I don't think about rules at all. Split infinitives and so forth? I split infinitives all the time. I don't care much about that stuff. I try and write aggressively, with purpose. I try and write so that you want to read it. And the rules don't fit into that. Use the active not passive voice is probably pretty good advice. So is avoid adjectives, but I break those rules, too. My goal is to do whatever I must to make my writing more clear and concise."**
>
> Marcus Buckingham, author of
> *First, Break All the Rules*
> (from his interview in Part II)

The Keep-It-Simple Principle

While learning how to write well is not easy—it takes time, practice, and patience—it's not as hard as most writing instruction and writing books imply. The Plan Then Write approach is successful because it's based on a universal concept: Keep it simple and doable. Here's a true story that proves my point. A good friend of mine, who is also a good athlete, signed up for a weeklong basketball camp run by a star in the National Basketball Association (NBA). My friend, I'll call him Bob, set two goals: to be the top scorer and the top rebounder at the end of the week. But by the end of the first day, Bob knew his goals were out of reach.

There were lots of good players in camp, and no matter how hard he tried, scoring points and grabbing rebounds wasn't easy. The pro took Bob aside and told him he was working way too hard. He told him to forget about scoring and rebounding and focus instead on being first under the basket each time down the court.

That was it. That was the grand strategy, the insider advice from one of the top players in the NBA: Be first under the basket. It seemed too simplistic. But it worked. At the end of the week, Bob received the trophy for top scorer and second place for rebounding. Here's why.

One Thing at a Time

Scoring points while five opposing players are trying to take the ball away from you requires mastering a variety of skills: working through a double-team, dribbling in a crowd, making hook shots, fadeaways, screens, and much more. Your mind is processing a million thoughts a second. The game becomes fast and confusing.

Scoring points with no opposing players around you involves two skills: wind sprints (so you can be first under the basket) and layups, the easiest shot in the game. The pro reminded my friend to focus on the simple and doable.

The same is true in writing. Experienced writers simplify the writing process by focusing solely on their message—that is, thinking clearly and concisely on paper. Writing while thinking about rules is like trying to write while surrounded by five English teachers telling you what to do. No magic here—anyone can learn this approach. Linda Flower touches on the simple and doable concept in her article, "Revising Writer-Based Prose."

Writing forces people to juggle a number of constraints or demands at the same time. When the task is familiar, or the skill well learned, we can handle multiple demands simultaneously—handwriting, spelling, grammar, syntax, connections between ideas, our rhetorical plan, and even the audience. But for novice writers, producing correct grammar, much less considering the audience, may be an excessive demand. It may, in fact, create what psychologists call a cognitive overload.[6]

Cognitive overload is exactly what happens to basketball players who allow themselves to become surrounded by the opposing team, all five of them—that's ten hands!—simultaneously swatting at the ball. Cognitive overload is also one of the biggest problems facing many business writers. When you approach writing as a complex process, it becomes a complex process. And simply thinking that writing is complex can trigger writer's block, which in turn causes you to procrastinate and put off the project until it becomes a do-or-die assignment. As a result, you end up writing it under duress without sufficient time to think clearly and reason out your argument. You turn in the piece knowing it's not your best work and dreading the next writing project on your to-do list.

A Common Problem Among Business Writers

I see cognitive overload all the time during my courses and workshops. Students tell me they don't know where to begin the writing process, that there are just too many things to think about—too many things they don't know and will never know—and they're defeated before they touch their keyboards.

Once, after I taught a workshop for a group of technical businesspeople, several participants commented that one of the most helpful bits of advice was the one about viewing writing as simple and doable. Their common sense told them it was the right approach. They also liked it because all it required was a change in attitude, which is much easier than mastering and remembering dozens of grammar rules. In short, they found the simple and doable approach to writing very simple and doable.

One Rule Covers Them All

Another reason the Plan Then Write approach works is that the majority of writing rules that govern style all boil down to one concept: Write clearly and concisely. Think about it. The rules that govern writing style (e.g., delete words that don't add to your meaning, use simple not formal language, do not overwrite, etc.) all point to that one simple piece of advice: Be clear and concise. That's all you need to keep in mind as you write.

A Time and a Place for Rules

There's a time and a place for thinking about writing rules: when you have a final draft in hand and it's time to proofread. Look what happens to a college freshman who doesn't follow that advice.

> In high school, Ruth was told and told again that a good essay always grabs a reader's attention immediately. Until you can make your essay do that, her teachers and textbooks putatively declaimed, there is no need to go on. For Ruth, this means that beginning bland and seeing what emerges as one generates prose is unacceptable. The beginning is everything. . . . Ruth operates with another rule that restricts her productions as well: If sentences aren't grammatically "correct," they aren't useful. This keeps Ruth from toying with ideas on paper, from the kind of linguistic play that often frees up the flow of prose. These two rules converge in a way that pretty effectively restricts Ruth's composing process.[7]

Nonblockers Rule

In the previous example, Ruth isn't the writer's name. Mike Rose, who is currently professor of education at the University of California, Los Angeles (UCLA), changed the names of the ten UCLA students he interviewed to write his article, "Rigid Rules, Inflexible Plans, and the Stifling of Language: A Cognitivist Analysis of Writer's Block." In Rose's paper, the five students with writer's block follow a rules-based writing process that prevents them from writing well. The other half of his study examines five nonblockers, students who do not suffer from writer's block. These experienced writers learned or taught themselves another way to write.

> These nonblockers operate with fluid, easily modified, even easily discarded rules and plans . . . that are sometimes expressed with a vagueness that

could almost be interpreted as ignorance. There lies the irony. Students that offer the least precise rules and plans have the least trouble composing. . . . The five students who experienced blocking were all operating either with writing rules or with planning strategies that impeded rather than enhanced the composing process. The five students who were not hampered by writer's block also utilized rules, but they were . . . few and functional, . . . less rigid ones, and thus more appropriate to a complex process like writing. Also, the plans these nonblockers brought to the writing process were more functional, more flexible, more open to information from the outside.[8]

Real-World Consequences

Everything that Rose's study says about student writers applies to business writers. For example, Rose notes that writer's block "usually resulted in rushed, often late papers and resultant grades that did not truly reflect these students' writing ability."[9] Businesspeople do not receive a letter grade on their writing projects, but those who write poorly probably wish they did because the real-world consequences can be much harsher: a few demerits on an annual review that could affect a promotion or pay raise.

The domino effect of a rules-based approach to writing causes even more damage. As Rose notes, besides writer's block "there were other less measurable but probably more serious results: a growing distrust of their abilities and an aversion toward the composing process itself."[10] In short, the writing confidence of Rose's inexperienced writers was shattered, and no one can improve their writing skills without first improving their confidence.

Few businesspeople would guess the two sources that Rose cites as the cause of his blocker-students' problems: "Blockers may well be stymied by possessing rigid or inappropriate rules, or inflexible or confused plans. Ironically enough, these are occasionally instilled by the composition teacher or gleaned from the writing textbook."[11] This is not to say that writing textbooks are bad and composition teachers inept. The key word Rose uses is *instilled*. Whether textbook authors or teachers realize it, the impression many students get from their books and instruction—as Rose's study makes clear—is that writing follows a rigid set of rules. If writing texts and instructors explained

that the rules they teach are flexible guidelines open to interpretation—
and show students how to apply them as such—a major cause of bad
writing would be well on its way to being solved.

**"[Procter & Gamble offers] a Basic Writing Skills course and a
more advanced Leading Management Thinking Through Writing class. The first course teaches the P&G process of writing and
explains why the process makes sense. When people come out
of the first course, you see a lot of standard formatted memos.
That's good because it means they're practicing what they
learned. The advanced course takes their skill to the next level.
Once they understand the basics, we teach people how to tailor
what they write to even more effectively deliver against their
communication objective and target audience's specific needs.
We teach the rules and then we teach people how to break the
rules to optimize communication. That's how the basic and advanced courses fit together."**

Ed Burghard, marketing director,
Procter & Gamble
(from his interview in Part III)

Writing Is a Problem-Solving Process

Following a list of school-taught writing rules to produce a good piece
of writing doesn't work because writing is a problem-solving process,
which is always trial and error and therefore defies rules. The moment
writers touch pen to paper, they begin a nonstop problem-solving
roller-coaster ride. You start by asking yourself a question that poses a
problem, "How do I begin?" The answer to that question triggers another question that poses another problem: "I have three ways I think
I can open the letter, which is the best?" The answer to that question
triggers yet another problem—"Is my second choice really the best
one?"—and on you go.

Writing is not a neat linear process; it quickly branches out like a
spider's web. One question often triggers two or three problems, some
of which have implications about what you will write in the middle and
end of your letter or report. Like chess, you're often thinking several
moves ahead. This is why writing can be such a brain drain.

Few managers have to solve as many problems, in so short a time,
as a large and difficult writing assignment throws at them. Obviously,
some writing projects are a bigger brain drain than others. Most people

dash off replies to e-mails and short memos without straining a single gray cell. Writing problems range from the exceptionally easy, "Let's see, how should I begin? Oh, yeah, 'Dear Lucille,'" to the exceptionally hard, "How do I make a logical transition from the diamond mine strikes in South Africa to the cost of legumes in southern France in my economics report? The explanation will take five pages and I have to write it in one!"

All problem solving—whether it's a writing problem, a relationship problem, a find-a-job problem—is trial and error. You try one solution. If it doesn't work, you try another, and continue the process until you finally stumble across one that does the trick. Writing isn't hard because it's writing. Writing is hard because it's a problem-solving activity, and problem solving is hard.

Flexible Guidelines

Experienced writers view all the writing rules taught in school, and even some of the mechanical rules, as rules of thumb—that is, flexible guidelines that can be bent, broken, or thrown out while transferring their jumbled, chaotic thoughts onto paper. Rose touches on this point in his article:

A lgorithms are precise rules that will always result in a specific answer if applied to an appropriate problem. Most mathematical rules, for example, are algorithms. . . . [However,] most often we function with the aid of fairly general heuristics or "rules of thumb," guidelines that allow varying degrees of flexibility when approaching problems. . . . In a world where tasks and problems are rarely mathematically precise, heuristic rules become the most appropriate, the most functional rules available to us: A heuristic does not guarantee the optimal solution or, indeed, any solution at all; rather, heuristics offer solutions that are good enough most of the time.[12]

A helpful way to view the roles of rules and rules of thumb is to look at them in the context of art vs. science.

The Art vs. the Science of Writing

Writing rules can be divided into two categories: stylistic and mechanical. Style rules govern the way you compose your message: Avoid long sentences, use the active not the passive voice, omit needless words, etc. Mechanical rules, as already mentioned, govern the form of the message: grammar, spelling, and punctuation. The mechanics represent the science side of writing because these rules are, for the most part, straightforward and unbreakable, just like the laws of science. For example, just as there is one and only one solution to the equation 2 + 2, there is one and only one way to spell the word *business.* You can never spell it *buziness* or *bisiness.* There is one and only one way to say "I do." There is never a situation where "I does" will be correct. There is one and only one way to punctuate a question. "Why me;" is always wrong; "Why me?" is always correct. You can find the answers to any rule on the science of writing in a dictionary or in a grammar or punctuation guide.

I said these rules are unbreakable "for the most part," because they do change over time. In the Middle Ages, the word *today* was spelled *to day* and later became *to-day* before finally taking its current shape. Also, *ain't* is now an acceptable grammar form.

The style rules represent the art side of writing, because these rules are not straightforward or unbreakable (see Figure 2-2). Applying them always requires a judgment call. For example, how long is a long sentence and how many long sentences are too many? You can't find the answer to either of those questions in a book. Both require the writer to make a judgment call, and that call will be different depending on each writing situation and assignment.

The rule "write as you speak" assumes everyone knows how to talk in an acceptable, conversational way. If a person uses terrible grammar when speaking, is it okay to use terrible grammar when writing? Of course not. What's "acceptable"? What's "conversational"? Both words are open to interpretation. Your writer's intuition plays a crucial

Figure 2-2. Art and Science.

THE ART OF WRITING	THE SCIENCE OF WRITING
Style rules	Mechanical rules
Examples: use active voice, delete needless words, write the way you speak, etc.	All grammar, spelling, and punctuation rules

and decisive role in making these judgment calls. But this is enough of an overview for now. I'll explain more about the art and science of writing and the role of writer's intuition in Chapters 5 and 6.

Common Sense, Not Creativity

On a final note, don't let the word *art* fool you. You don't have to write like Maya Angelou or John Updike to produce a well-written memo. Use your common sense. Got a good idea? Write it down the way you would want to receive it. You don't have to be Eudora Welty to do that.

"I'm not a good writer because I'm not creative." That's a common complaint I hear in workshops and seminars. The root of this problem goes back to elementary school, where students are often required to read literature in their writing classes. Classic works from the English novelist George Orwell to the American poet Emily Dickinson can be found in many textbooks. Passages from such authors are, in turn, used as examples of good writing. There is nothing wrong with teaching literature in writing courses, but teachers should make it clear that their students do not have to be creative like Orwell or Dickinson to learn how to write well. And that's clearly the message many students take away from their writing/literature courses and carry with them into adulthood and their careers.

Equal time should be given to the type of writing students will face once they graduate. Teachers should give students business reports, articles, and letters as reading material and writing assignments. In addition, teachers should point out that "academic writing" is a distinct and separate genre. The implication is that the way students are taught to write for their teachers is the common or generic way to write. That's not true. Academic writing has its own style. For example, the tone is more prim and proper than journalism or business writing.

Again, I find nothing wrong with learning the academic style as long as teachers 1) explain how it differs from other genres and 2) teach other genres. The bottom line is that all writing instruction transfers. That is, if you do a lot of letter or diary writing, the skills you pick up doing that type of writing will help make you a better business or academic writer, too.

One important step in your education as a business writer is to realize that your basic common sense is all you need to write well. If you can discern which idea should logically follow another, you have all the brainpower you need to be an excellent business writer. Creativity is a nice plus, but by no means is it a requirement.

CHAPTER 3

FORMATS AND TEMPLATES HELP YOU WRITE SMARTER AND FASTER

No businessperson should open a blank word-processing file when writing routine correspondence such as bids and reports. That's the theme of this chapter, which explores the first step in the planning stage of the Plan Then Write process (see Figure 3-1). Blank pages are intimidating and can lead to writer's block. Opening a preformatted template is a big help because formats point you in a specific writing direction and dictate tone and style. Choosing which format to use for each writing assignment is an important first decision for every writer. For example, when you think of writing an e-mail, you know it will be informal in tone and style. In addition, e-mails are mainly used for casual correspondence—think of e-mails as substitutes for phone calls—such as quick replies to colleagues, friends, and clients. However, you wouldn't think of using the e-mail format to write a bid or a sales report.

Choosing the Right Format

It's not uncommon to read stories about writers who worked on the draft of a novel for several months before suddenly realizing that what they were writing was really a play or a movie script, not a novel.

Fortunately, in business writing, choosing a format is fairly easy

Figure 3-1. Step 1. Plan: Format.

PLAN THEN WRITE

> **1. Plan**
> • **Format**

2. Write and Rewrite

3. Edit 1

4. Edit 2

and fast. In fact, when you sit down to write, the format usually chooses itself. If someone sends you an e-mail, chances are you'll respond with an e-mail. If you must write a customer for any reason, etiquette dictates a formal letter is most appropriate. If your boss tells you to write a report or proposal, that's what you write. If you're not sure which format to use, ask a colleague who's been around longer than you. Different companies have different requirements depending on the purpose of the document.

Businesses can use formats to help their employees write faster and smarter by creating templates that spell out which information needs to go where. I'll explain the benefits of templates in a moment. First a few basics.

What's a Format?

Webster's definition of *format* is: the outline, layout, or presentation of a document or other publication; the way in which something is presented, organized, or arranged. Here are two sample formats—a typical e-mail and a typical letter.

E-Mail

> Date:
> To:
> From:
> Subject:
> Cc:
> Bcc:
> Attachments:
> (Your message)

_____

_____

_____

Letter

> Date
> Return address
> Salutation or greeting
> Body of the letter
> Close
> Signature block

Templates Speed the Writing Process

Every type of business correspondence has a particular structure that acts as a guideline to help organize your thoughts. Experienced and inexperienced writers alike can benefit greatly from using prebuilt format templates with descriptive subheads that prompt them for the information they will need to include. There are several advantages of using templates:

◆ *They help prevent writer's block.* Writers can jump around the format and choose the subhead for which they have the most information and start writing immediately.

◆ *They speed the writing process* by establishing the logical flow of ideas and information. No need to sit and ponder, What should I write next? or, Do I need to add more information here? or, How do I transition from this section to the next? When you are done filling in the subheads, you are done writing.

◆ *You know which types of information* to gather and where to put them in the document.

◆ *Since each section in the template* acts as a prompt for the data you need, templates guarantee your documents will always be complete and that you never leave out important information.

◆ *Your readers know what to expect* and where to quickly find information in the document.

◆ *Templates help eliminate wordiness.* Once you've covered the information the subhead requires, you know it's okay to move on. Wordiness is usually the result of not knowing when to stop writing and "feeling" as if your report or letter needs to be longer.

Templates mean you never have to open a blank computer file. That's important because blank files look too much like blank movie screens, inviting you to sit and wait for something exciting to happen. A blank white page is mesmerizing and promotes writer's block. An added benefit is that when you open a template, the prewritten subheads give the impression you've started the writing process already. Confidence is half the battle.

A Word of Caution

Every document has a format, but not every format can be turned into a template. As a general guideline, documents that are produced on a

> **"A big part of learning to write well is learning the frameworks or formats for the letters, memos, and other correspondence you write, and dropping your words into those frameworks. People have a sense that learning to write well is different from learning other business skills. It's not."**
>
> Roger Conner, vice president of
> communications, Marriott International
> (from his interview in Part III)

regular basis and contain types of information that must be included in each iteration are excellent candidates for templates. Correspondence that includes information that changes every time you create it will never fit a template.

Reverse Engineering

Here's how to create templates for routine documents. Simply work backward and reverse engineer the template from old reports, letters, or memos. For example:

1. Gather the last two years' worth of quarterly inventory reports.
2. Read each one carefully.
3. While reading, draw brackets in the right-hand margin next to groups of sentences or paragraphs that represent blocks of required information that each report must include.
4. Next, create a template. Open a blank word-processing file on your computer. Create an appropriate name for a subhead for each block of required information and type the subhead in the blank template.
5. To keep the template flexible, type in two blank subheads that writers can use for information that wasn't anticipated or that changes each time the document is written. Report writers can delete these subheads if not used.
6. Modify the template as needed over time.

Keep in mind that the best opening for any piece of business writing is your main point and what you want your reader to do. The best close is a summary that repeats your main point, your most important supporting details, and your call to action. Also, template subheads must be brief, straightforward, and describe the type of information that section of the document must include. Don't write creative or vague subheads. The beauty of reverse engineering is that you are guaranteed to custom-develop a format that meets your exact needs.

Templates Are Not Straitjackets

If your monthly personnel report requires the same data time after time, it will be easy to create a template for it with fixed subheads. For example, one subhead might be "New Hires, Layoffs, Retirements." Each month, you simply update the numbers in that section and add any needed explanations or comments.

However, you can't anticipate all the information each type of written communication will require and create a template with subheads to fit it. For example, letters responding to a customer complaint or request for information defy subheads like the one for the personnel report. But you can replace subheads in letter templates with general guidelines for writers to follow such as:

- ❑ Open each letter by thanking the customer for writing and then rephrasing his complaint or request.
- ❑ After the open, immediately address the customer's complaint or list the information requested.
- ❑ Conclude each letter by thanking the customer for writing, including the company's toll-free 800 number, and inserting a discount coupon.

These guidelines have the same effect as subheads and aid fast, smart writing. Writers know which information to gather, how to start the letter, what to say in the middle, and how to end it.

CHAPTER 4

HOW SUBJECT, AUDIENCE, AND PURPOSE KEEP YOUR WRITING CLEAR AND CONCISE

The next three steps in the plan stage of the Plan Then Write process—subject, audience, and purpose (SAP)—represent the starting elements of every type of writing, whether it's a business letter, Christmas list, graffiti, or billboard (see Figure 4-1 below). Here's what they include.

Starting Elements

◆ **Subject.** The topic you will write about. The subject element includes the main point and supporting points. (For example, the subject of this book is business writing. The main point is to prove that you can become a better writer by learning the Plan Then Write process, not by memorizing more rules. For supporting points, see the individual chapter headings under Part I in the table of contents.)

◆ **Audience.** The individual or group who will read what you write. You must always take into consideration the reader's level of experience and knowledge about your subject. (The audience for this book is anyone with a minimum of a high school degree or equivalent

Figure 4-1. Step 1. Plan: SAP.

PLAN THEN WRITE

1. Plan • Subject, Audience, Purpose

2. Write and Rewrite

3. Edit 1

4. Edit 2

writing experience. Because writing instruction begins about the third grade, everyone in this audience has at least a decade of writing experience, in and out of school, and received enough academic training to have an understanding of the basic writing principles.)

♦ **Purpose/Call to Action.** Why are you writing? What do you want your audience to do? These two questions are so closely related— often your purpose is your call to action—that I included them under a single subhead. (In this book, I am writing to introduce and explain the Plan Then Write process. I want readers to improve their writing skills by learning and applying the method experienced writers use.)

For quick e-mails, memos, and other short writing projects, SAP often takes little or no thought because it is so clearly implied. Bigger projects, such as annual reports and white papers—along with sensitive or important correspondence such as a letter to your customers explaining why your company is not liable for incidental damage caused by your product—require a careful consideration of SAP. Here's why.

SAP Is Your Guide

By thinking about all three elements before you begin to write, and keeping them in mind as you write, SAP will focus your writing and tell you when you are straying from the topic, being wordy, overwriting, including irrelevant or confusing information, and more. Consider SAP the virtual writing coach of the clear and concise writer. This is an extremely important use of SAP, one that experienced writers rely on every time they write, but inexperienced writers rarely consider.

SAP at Work

Let's say your boss asks you to write a letter to your company's board of directors explaining why last quarter's sales were 5 percent lower than the previous quarter. Writing out your subject, audience, and purpose will not only force you to think about details that will make your letter effective, it will also force you to construct the mental guideposts that will keep you focused while writing. Begin by freewriting or brainstorming (i.e., writing whatever comes into your head without regard for logic, grammar, spelling, or punctuation). Here's an example of freewriting on the above-mentioned topic:

Subject: main point: sales 5% lower; supporting points: recession hit, manufacturing snafus, competitors came out with a new product; these all sound like excuses, what are the positives? Sales force was reduced 20% since last quarter but productivity increased 28% per salesperson. Restructuring made sales force leaner and meaner . . . before restructuring, we expected a 10–15% loss. New main point: 5% loss shows that our restructuring is already having an affect. Main point is now: how effective our restructuring is . . . the 5% loss is now a supporting point, albeit a negative one. So instead of dwelling on the loss, 90% of my letter will be emphasizing the steps in our restructuring effort and how promising it looks already.

Audience: board of directors. What do they know about this type of problem and the reasons for it? A lot. As current or retired CEOs of big companies they've seen sales drop before . . . they'll understand a reasoned explanation . . . they've weathered restructurings before. Must downplay the reasons for the loss and show how hopeful the future looks. Research each person on the board, check out our last annual report for their bios. I may find that one was once CEO of a company that experienced our exact same problem and then saw his company bounce back, I might find some nuggets of information in that board member's bio that I can use in the letter. Don't sound panicked . . . this group will pounce if they think I'm panicked or making excuses . . . be straightforward, don't mince the facts, but cover the loss quickly and move on. They'll understand.

Purpose: to inform the board that sales were 5% lower, yes, but that's bad news. I need to placate soothe reinforce, assure them that the restructuring is complete and already showing positive results. Yes, that's my purpose, to assure them. Sound supportive and positive.

Backing into the Writing Process

Brainstorming SAP helped me to discover a more positive approach to take in the letter—that is, I'm now focusing on the benefits of restruc-

> "If you get four paragraphs or four minutes of speech time with a decision maker or potential client, the value of the written word at that moment is immeasurable. . . . Terrible writing forms an immediate and indelible bad impression. People think their idea is all that counts, not how they present it. They couldn't be more wrong. When you're competing for a few moments of the chairman's time, a very small and valuable window of opportunity, a rambling four-page proposal that could easily have been written in one page, if the person simply took the time, will end your chances in a heartbeat. Poor writing says a lot about you and certainly enough to sink a proposal on first impressions alone."
>
> Ken Sternad, vice president of
> public affairs, UPS
> (from his interview in Part III)

turing, not the loss in sales. The new angle increased my confidence because I'm delivering more good news than bad. In addition, the free-writing produced 1) an outline consisting of my main point and several good supporting points that I can use to start a rough draft, 2) a new purpose that's in line with my new "restructuring" subject, and 3) a better understanding of my audience, although I need to do more research on them.

Here is an outline that I cut and pasted from my freewriting session:

Subject: inform board of restructuring gains and the 5% loss
Main point: how effective our restructuring is
Supporting points:

- sales force was reduced 20% since last quarter
- restructuring steps
- 5% loss shows that our restructuring is already having an effect
- productivity increased 28% per salesperson
- we expected a 10–15% loss

Audience: board of directors (It's too limiting to reduce a description of my audience down to a sentence or two, so I'm just going to keep the "idea" of my au-

dience in my head. I can always reread what I wrote
about them in my freewriting, if needed.)

Purpose: assure board that the restructuring is complete and already showing positive results.

Keep an Open Mind

This outline is not complete, but it's more than enough to allow me to
begin writing and fend off any procrastination or writer's block that
may otherwise set in. I'll add supporting points as I write and discover
more about my topic, plus I'll keep an open mind: My subject and purpose changed once already and may change again while writing my
draft and uncovering new ideas. As Stephen Krashen notes, "Not only
do good writers plan more, they also have more flexible plans—they
are more willing to change their ideas as they write and to revise their
outline as new ideas and arguments emerge."[1]

SAP as a Sounding Board

While writing the letter to the board of directors, I'll use SAP in the
latter part of my rewriting stage to write tight, crisp, logical sentences.
For my first draft, however, I need to put SAP in the back of my mind
and concentrate on putting words on the page that I can later form into
a final draft. For instance, here's a first draft of my first supporting
point:

> The sales force was reduced 20 percent because
> cash flow started to go in reverse and our product
> received a bad review by a big-time analyst, even
> though three other big-time analysts gave it a good
> review. Morale started to sink in our southwest office
> and that didn't help sales, either. Forecasts predict
> that the 5 percent could increase to 7 or 8 percent
> next quarter, but that's without taking into consider-
> ation our new pricing policy, which won't be an-
> nounced until the end of this month . . . we're also
> going to announce a month-long booster pack special
> that will certainly help sales, but how much no one
> knows. The 20 percent sales force reduction is a good
> thing because it lowered overhead and got rid of un-

derperformers; but it is bad because we have fewer salespeople out there selling, and those who are left feel overwhelmed at this point from the extra work they now have to do and the uncertainty of who might be next to go.

My first impression after rereading this draft is that it sounds depressing. Should I keep this paragraph? Delete it? Save part of it (and if so, which part)? I'll use the three elements of SAP as an adviser to guide my decisions.

1. **Subject:** Which ideas in the paragraph support my new subject of "effective restructuring"? Sentence number one supports it, sentence two does not. Sentence two is also one of the points that makes the paragraph sound depressing, plus the morale of the southwest office is not relevant. Sentence one needs more work to make it concise and read more clearly, but I'll worry about that in another edit. I don't want to stop and fine-tune the draft at this stage, but it is helpful to stop and clean up parts from time to time so I can see where I'm going.

> **"Because my book is such a long project, I usually stop and edit what I've done about halfway through. I need to polish it so I can see where I need to go next. I compare writing a book to a walk in the woods. You go down a path and you're not sure where it's taking you. Suddenly you come to a fork in the path, and you can't figure out which one you should take. So you turn around and look back to see where you've come from, to get your bearings and help you decide which fork to take. Stopping to edit halfway through a book is like turning around and looking back to see where you started, so you can get a better idea of where to go next."**
>
> Richard Bolles, author of
> *What Color Is Your Parachute?*
> (from his interview in Part II)

2. **Audience:** The board members are very savvy, but they probably won't know the meaning of the phrase that marketing created: "booster pack special." I either have to define it or delete it. Even if some board members do understand the phrase, the fact that all of them may not forces me to define it. Also, you can never go wrong

by defining a term in your copy. As long as you're not talking down to your audience, the explanation will be appreciated.

3. **Purpose:** My purpose is to assure the board that the restructuring is going well. I can't delete all the bad news from this paragraph, but I need to keep it to a minimum so they know things are getting better. I decide to leave out the part about the uncertainty regarding the effectiveness of the "month-long booster pack special," but keep the point about laying off underperformers. My reasoning is that the booster pack is a positive step for the company, and I don't want to temper the good news with a pessimistic reminder the initiative could fail, which they know is a distinct possibility with any new initiative. Also, they are well aware that letting underachievers go is good for several reasons: Employees who consistently fail to meet their goals are probably in the wrong profession and need a push to reevaluate their careers. Also, keeping underachievers on the payroll lowers the morale of the rest of the group.

Using SAP as an editor, this is what a quick rewrite looks like:

> The sales force was reduced 20 percent because cash flow started to go in reverse and our product received a bad review by a big-time analyst, even though three other big-time analysts gave it a good review. Forecasts predict that the 5 percent could increase to 7 or 8 percent next quarter, but that's without taking into consideration our new pricing policy, which won't be announced until the end of this month . . . we're also going to announce a month-long booster pack special where customers receive one free product when they purchase four, which should help sales. The 20 percent force reduction is a good thing because it lowers overhead and weeds out underperformers.

The paragraph is becoming clearer and more concise after just one simple and fast rewrite using SAP as a guide. This is enough editing to prove my point, so instead of taking this paragraph to final draft form, I'll move on to another important point about audience.

Writing to a Specific Audience

One of the biggest problems I see in business writing concerns audience. Too often, people fail to take their readers' needs into consideration and leave out important details that aid a reader's understanding. The following two paragraphs, which open a report on team building, read like hastily written class notes or diary entries. The paragraphs mean something to the person who wrote them because he can recall the missing information as he reads. But to an objective reader—anyone not present at the meeting this report is based on—the piece is nearly gibberish.

This report is about insight into effective marketing groups and how important living a clear mission statement is. First, marketing directors need to know the mission better than anyone. Highly cooperative groups can most easily be created through systems, most difficult through cultural associations and require individual commitment. Teamwork is the cooperative use of resources for people who must work together to achieve common marketing goals.

There are significant differences between marketing tasks that are focused at events and organizational objectives that instill high individual standards. The task level is what groups accomplish and the process level is how standards are accomplished. Group marketing building requires a plan. In each group meeting, the need is stressed for an opportunity when each group member can express how they perceive each other's goals. This keeps the group on track to support their mission statement and clarify any shortcomings.

Writer-Based Prose Defined

This is clearly an example of bad business writing. The ideas are so muddled that another communication is required to explain it. Linda Flower calls this type of writing "writer-based," and she defines it as follows:

The distinction I wish to make here is between reader-based prose, which takes the reader into account, and what I call writer-based prose, [or] prose in which the writer is essentially talking to himself. . . . Writing to oneself is better understood as merely an easier, highly available mode of thought. Reader-based prose is, by contrast, often quite difficult to do. Furthermore, being able to write reader-based prose often means being willing and able to revise—a skill many students lack. . . . Writer-based prose, then, is inadequate for the reader, but easier for the writer, and on difficult tasks it can represent an efficient first step in the writing process. . . . A critical skill in writing is learning how to transform writer-based prose into reader-based prose.[2]

How do you fix writer-based writing? During the rewriting stage, reread what you wrote from your reader's point of view and fill in any missing details or gaps in logic that your reader will need to make sense of the piece. It takes practice and patience. Spotting and fixing writer-based prose is difficult to do when editing your own work, but much easier when editing someone else's work because you don't have to pretend to be an objective reader—you are one.

Fixing Writer-Based Writing

Let's revise the first paragraph of the "team building" report. Here is the original again:

This report is about insight into effective marketing groups and how important living a clear mission statement is. First, marketing directors need to know the mission better than anyone. Highly cooperative groups can most easily be created through systems, most difficult through cultural associations and require individual commitment. Teamwork is the cooperative use of resources for people who must work together to achieve common marketing goals.

What do we as readers understand after reading the first sentence? That the report is about "insight into effective marketing groups" and "how important living a clear mission statement is." It sounds like a double topic, but after rereading both paragraphs, I think "living a clear mission statement" is a characteristic of an effective marketing group, not a second main point.

The first topic, "insight into effective marketing groups," is vague. What does the phrase actually mean? Will the report list insights about effective marketing groups, or will it describe effective marketing groups? What are these insights going to tell me? Why should I care about them? As a reader I'm not sure, specifically, what the main point is, which is why the paragraph is so confusing right off the bat. But again, after rereading both paragraphs, especially the third sentence that talks about creating groups, my educated guess is that the subject of this report is how to build effective marketing groups. "Insight into effective marketing groups" is an awkward, brainstorming, first-draft way of saying "how to build effective marketing groups." Based on the second sentence, my guess is that the topic is how marketing directors build these groups.

Because the writer is, as Flower says, basically talking to himself in this paragraph, I have to do a lot of detective work to figure out the message. The writer has given few supporting details that will help me make sense of the cryptic statements he's weaved into a paragraph.

Reading Should Be Easy, Not Hard

Based on my interpretation of the paragraph, one way to rewrite the opening sentence is: "This report explains how marketing directors can build effective marketing groups." That's much clearer, and as a reader, I now understand the subject of the report.

However, the second sentence confuses me as much as the first. It almost sounds as if it belongs in another report, one about "the importance of mission statements in businesses." But by reading between the lines again and linking it to the phrase *mission statement* in the first sentence, I come up with this for a rewrite: "This report explains how marketing directors can build effective marketing groups. A key first step to building effective groups is establishing a clear mission statement."

The third sentence is even more confusing to readers than the first two. The writer is going to introduce two new ideas: the easy way to create effective marketing groups and the hard way. The first part of the third sentence makes sense to me: "Highly cooperative groups can most easily be created through systems. . . ." Good, I'm going to find out how to create the best type of marketing groups, the highly cooperative ones. I don't know what the writer means by systems yet, but I assume I'll find out soon.

The rest of the sentence, however, is completely unintelligible: ". . . most difficult through cultural associations and require individual commitment." If I knew what the writer meant by cultural associations, I'd have some clue as to what he was trying to say. Obviously, the writer knew what he meant by this phrase and assumed his readers did too, which is another classic symptom of writer-based prose. The final part of the sentence, "and require individual commitment," comes out of the blue. I have no idea how it connects to the ideas in the rest of the sentence. Before attempting to rewrite this part of the third sentence, I'd have to talk to the writer. There simply aren't enough signposts to even hazard a guess as to what he's trying to say.

Reading Between the Lines

The fourth sentence injects yet another new idea, a definition of teamwork. The writer is talking about building effective groups, so it makes sense to discuss teamwork, but not at this point in the report. The writer must first stop and supply supporting details that clarify the ideas he has introduced in the first three sentences. Because I'm having such a hard time deciphering what he is trying to tell me, I don't get past the first paragraph before I stop reading the report.

The writer's thinking is unclear and therefore his writing is unclear. However, this paragraph—which the writer handed in as his final draft—makes an excellent first draft. Now all he has to do is rewrite it, keeping his readers' needs in mind.

Clear Thinking Requires Writing

This sample report shows why writing is an indispensable part of the thinking process. Thoughts come flying into our heads in a willy-nilly, crossword-like jumble. The best way to clarify or straighten them out is to write them down so we can free up our minds and make room for more ideas (you can only hold so many in your head at once). Also, putting them on paper gives you the luxury of spreading your ideas out on a large table so you can take all the time you need to physically rearrange them and work out the logic of your argument. Once your thoughts are captured on paper, they can't get away. I talk about the writing process being a problem-solving activity. Another way to describe it is the endless process of "think, write, think, write, think, write."

> "In technology-oriented companies like Cisco, the challenge is to take a complicated topic and make it simple and understandable. This is true for technology companies across the board. Also, there are different audiences who read our material. What we say to a CEO about the Internet and how a network operates is far different from what we would say to a network administrator. . . . So, in a company like Cisco, we have to make sure we match the style and level of complexity of the writing to the audience. In all cases, however, it's a matter of taking complicated subject matter and making it relevant to the reader."
>
> Jere Brooks King, vice president of
> worldwide marketing communications, Cisco Systems
> (from her interview in Part III)

The Best Solution

If a proofreader points out that you have a writer-based problem, you can fix it by asking the person to show you exactly where the copy doesn't make sense and keep asking her questions until it's resolved. The proofreader doesn't have to be an expert in writing or in spotting writer-based prose to detect a writer-based problem. A reader's common sense tells her when she doesn't understand a phrase or sentence, or when the logic of a paragraph skips a beat. That's all a proofreader has to tell you: "I don't know what's wrong with this paragraph or how to fix it, but I don't get it. I don't know what you're trying to say in the first sentence or the last half of the fifth one."

If you have to work out the problem on your own, carry on a conversation with yourself. It might sound something like this: "What is this report really about? Insight into effective marketing groups? No, not insight, but how to build effective teams. Yes, that's it. What does my reader know about effective group building? What does he or she need to know first?" This sounds like a haphazard approach, but that's the nature of the problem-solving process, which is discussed in more detail in Chapter 5.

Stating Your Purpose

Of the three starting elements, purpose is the easiest to determine. All you have to do is answer these two questions:

1. Why am I writing? (your purpose statement)

2. What do I want my audience to do? (your call to action)

Often, a single answer covers both. For example, the following purpose statement includes a clearly implied call to action: "I'm writing to invite the CEO and VP of manufacturing for Acme, Inc., to be my guests at this year's tradeshow in Las Vegas."

Your purpose is to invite your number-one client and her VP of manufacturing to your tradeshow. Your call to action is to convince them to accept the invitation.

Even though it's fairly straightforward, write down and think about your purpose and call to action. In this case, for instance, rereading your call to action may remind you that this client doesn't like tradeshows or doesn't like showing preference for one vendor over another, and that you will have to be extra careful when choosing details to persuade her to attend as your guest.

The main point to remember about purpose is to include a call to action in every writing assignment that requires one. Just as every salesperson must never forget to ask for the sale, business writers should never forget to tell their readers what they want them to do. Never assume.

SAP Is Often a Given

Unlike novelists, op-ed journalists, poets, and advertising writers, businesspeople rarely sit down to write a project without the subject, audience, and purpose either given to them or clearly implied, which makes that part of the writing process a little easier. When your boss tells you to write a report that summarizes the meeting you just attended and to make a copy for all the participants, your subject (what was discussed at the meeting), audience (your boss and colleagues in the meeting), and purpose (to document what took place and ensure everyone left the meeting with the same information) were told to you.

When you reply to an e-mail, your subject, audience, and purpose are often implied in the e-mail you received. Let's say that Marlene in sales wants to reserve the executive conference room this Thursday. In your response ("Dear Marlene, Yes, you may reserve the executive conference room this Thursday"), the subject (use of a room), audience (Marlene), and your purpose (to inform her) are clearly spelled out. You can write your response quickly and with little thought other than determining if the room is free on Thursday.

Fortunately, the same is true about much of the writing you do every day on the job. Being given the subject, audience, and purpose is a huge first step. It eliminates a lot of hard thinking—What do I write? Where do I start?—that can lead to frustration and writer's block.

How to Prevent Writer's Block

Writer's block is the inability to think of anything to write. Most businesspeople probably experience this "affliction" at least once in their careers. The problem has three common causes:

1. You don't know what to say.
2. You don't know how to say it.
3. You're paralyzed by perfection.

The solutions:

1. Gather more material, do more research.
2. Write something, anything. Get the writing process started by writing down whatever comes into your head, even if it has nothing to do with your subject.
3. Lower your expectations. Give yourself permission to write not just an imperfect first draft, but a downright terrible one.

When you feel writer's block coming on, stop and determine the cause and then apply the solution. Type-three writer's block—where you feel everything you write has to be perfect—is harder to fix because you can't turn those feelings on and off like a spigot; nonetheless, it's important to head off the problem early. Also, don't confuse procrastination with writer's block. Most people have to psyche themselves up to start a project that requires heavy thinking, and procrastination—filing bills, writing a poem, cleaning off your desk—is part of the psyching up process. Procrastination is good. It's a normal first step in most people's writing process. The bigger the project, the more time you need to rev your engines.

Charles Dickens, Victor Hugo, Winston Churchill, and many other past and present writers wrote at chest-high desks that allowed them to stand and walk around and gesture and role-play what they were writing. When you feel nervous energy storing up inside, either before you start or while you're writing, get up and walk around with a note pad and pen and think about what you want to say and write it down. Go to a park or walk around the block. Do something. You'll come back with plenty to write and be eager to start.

Here's one thing I do to procrastinate. While rewriting my drafts, I often break the "don't edit while you write rule" and look up the spelling and definition of words in the dictionary. Sometimes it's a waste of my time because I delete the words in a later revision, but it gives me a little break and keeps me working at my desk.

Tone and SAP

"It's not what you say, but how you say it." The "how you say it" part of this universal parenting principle refers to tone. How your words sound to people when they read them is a very important part of writing; tone is the voice or personality that comes through on paper. You can sound angry, awkward, happy, sad, mad, excited, bored, encouraging, disappointed, disgusted, mysterious—the list goes on. Reread the five sample memos in the Business Writing Standards section at the end of Chapter 1. Listen to the tone deteriorate as you read them in order. It goes from pleasant and professional to harsh and unpolished.

Tone is extremely important in business writing because the way you sound on paper is the way your audience perceives you and your company. If you sound stuffy and arrogant in your memos, colleagues will think you are a pompous bureaucrat. If a brochure sounds complex, boring, and aloof, that's the image customers will have of your company.

The problem with tone is that it's easy to hear and describe in other people's correspondence, but not always easy to detect in your own. Tone is too much a part of who we are and what we write. It's like hearing yourself speak on video or audio tape. Often, when we hear our own voice we think, That's not me!

All of us have given a letter to someone to proofread only to have that person ask if we really meant to sound so tough and demanding, or mild and wishy-washy, or uncaring and resentful. Our first response is, "I didn't mean to give that impression. Where do you see that?" And when he points it out, sure enough, it's there on the page. One reason for letting a document sit for a few days or weeks before sending it is to put some distance between you and the tone. That often isn't possible with business correspondence that's due in a matter of minutes or hours, but these tips will help you hit the right tone even when pressed by a tight deadline.

Different Tones for Different Purposes

Your average business document should sound pleasant, professional, and neutral in tone. One trick is to pretend you are talking to your very best friend while writing. Do this especially when you are upset, such as when writing yet another memo to the delivery driver who has disregarded your previous ten memos about where to leave packages. By pretending the driver is your best friend, you'll tone down the anger in your "writing voice."

Sometimes you will want to change your tone. And because tone is a decision you make when considering SAP, your choice of tones will depend on these three considerations, especially audience and purpose. For instance, if your collaborative writing group is getting behind schedule because petty turf wars are breaking out among members, your memo to them might begin with a disappointed tone when discussing the in-fighting and end with an upbeat, encouraging tone to motivate them to move on with the project.

How Would Jack Nicholson Write This Letter?

Changing tones from one writing project to another can be tough. It's hard to write a letter to a customer in a friendly business tone, then immediately switch gears to write a memo to a vendor complaining about a missed deadline in a tough-but-fair tone, and switch yet again to write a report to potential investors in a formal, pleasant tone.

Here's a tip that works. An easy way to change tones is to role-play while writing. If you have to write a smoothly persuasive letter to someone, think of a smoothly persuasive movie or television actor (Jack Nicholson or Denzel Washington?) or actress (Judi Dench or Sandra Bullock?) and step into his or her shoes while writing the e-mail, letter, or memo. For a lighthearted tone think Meg Ryan or Billy Crystal. The possibilities are endless, and there is a celebrity role model for every type of tone you will ever need to use in your business writing assignments.

A Final Note on Tone

The tone of your business correspondence is a subtle yet powerful part of your message. When you are writing a friendly letter but mistakenly use an unfriendly tone, your reader will pick up on the hostile tone, not your good-natured intent. That's why you should rarely if ever use humor in correspondence with someone you don't know well. Comedy is not easily conveyed in writing. For example, irony usually requires a wink of an eye or some other body language to help the audience realize that you mean the exact opposite of what your words convey. You can't wink on paper.

Use the wrong tone and you could lose a client or a promotion. You can guard against this by remembering to let a colleague or professional proofreader check what you write before sending it, especially if it's a public or promotional piece, to make sure the tone is not off-key.

CHAPTER 5

THE ART OF WRITING

How to Solve Problems Using Your Writer's Intuition

The second step of the Plan Then Write process—write and rewrite until you have a final draft—is the most important. This is where your message gets hammered out, where the real work takes place as you struggle to put your thoughts on paper.

The 90-10 Rule

As mentioned in Chapter 2, I divide the writing process into two parts: the art of writing and the science of writing. The art side includes everything associated with communicating your message, which coincides with steps 1 and 2 in Plan Then Write. The science side covers everything associated with making your message mechanically correct and correlates to steps 3 and 4.

Ninety percent of the actual work of writing falls under the art of writing, and 10 percent falls under science. These are my estimates. They're not based on any survey. I guesstimated them based on the fact that all the sweat associated with writing—the problem solving and the effort to produce a clear, concise message—takes place in step 2 (see Figure 5-1).

Figure 5-1. Step 2. Write and Rewrite.

PLAN THEN WRITE

1. Plan

2. Write and Rewrite

3. Edit 1

4. Edit 2

Science Is Easier Than Art

I assigned 10 percent to the science side of writing because, compared to step 2, you really don't have to do much thinking to make your drafts mechanically perfect. Choosing the easiest solution—giving your final drafts to a professional proofreader—requires no effort at all on your part. The second easiest solution is to give your documents to a colleague who is good at proofreading. Chances are the person won't catch every mistake and you'll have to spend time proofreading it too, but a second opinion always helps. The hardest solution is to figure out the mechanics by yourself with the aid of your computer spell checker or a handy dictionary, grammar, and punctuation guide.

If you equate the science side of writing with memorizing the thousands of grammar, spelling, and punctuation rules listed in style manuals, dictionaries, and other reference texts, then, yes, the mechanical side of the writing process will be extremely difficult. But that's the wrong approach to take, and an impossible one. Even professional proofreaders can't memorize all the rules. Take a tip from experienced writers and expend your brainpower on composing your message, and use proofreaders or do the best you can with writing reference guides to clean up any mechanical problems you find in your final draft.

The most important factor in my decision to assign only 10 percent of writing work to the science side is that the effectiveness of your message is judged by how clearly you communicate your thoughts, not by how well you know grammar, spelling, and punctuation. Now, if your mechanics are so bad they cause your message to be unclear, then that's a big problem. But all that tells me is that you overlooked, at your own peril, steps 3 and 4 in the Plan Then Write process.

When it comes to the writing and rewriting stage, the most important tool you have at your disposal is your writer's intuition, the main topic of this chapter.

Using Your Writer's Intuition

The hunter ran out of the tent and shot the elephant in his pajamas.

Anyone educated in America after 1960 has probably read this sentence in an English class textbook or on a classroom chalkboard. It's a classic example of how not to write a sentence.

What's wrong with it? The answer is obvious: Elephants don't wear pajamas. The sentence doesn't make logical sense and must be rewritten so the phrase "in his pajamas" describes the hunter.

How did you know what was wrong and how did you know how to fix it? You used your writer's intuition. The textbook explanation of the problem is that "in his pajamas" is a dangling modifier that "violates the fundamental grammatical principle that adjectives or words that function like adjectives should modify specific nominals."[1]

Such academic explanations only reinforce the false impression we get in school that if only we were master grammarians, expert spellers, and wizards at punctuation we would be better writers. That's not true. In the first place, there is much writing in the business world that is error-free but makes no logical sense. Second, and most important of all, you don't need to understand dangling modifiers, coordinate conjunctions, and indefinite pronouns to recognize bad writing and fix it.

> **"Following the rules doesn't guarantee success. One of the best reporters at *USA Today*, a terrific writer, will write sentences that don't have a subject or a predicate. His writing is very conversational. He'll write the way he speaks. One of the reasons he's so good is that he's developed a style that's not shackled to the rules that we grew up with. His style communicates extremely well. The point or argument he's trying to make is never in doubt, it's always clear to the reader. Grammar, punctuation, and spelling do aid effective communication, but keep in mind the ultimate goal is to clearly communicate a thought, an idea— not to write an article or letter that has zero errors."**
>
> Greg Farrell, journalist,
> *USA Today*
> (from his interview in Part II)

Writer's Intuition Defined

Your writer's intuition will help you identify and fix bad writing. Writer's intuition is an instinct for what is correct or "works" in every assignment. We all have a writer's intuition. It consists of our innate logic, common sense, and everything we've internalized about writing and reading after doing both—almost daily—since the age of five.

Writer's intuition is the most important concept in this book. It's the missing link in writing instruction, the secret knowledge that students think instructors are holding back: "In my last paper you told me not to write this way, now you say it's okay. Why won't you tell me how to write correctly all the time?"

The simple answer is that there is no single rule or group of rules that, once memorized, will tell you what is correct in each situation. As pointed out in Chapter 2, writing is a problem-solving activity and must be approached by trial and error using your instincts—your writer's intuition—as a guide. Writer's intuition is your most powerful problem-solving weapon. It's the one tool experienced and professional writers use to get them through the toughest parts of each writing project.

Dialing in Your Instincts

I knew a manager at a large credit card company who had a problem with a group of employees using the office phone for personal calls. He sent memos around, held meetings every few weeks, made surprise visits—yet nothing worked for more than a few days at a time. Finally, he put the worst offender in charge of the phone. The problem cleared up overnight. The worst offender not only stopped making personal calls, but stared down anyone who as much as looked as if he were going to make a personal call.

The manager followed his "manager's intuition" and finally, after many failed attempts, hit on the right solution. But that doesn't mean the next time a similar situation arises, it can be solved the same way. Next time, the worst offender might take advantage of being in charge. There's no way of knowing until you try.

The same trial-and-error process applies to writing. You must try several solutions—that is, rethink and rewrite words, sentences, and whole portions of your drafts—until you hit on a revision that solves the problem. Let's look at an example. Here's a paragraph from a letter written by a psychologist to a manager at a large corporation. The psychologist wants to persuade the manager to hire him to reduce stress in the manager's department:

Typically, approaches to dealing with stress in the workplace often focus only on identifying symptoms and their relief. This is not good. Stress is usually thought of as "bad" and to be ameliorated. Experts most often use corrective action and mediation to point out hidden symptoms and "remove" the stress. Effectively understanding the nature of stress requires an analysis of root causes. This can sometimes be difficult. The experts can then take multiple actions once a true picture of the stress is established. One action is to show how stress can be beneficial. Other actions are possible.

This paragraph needs serious editing. It rambles and forces the reader to work hard to decipher its meaning. I'll use my writer's intuition to show you how I would rewrite it. Keep in mind, however, that there are many correct ways to revise this paragraph. My revision is simply one of many. I could ask ten experienced writers to revise the passage and they would use their writer's intuitions to write ten excellent but different paragraphs. Before walking you through my revision, however, I want to discuss a few important points about rules and how to apply them when revising drafts.

Rules of Thumb and Writer's Intuition

I defined rules of thumb in Chapter 2; now it's time to connect the concept to writer's intuition. I'll use an example. "Neither a borrower nor a lender be." This advice by Polonius to his son, Laertes, in the play *Hamlet* is presented as a command, something his son should never do. But it's clearly a rule of thumb, not an unbreakable law. No one can go through life without borrowing or lending money—a quarter for a parking meter, a few dollars for lunch, thousands for a car, etc.

Polonius knows this. He's simply stating his advice as an inflexible rule to impress upon his son the importance of hanging on to his money. All the old man can do is hope that Laertes will use his good judgment (read intuition) to determine when he should borrow or lend, and do so wisely.

Writing style rules, like Polonius's advice, are presented in schools and in writing guides as commandments set in stone, when they should be presented as flexible guidelines that are applied using your writer's intuition. This is the secret knowledge experienced writers discover on their own by writing and reading a lot. Going back to Michael Rose's study, this is what his experienced writers think about rules.

[T]hey] do express some rules with firm assurance, but these tend to be simple injunctions that free up rather than restrict the composing process, e.g., "When stuck, write!" or "I'll write what I can." And finally, at least three of the students openly shun the very textbook rules that some blockers adhere to: e.g., "Rules like 'write only what you know about' just aren't true. I ignore those." These three [students], in effect, have formulated a further rule that expresses something like: "If a rule conflicts with what is sensible or with experience, reject it."[2]

How to Apply the Rules

All stylistic writing rules—and some mechanical rules—require the application of your writer's intuition. Take the "delete unnecessary words" rule. How do you determine which words are necessary and which are not? By using your writer's intuition. No writing guide can help you because the answer changes from one situation to the next. While stylistic rules describe what your final draft should look like, they don't tell you how to get there, which is why learning the correct writing process is so important.

Here's another common writing rule: Use simple language. That's good advice, but how do you define simple language? Again, no writing guide has a single, definitive answer to this question. For starters, the definition of "simple language" changes depending on the education level of your audience. Every time you edit a draft, you have to decide what you think is overly complex or sophisticated language. The huge gap between memorizing a rule and actually applying it is one root cause of frustration, panic, and fear of writing among writers.

The Chicken or the Rule?

Which came first, writing or writing rules? Unlike the chicken and egg riddle, the answer to this question is obvious: Writing came first. Aeons ago, someone with the intelligence of an Aristotle or a Leonardo da Vinci did not sit down and create dozens of writing rules and then invent the art of writing. The reverse happened. The first writers taught themselves to write, and when it became important to teach the craft to others, someone sat down and reverse engineered rules from documents that were generally accepted as being well written: Most well-

> "When I write, I focus on what I want to say, not rules. A big part of my writing process is that I live with a project for a while. Often, ideas for starting an article come to me when I'm falling asleep or just waking up in the morning, when I'm totally away from my notes, which I have all over the place. I simply sit down and write, not from memory, but after having thought about my topic for a long time. I sit down and write what I know. If I come to a part I don't know or haven't thought about much, I'll leave a place marker. . . . I don't want anything to interrupt the flow of writing down what I do know about my subject. I don't stop to capitalize words or fix other errors. I write what I want to say and then I go back and fill in the details later. I don't want to slow down or stop my thought process in any way while writing a first draft."
>
> Humberto Cruz, syndicated financial columnist,
> Tribune Media Services
> (from his interview in Part II)

written documents omit needless words, use active not passive voice, avoid long sentences, etc. I've just listed a few "modern" rules of writing, the ones that have evolved over time to describe what we consider good writing today. I say "today" because writing styles and rules change over time. For a look at what was once considered the epitome of good writing, read the opening to James Boswell's book, *The Life of Samuel Johnson,* written in 1791.

To write the Life of him who excelled all mankind in writing the lives of others, and who, whether we consider his extraordinary endowments, or his various works, has been equaled by few in any age, is an arduous, and may be reckoned in me a presumptuous task. Had Dr. Johnson written his own Life, in conformity with the opinion which he has given, that every man's life may be best written by himself; had he employed in the preservation of his own history, that clearness of narration and elegance of language in which he has embalmed so many eminent persons, the world would probably have had the most perfect example of biography that was ever exhibited.[3]

Today, this paragraph would be criticized as wordy, unclear, and a good example of convoluted thinking.

eBay or EBay?

Even mechanical rules are open to interpretation. Take the rule that every sentence must begin with a capital letter. What situation could possibly arise that would cause a writer to break this rule? Here's one: When writing an article about the online auction Web site eBay, and the company name starts off the sentence, do you write eBay or EBay? EBay looks unnatural and awkward. It draws attention to itself. eBay looks normal and natural, even at the beginning of a sentence. I would leave the *e* lower case. My writer's intuition tells me it's more appropriate to write the name of the company the way the company trademarked it.

And what about the comma? People have the impression it's governed by a strict set of laws, and even *The Chicago Manual of Style* lists forty-two rules on comma usage, but here's how that same text introduces its section on the comma.

The comma, perhaps the most versatile of the punctuation marks, indicates the smallest interruption in continuity of thought or sentence structure. There are a few rules governing its use that have become almost obligatory. Aside from these, the use of the comma is mainly a matter of good judgment, with ease of reading the end in view.[4]

Comma rules are "almost obligatory" and comma placement is "mainly a matter of good judgment" or intuition. In other words, you can actively engage your writer's intuition and let the rule of thumb "ease of reading" be your guide when sticking commas in a sentence.

The next time you run into a problem while writing and aren't sure which writing rules apply, don't freeze up or curse your English teacher for not forcing you to memorize the hundreds of writing rules in *The Chicago Manual of Style*. Stop and use your writer's intuition to solve the problem: make a choice and continue writing.

Rewriting

Here are four rules of thumb I follow every time I write, and the ones I'll apply most when revising the aforementioned "stress in the workplace" letter written by the psychologist. These aren't the only four rules I use, but they are the ones that come into play most often.

1. ***Delete unnecessary words.*** Spending ten minutes revising a paragraph only to delete one word, even if it's just the word *a*, is a worthwhile effort because the fewer words in a sentence, the easier it is for your readers to read.

2. ***Listen to the way words, phrases, and sentences sound; it's important.*** Experienced writers break rules to make their sentences "sound right."

3. ***Rethink the wording and structure of sentences.*** Sometimes deleting words isn't enough. You have to find a different way to say what you mean.

4. ***Use SAP as a sounding board for every word you write.*** An unnecessary word, for instance, is one that does not in some way support the subject or purpose of the piece you're writing or make sense to your audience. (See Chapter 4.)

It's only in retrospect that I know I apply these four rules of thumb while writing. I made this list after sitting down and analyzing my writing process. Rules never play a conscious role. I only focus on what I'm trying to say. When reading a sentence I may tell myself, "That's not clear. Rethink that phrase. That's not what I mean. How can I say that better? My readers won't understand that."

Now I'll use these four rules of thumb and my writer's intuition to solve the writing problems in the psychologist's letter, which for convenience I'll repeat here.

Typically, approaches to dealing with stress in the workplace often focus only on identifying symptoms and their relief. This is not good. Stress is usually thought of as "bad" and to be ameliorated. Experts most often use corrective action and mediation to point out hidden symptoms and "remove" the stress. Effectively understanding the nature of stress requires an analysis of root causes. This can sometimes be difficult. The experts can then take multiple actions once a true picture of the stress is established. One action is to show how stress can be beneficial. Other actions are possible.

The subject of the letter is stress in the workplace. The purpose is to convince the manager to hire the psychologist to lower stress. To see if this passage supports the subject and purpose, I ask, "What's the main thought in the paragraph?" The answer: Stress is bad and must be reduced. An unfinished idea at the end alludes to the fact that some stress is good. So the paragraph passes the subject and purpose test.

The psychologist is taking an effective approach in his letter. When trying to convince someone to hire you, it's best to remind him of the problem and state the solution you can provide. However, this paragraph does not state the consultant's ideas clearly and concisely. To solve this problem, I'm going to use SAP—subject, audience, and purpose—as a guide and cross out all the unnecessary words that don't support the purpose.

Faster Than It Looks

First a warning: Over the next few pages, I explain every facet of the reasoning behind each edit I make. While it's helpful to see how I exercise my writer's intuition, there is a risk that the detailed explanations will make the revision process seem long and difficult. The actual revisions only took a few minutes. It's like writing out the process of blowing a bubble. You can blow the bubble in one one-hundredth the time it takes to read the description. Here goes:

Typically, approaches to dealing with stress in the workplace often focus only on identifying symptoms and their relief. ~~This is not good.~~ [THIS POINT IS OBVIOUS TO THE READER] ~~Stress is usually thought of as "bad" and to be ameliorated.~~ [AGAIN, OBVIOUS TO THE READER] Experts most often use corrective action and mediation to "remove" the stress. ~~Effectively understanding the nature of stress requires an analysis of root causes.~~ [INFORMATIVE, BUT DOES NOTHING TO PERSUADE OR ADVANCE

THE WRITER'S PURPOSE] ~~This can sometimes be difficult.~~ [OBVIOUS STATEMENT, DOESN'T PERSUADE] The experts can then take multiple actions once a true picture of the stress is established. One action is to show how stress can be beneficial. ~~Other actions are possible.~~ [OBVIOUS STATEMENT, DOESN'T PERSUADE]

Here's what's left:

Typically, approaches to dealing with stress in the workplace often focus only on identifying symptoms and their relief. Experts most often use corrective action and mediation to point out hidden symptoms and "remove" the stress. The experts can then take multiple actions once a true picture of the stress is established. One action is to show how stress can be beneficial.

This is better, and I haven't done any serious revising yet. I simply deleted words that I thought, using my writer's intuition, were unnecessary. But this paragraph can be whittled down even more. Let's look at the first sentence.

Typically, approaches to dealing with stress in the workplace often focus only on identifying symptoms and their relief.

Who typically deals with stress in the workplace? Managers. I'll make that the subject of the sentence.

Managers typically deal with workplace stress by identifying and removing the symptoms.

Replacing the word *approaches* with *managers* allows me to make a human being the subject, which is more interesting and concrete than the wispy, abstract noun that you can't visualize. As you can see, I also made a few other edits to this sentence. Changing the subject lets me turn the word *dealing* into the verb *deal;* simply cutting off the *-ing* gives the sentence more snap and makes it easier to read.

I also changed the phrase *stress in the workplace* to *workplace stress,* because that eliminates two words, and I think the shorter phrase sounds better. (As a side note, I've often done the opposite: change a phrase like *business principles* to *principles of business* because I thought the sentence needed the extra beat provided by the word *of* to make it flow more smoothly and sound better.)

I shortened the rest of the sentence. So, *often focus only on identifying symptoms and their relief* becomes *by identifying and removing the symptoms.* The words *often focus only on* are unnecessary. Deleting them does not change the meaning of the statement. And the phrase *identifying symptoms and their relief* is an awkward, shorthand way of saying *identifying symptoms and identifying their relief.* This last phrase, *identifying their relief,* is a roundabout way of saying *removing the symptoms.* The revision, *identifying and removing the symptoms,* is more concise, clear, and easy to read.

Finally, I've reduced the last three sentences in the paragraph from:

> Experts most often use corrective action and mediation to point out hidden symptoms and "remove" the stress. The experts can then take multiple actions once a true picture of the stress is established. One action is to show how stress can be beneficial.

to:

> However, experts can point out deeper, often-overlooked symptoms and even show how stress can be a productive tool.

Here's my reasoning. The terms *corrective action* and *mediation* are "consultant speak." We lose nothing by deleting them and gain a lot by improving readability, which is also true about deleting the three words *most often use.*

When Brevity Is Not a Virtue

Next, I replaced the single word *hidden* with the words *deeper, often-overlooked*. This appears to break my rule of thumb, but 1) rules of thumb can be broken, and 2) the rule of thumb is not "delete words" but "delete unnecessary words." Brevity in and of itself is not a virtue when it comes to writing. The goal is to delete words that do not support your subject or purpose or make sense to your audience. Sometimes, a twenty-page brochure is the most concise way to communicate what you have to say.

Also, my writer's intuition told me to replace one word, *hidden,* with three words, *deeper, often-overlooked,* because this phrase highlights a talent the psychologist has that the manager does not—an ability to ferret out deep symptoms that cause stress, which is a big reason to hire the psychologist, which is the purpose of the letter.

I threw out the second sentence, *The experts can then take multiple actions once a true picture of the stress is established,* because it seems obvious that experts would take some type of action once they found the cause of the stress. However, I can see how another writer would find this information important and include it in his final draft. It wouldn't be wrong to leave it in, just as it's not wrong for me to take it out. We would each follow our writer's intuition and come up with different but equally correct results.

Using Audience as a Sounding Board

Finally, I looked at the main idea in the last sentence, *to show how stress can be beneficial,* and tried to think of a more specific term to replace the word *beneficial.* I wanted something the reader could relate to immediately because my writer's intuition told me it would be more persuasive and convincing. Managers are always looking for ways to improve productivity; it's a very positive word. Hence, I chose the term *productive tool.* The result:

> Managers typically deal with workplace stress by identifying and removing the symptoms. However, experts can point out deeper, often-overlooked symptoms and even show how stress can be a productive tool.

We started with a nine-sentence, ninety-seven-word paragraph and ended with a two-sentence, thirty-word paragraph. I cut more than two-thirds of the text. But the main point is not simply to cut words, but to make the thinking clearer by making the writing clearer.

The two sentences form a nice one-two punch. The first punch reminds the manager about the problem, workplace stress, and his typical solution to it: identify and remove the symptoms. The second punch drives home the main purpose of the letter: that experts can find problems managers might overlook. The implied message here, of course, is, "Hire me to do this!" The second sentence also ends with a surprise hook: The consultant can show the manager how something he'd always considered bad, stress, can actually be turned into something good. It's like fighting fire with fire. If I'm the manager, I finish reading the paragraph thinking this consultant has something new to tell me and at the very least merits an interview.

Confidence Is Half the Battle

Actually, it's more than half the battle; in some cases, it's the entire war. If you don't think you can do something well, you will struggle with it forever. Many businesspeople I meet are better writers than they think they are. Their biggest obstacle to writing with ease and fluency is themselves, or as a famous line from a Pogo cartoon puts it, "We have met the enemy and he is us."[5] A businessperson in the financial industry once asked me to evaluate his writing skills to see if he needed to enroll in a writing course. After analyzing many samples of his on-the-job writing assignments, I told him he was an excellent writer. The first thing he said was, "I thought so. I just wanted to make sure."

Confidence—knowing how to do something and knowing you do it well—puts you in control and eliminates fear. In this case, the fear of writing. In his article, "Can Professors Influence the Writing Confidence of College Students?" Dr. Gio Valiante explains a study he conducted that found a direct correlation between writing ability and confidence. He opens his article with a statement about the role confidence plays in students' lives.

> Students' beliefs about their capabilities to successfully perform academic tasks . . . powerfully influence how they perform in academic endeavors. Because people behave in accordance with what they

believe, rather than in accordance with their actual capabilities, it is individual beliefs about their capabilities, rather than their actual capabilities, that accurately predict performance attainments. . . . [Lack of confidence explains] why capable students often perform at levels below their capabilities. Without believing they are capable of influencing outcomes that affect their lives, individuals have little incentive to act [or write!].[6]

How to Boost Your Writing Confidence

But there is hope. Valiante lists several ways that, according to social cognitive theory, people attain confidence. I'll paraphrase three of them that pertain specifically to writing.

1. **Past Experience.** When people try something, they learn from the experience even if it isn't a success. They know what to expect and gain confidence from that hands-on knowledge.
2. **Vicarious Experience.** Watching others perform a skill also builds confidence. We've all seen someone perform a task we've never tried and said, "I can do that!"
3. **Encouragement.** Praise for a job well done, or just for trying, builds confidence.[7]

Even though we have all been writing for years, the "past experience" solution doesn't apply to those of us who, like the finance person in my previous example, are not sure if we have been writing "correctly" all those years. Most inexperienced writers think that writing is a neat, simple, linear process because that's what the end product—an article in *The Wall Street Journal,* a book on leadership, an annual report—written by a professional writer looks like. Inexperienced writers think published writers do not struggle with the writing process; therefore, because they do struggle, novice writers assume they are doing something wrong.

The author interviews in Part II—in which, among other things, each author talks about how hard it is to write—will help businesspeople confirm that struggling while writing is part of the normal process; the interviews will validate their past writing experiences and help build their confidence. The interviews also double as vicarious experiences, the second way to increase writing confidence, because interviews are the closest most of us will get to actually looking over the shoulder of an author while she works on the draft of her next article or book.

When you read the interviews in Part II, one common attribute that comes across is the authors' confidence in their abilities. They know the writing game inside and out. They aren't afraid to buck the establishment, break rules, and do what they think is right regardless of what others, even supposed writing experts, think. That's confidence.

A Kind Word Makes a Big Difference

Managers, supervisors, and bosses of all stripes can improve the writing confidence and productivity of their entire team by tossing out a few sincere compliments from time to time at meetings, when walking past an employee's cubicle, or sharing a shuttle to a rental car agency: "I'm nominating your white paper for a Pulitzer. Excellent writing!" "Great letter, Chris! Wish I had written it." "I'm saving your memo as an example, to show new employees how to do it right. Super job, Jeanne."

Too often, people in supervisory positions do not realize the huge impact a hale and hearty "job well done!" can have on employee morale and writing productivity. For whatever reason, they find it hard to dish out compliments. If nothing else, they should consider the business benefits, in time and money saved, that a few kind words can have. It's not uncommon to hear stories about how one or two poor writers cause an entire group to miss deadlines and force their boss to work late rewriting their reports. A well-placed compliment praising even a single paragraph that is well written may not be the only fix needed in these cases, but it is an inexpensive one that can only help.

Also, keep in mind that e-mails, letters, and memos don't have to be perfect specimens to warrant a compliment. Review the writing standards in Chapter 1. Any project that falls between the excellent and borderline business writing standards deserves praise, and don't devalue the compliment by following it with a comment like, "But you do need to get help with that run-on sentence problem you have." Save any criticism for later if the problem doesn't take care of itself. Also, look for anything—a well-turned phrase or excellent word choice—in bad and bottom-line bad writing. When your eight-year-old scores one out of five goal attempts at her soccer game, you don't dwell on the four missed goals; you boost her confidence by praising the one.

Writer's Intuition, Confidence, and Problem Solving

Writing confidence is an extremely important part of the writing process and key to becoming an experienced writer. Think back to the first few weeks on a new job when you didn't know where to get office supplies, how to work the copier, or what you should or shouldn't say in a meeting—that is, you didn't know the process to follow at work. You were tentative, lacked confidence, and it showed. The same applies to writing. Once you understand and become comfortable with the process, writing will be easier (not necessarily easy, but easier) and less frustrating, and your memos and reports will be more clear and concise.

Confidence and writer's intuition support and nurture each other. Confident writers have well-developed intuitions that help speed the problem-solving aspect of writing and also help make the solutions more effective. These elements work in unison and create a whole that's bigger than the individual parts. Armed with the correct process and your writer's intuition, you will have the confidence and power to solve all writing problems on your own and become an excellent writer.

One More Example

This sentence appears in the introduction to a book:

> Fresh examples have been added to some of the rules and principles, amplification has reared its head in a few places in the text where I felt an assault could successfully be made on the bastions of its brevity, and in general the book has received a thorough overhaul—to correct errors, delete bewhiskered entries, and enliven the argument.[8]

I'll use one of the best-selling writing guides ever written, *The Elements of Style* by William Strunk, Jr., and E. B. White, to critique this sentence. For starters, it's extremely long: fifty-nine words. In addition, the sentence breaks several key rules found in Strunk and White:

❑ **Use the active voice.** Passive voice appears three times in the sentence (. . . examples have been added . . . , . . . an assault could successfully be made . . . , . . . the book has received a thorough overhaul . . .).

- ❑ **Omit needless words.** A case could be made that the words "successfully," "the bastions of," and "in general" are unnecessary.
- ❑ **Do not overwrite.** It could also be argued that the entire sentence, being fifty-nine words long, is overwritten.
- ❑ **Avoid fancy words.** "Reared its head," "bastions of brevity," and "bewhiskered" fall into this category.

The Kicker

The fifty-nine-word sentence I just critiqued was written by E. B. White and appears in his introduction to the third edition of *The Elements of Style.* How do you reconcile the fact that White, one of the finest essayists and storytellers of the twentieth century, broke several major rules that appear in his own guide?

Like all experienced, professional writers, he views rules as flexible guidelines. He doesn't stop to count the number of words in his sentences, or worry about active vs. passive voice, or sweat any other rules. This is not to say White adopted an "anything goes" style. What he did was rely on his writer's intuition to lead him down the path to clear and concise writing.

Reread White's long sentence. While his tone is playfully pompous, that's his style here—the sentence is eminently readable and clear. He made his point with panache, even though he broke some of the rules in his own writing guide along the way.

You're Hired for Your Ideas

Don't lose sight of the fact that writing is a means to an end. Your company hired you, above all, for your excellent ideas, and there are two ways you can convey the thoughts in your head to a fellow human being: writing or speaking. We also communicate through paintings, sculptures, songs, and other media. For example, when Michelangelo wanted to express his idea of the perfect male form, he chose to chip David out of a rock instead of writing a poem or going from corner to corner giving a speech about male anatomy. But in the business world, writing and speaking are king.

No Magic Potion

Writer's intuition is not infallible. Experienced writers make wrong decisions all the time. Usually, they'll catch and correct the problem in

> **"An amazing thing happens as you mature as a business writer, as you progress and get better and better. We all start out writing on a basic or tactical level: pumping out e-mails and reports and speeches and articles. Then slowly and naturally you ratchet up your writing, which ratchets up your thinking. You start to think at a higher level about strategy: What are the key messages my company must convey to the outside world? Now writing has taken you from the content-creator level to the strategic-thinker level. That's how writing kicks you up the corporate ladder."**
>
> Nick Balamaci, director of internal
> communications, Citigroup
> (from his interview in Part III)

the revision stage, or an editor or proofreader will spot the mistake. But not always. Here's a story E. B. White tells about his mentor and coauthor of *The Elements of Style*, William Strunk, Jr. It illustrates how an experienced professional writer can be led astray by his writer's intuition.

[S]trunk] had a number of likes and dislikes that were almost as whimsical as the choice of a necktie, yet he made them seem utterly convincing. . . . He despised the expression *student body* . . . and made a special trip downtown to the *Alumni News* office one day to protest the expression and suggest that *studentry* be substituted. . . . It's not much of an improvement, but it does sound less cadaverous, and it made Will Strunk quite happy.[9]

You won't find *studentry* in the dictionary. It never caught on. But it's a good example of Strunk's writer's intuition at work. He confronted what he considered a writing problem and, following his instincts, created a solution—he coined his own word, *studentry*. In this case, his solution fizzled, but the lesson here is to keep using, trusting, and developing your writer's intuition. The stronger it becomes, the better your writing will be.

Writer's Intuition Will Improve Your Mental Health

Learning to recognize and use your writer's intuition will save your sanity and make all of your on-the-job writing assignments easier by freeing you from the paralyzing concept that you must write according to an endless list of rules that you can never hope to memorize and learn how to apply. Writer's intuition gives you the power to solve your own writing problems and helps you to write smarter and faster. That's a lifesaver for any businessperson, because the vast majority of business writing takes place in isolation, under duress, and with impossible deadlines. When you're tired, alone, and struggling to knock out a letter to a client at eight o'clock at night, your writer's intuition is all you have to rely on. Fortunately, it's more than up to the challenge.

THE SCIENCE OF WRITING

When and How to Apply Writing Rules

When you finally arrive at steps 3 and 4 in the Plan Then Write process—Edit 1 and Edit 2—you can breathe a sigh of relief. The worst is over. The problem solving and struggle with putting your thoughts on paper are finished. All that's left is cleaning up any mechanical problems in your final draft. You can take off your thinking cap to do that, because the answers to those problems are waiting for you in a book.

Run Iliphant Run!

The hunter run out of, the tent and shot the iliphant in his pajamas.

What's wrong with this sentence and how do you fix it? As pointed out in Chapter 5, your writer's intuition spotted the main problem. The message is confusing and reflects muddy thinking: elephants don't wear pajamas. The sentence must be rewritten so the phrase *in his pajamas* describes the hunter. You have to rely on your writer's intuition to make the correction because no writing guide can tell you exactly how to fix it. As with most style problems, there are many ways to revise the sentence, and each one is correct.

For example:

The hunter, in his pajamas, ran out of the tent and shot the elephant.
Wearing only pajamas, the hunter ran out of the tent and shot the elephant.

The elephant was shot by a hunter wearing pajamas.
The hunter ran out of the tent in his pajamas. He then
shot the elephant.

What about the mechanical problems? There's a grammar error (*run* is the wrong verb tense), a punctuation problem (the comma, which makes the reader pause in an unusual place and therefore causes momentary confusion, is not even necessary), and a spelling mistake (iliphant). Unlike the message problem, you can open a grammar book, punctuation guide, and dictionary to find the one, and only one, correct solution to these three mechanical errors.

Mechanical problems rarely involve choices. Message problems always involve choices. In the third century B.C., Aristotle made a distinction between the sciences (physics and mathematics) and the arts (pottery and poetics). His approach, explained by Edward P. J. Corbett in the introduction to *The Rhetoric and the Poetics of Aristotle,* gets at the heart of the distinction I make between the art and science of writing.

The sciences dealt with the necessary, with the invariable, with what had to be; the arts dealt with the contingent, with the probable, with those areas where there were choices to be made.[1]

Writer's intuition (like a poet's intuition or a sculptor's intuition) helps you make the many decisions you face when writing business correspondence. The choices are rarely black and white as they are in the world of science.

Step 2 of the Plan Then Write process—write and rewrite—is where you should catch and correct any problems with the message. If by chance you find and fix mechanical mistakes during step 2, that's a nice bonus. But don't waste your time, energy, or—most important of all—your mental focus on the mechanics until you have a final draft in hand.

Edit 1 and Edit 2

The last two steps in the Plan Then Write process (see Figure 6-1) are important, but they are second in importance to step 2, where you actually create your message. The quotation from William Oliver on the facing page points out why this is true.

Figure 6-1. Steps 3 and 4. Edit 1 and 2.

PLAN THEN WRITE

1. Plan

2. Write and Rewrite

| **3. Edit 1** |
| **4. Edit 2** |

Error-Free Writing Is Not the Goal

Results, not zero mechanical errors, are the primary goal of every business writer. No one is going to congratulate you for writing a clear, concise, and flawless memo about an inane idea. Perfect, error-free writing is a nice idea to keep in the back of your mind, but that's not why you were hired (unless you're a professional proofreader). Your company will reward you for making excellent decisions, developing innovative products and services, solving customer problems, and attracting new clients. All of these achievements require you to think clearly then translate your thoughts and ideas onto paper so they can be distributed and shared with others. If you can do that, you will be rewarded and promoted—whether you know how to spell or not. Again, that's not to say that grammar, spelling, and punctuation don't matter. They play an important role in the writing process, just not the lead role.

To recap what I've explained about the science of writing in Chapter 2, mechanics for the most part are a matter of memorization, while the art or message of writing is a matter of judgment and instinct.

> "Ultimately, the final proof of writing quality is its effect. Was the message clearly received by its intended target audience? That performance standard is the same whether we're talking about a memorandum sent to 130,000 employees or a page from the annual report sent to our 3 million shareholders. We do periodic research to determine how well the messages we're sending out are being received and understood by individuals. So the test of good writing is the results it gets."
>
> William Oliver, vice president of
> public relations, AT&T Corp.
> (from his interview in Part III)

Communication takes place on the art side; cleaning up the form of that communication takes place on the science side. If you spend enough time memorizing the rules regulating grammar, spelling, and punctuation, you will excel at proofreading. But becoming an excellent proofreader does not automatically make you an excellent writer. There are plenty of examples of incomprehensible, error-free writing floating around cyberspace and office mailrooms.

Once you have a draft with a clearly written message in hand, it's time to proof it for mechanics. Remember the 3P Principle: private, public, promotional. If your message is a memo to colleagues and you know you're a good proofreader, edit the memo to the best of your ability before sending it. If you know you have weak proofreading skills, give the memo to someone who is a good proofreader, and follow the tips later in this chapter that will help you improve your editing skills.

A letter signed by your CEO and your résumé are two examples of public and promotional documents that should be checked by a professional proofreader. Typos and poor writing on a résumé are two criteria many executives use to immediately disqualify candidates. And if customers catch a typo in a letter from the CEO, your company will lose at least some credibility in their eyes. It's up to you to take the appropriate editing steps, based on whom your audience is, to make sure you always look good on paper.

Edit 1 Made Easy

Once you've completed steps 1 and 2 of the Plan Then Write method and you've said everything you want to say as clearly and succinctly as possible, it's time to proofread your final draft. Here is a new proofreading technique based on the art vs. science concept. This process breaks down all writing problems into just two types, simplifying the proofreading process and improving your chances of catching and correcting writing errors.

The Art/Science Editing Process

When you run across a writing problem in your own draft or someone else's ask yourself:

1. Is it an art problem or a science problem?
2. If it's an art problem—confusing logic, writer-based prose, rambling sentences, etc.—use your writer's intuition to solve it.

3. If it's a science problem—grammar, spelling, or punctuation—look up the answer in the appropriate reference book or ask an experienced proofreader for help.

If It's an Art Problem . . .

Print out and proofread the draft just for art errors. Use a pen to circle any issues with clarity and logic. Is the argument coherent? Are there any words the audience may not understand? Is the call to action ambiguous? Which phrases, sentences, or paragraphs do not make sense? Check for all the points associated with steps 1 and 2 of the Plan Then Write method. Use your writer's intuition to help you fix mistakes. For instance, if you find a sentence fragment, don't automatically rewrite it as a full sentence. Ask yourself, does the fragment "work"? Does it make the piece more readable and clear? If so, keep it.

When proofing something you've written, perform this art edit at the end of step 2: write and rewrite. Make it the final stage of your rewriting process. However, if you have time, feel free to perform this procedure even after you've proofed for mechanics. Many professional writers tweak their message up to the moment their publishers pry the draft from their hands for printing.

If It's a Science Problem . . .

Once you've fixed the art problems, print a new version of the draft and read it for mechanical errors. Underline grammar, spelling, and punctuation errors, then look up the correct answers in a reference guide.

You can do the art and the science edits on the same printed pages, but reprinting the document after the art edit works best because it lets you focus on one type of problem at a time. Also, by reprinting the document, the written comments you make when doing the art edit won't cover up or distract you from looking for mechanical errors.

The following tips and suggestions will help make the Edit 1 step easier to perform.

Art Proofreading Tips

1. Read your draft out loud. You'll be surprised at the number of errors you catch this way. If you stumble through a phrase or sentence, rewrite it so it reads smoothly. If you don't understand something you wrote, neither will your audience—rewrite it.

2. If time permits, set the document aside for a few hours or days and then proofread it again with a fresh set of eyes.

> **"If you use terrible grammar, people will think you're uneducated, but grammar is not a law. Grammar is an evolved tradition and you can deal with it as you want to deal with it. Some rules of grammar are better founded in reason than others. I think it's useful when subjects and verbs agree, but I don't think rules like 'never end a sentence with a preposition' are terribly useful. It's rare that I catch a grammar error that I didn't intend to make. Usually I don't care all that much about grammar, and if I break the rules it's because it made it easier for me to say the things I wanted to say."**
>
> Michael Lewis, author of
> *The New New Thing*
> (from his interview in Part II)

Science Proofreading Tips

1. *Use your computer's spelling and grammar checkers.* While this seems an obvious first step, I'm surprised at how often I hear the excuse, "Yes, but if I meant to write *their* but typed *there* instead, the computer won't catch the error, so I don't bother to spell check at all." That's the wrong attitude because the computer will tell you when you typed *kan* instead of *can* and *cleint* instead of *client.* Your readers are likely to miss a *their* instead of *there* mistake, or if they do catch it they'll instantly recognize it as a typo and forgive you. But they won't forgive misspellings like *kan* or *cleint.* The mistake shows you didn't bother to do even a lightning-fast proof of your document, which gives the impression you don't care about them or how you look on paper. Computers aren't perfect, but they are your first line of defense when proofreading.

2. *Call the English department at a local college.* Tell the receptionist you have a writing question and ask to speak to a teacher. If one isn't available, ask the person to transfer you to the writing center. Most two- and four-year colleges have one.

3. *Call or e-mail a writing hotline.* Do an Internet search for "writing hotline" and you'll find services, many free, that will answer any question you have about writing.

4. *Read your document backward, from right to left, starting with the last word.* This way your mind is forced to consider every word individually and out of the normal flow or context in which it was written. "Can seen be" (instead of "can be seen") might slip by when you proofread normally—that is, the way you wrote it, left to right starting

with the first word. But the error will stand out like a sore thumb when you proofread backward.

Proofreader's Marks

When proofreading your own or another person's writing, you can save a lot of time by using the professional proofreader's shorthand to note corrections. Figure 6-2 is a list of proofreader's marks. Refer to the chart as often as you need to. You'll end up memorizing the most-used symbols, like the insert caret and delete marks, through constant use.

Figure 6-2. Proofreader's Marks.

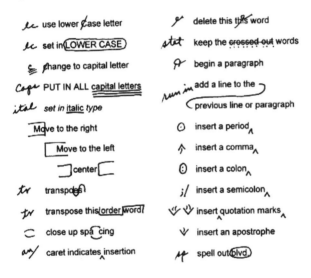

General Tips

1. ***Proofread for your known art and science problems.*** After writing in school and on the job for several years, you've received enough feedback to know some of the writing errors you consistently make. Starting now, keep a list of these mistakes in a little notebook or computer file labeled Edit 1 Notebook. For each project you write, proofread once specifically for these known problems. Chances are you will have caught these mistakes in the art/science editing process, but it's an excellent double-check.

2. ***Proofread your document several times.*** Perform the art/science editing process as often as time allows, preferably with a few hours break in between. Depending on the size of the document, don't expect to catch everything in one or even two proofreadings. If you only have

time to perform one proof, then that's the best you can do. But the more important the project, the more proofreading time you should build into your schedule.

3. **Focus on the art problems.** If you don't have time to let your draft sit for a few hours or to proofread it several times, do the best you can in the time allowed and spend most of your effort on the art problems. Your readers will overlook or not even notice a few minor mechanical problems, but problems with clarity, understanding, and logic could make your message unreadable.

4. **Constantly work to improve your proofreading skills.** This will take time, so don't plan on becoming an expert in a few weeks. The best first step in this learning process is to keep your Edit 1 Notebook up to date. Most writers make the same handful of mistakes over and over. By discovering and learning how to correct these errors, you will be well on your way to improving your writing and proofreading skills. Also, read *Time, The Wall Street Journal, Fortune, The New York Times,* and other well respected magazines and newspapers, with a pocket dictionary close by. As you read, circle any words you don't know. After reading the article, look up the definitions and write them down. By doing this, you will keep abreast of the latest business news and current events, improve your vocabulary, and develop a sense for good grammar and punctuation by reading well-written articles that have the same tone and style most good business correspondence should have.

If you slept through all of your English classes and know (or have been told by a friend or colleague) that your proofreading skills are extremely weak, you should take a refresher course in mechanics and then follow the other tips in this section to maintain and improve your skills.

5. **Seek out a professional proofreader who may be just down the hall.** Your marketing and public relations departments are staffed with excellent writers. If it's not feasible to send documents to those groups, do a little survey of your workplace and create a list of good proofreaders. The mailroom clerk may be working on a masters in journalism and the new sales rep might be publishing articles on the side.

Edit 2: Professional Proofreading

In the best of all possible business worlds, once you've proofread your own draft, you should pass it to a professional proofreader or equivalent, such as a colleague who is known for her attention to detail and proofreading skills. But more often than not, you won't have time to take this step or a professional proofreader will not be available. Again, keep the 3P Principle in mind. If it's for private eyes, and you did a good job on Edit 1, your draft will in all probability leave your desk in great shape even though you skipped Edit 2. However, if the document is for public or promotional use, you must find a professional to check it or accept the risk associated with bypassing this step. Companies spend hundreds and sometimes thousands of dollars to ensure that annual reports, letters to shareholders, press releases, company brochures, and other public and promotional documents are carefully scanned by at least one professional proofreader, often more. The stakes are just too high. Incoherent sentences and typos are a signal to shareholders that you do not pay attention to details and do not think they are important enough to take the time to create a well-written message. This spreads ill will, and the image of your company suffers.

> **"While I think that my grammar is mediocre and my spelling is terrible, I won't interview somebody who applies for a job with a typo on her résumé. You don't have to be an expert in the formal aspects of writing; there's no way to master it all. But you can find someone who is an expert. That shows me you pay attention to details. You don't have to be a good speller, but you should know where good spelling is available and make sure you get it."**
>
> Gail Evans, former executive vice president of
> Domestic Networks for the CNN Newsgroup and author of
> *Play Like a Man, Win Like a Woman*
> (from her interview in Part II)

You're Your Own Worst Proofreader, But You're All You've Got

This subhead needs a good edit. There are no mechanical errors, but the repetitive "you" forms—your, you're, you've—make it read a bit clunky, awkward, funny. However, I like the crudeness of the expression and the impression it leaves (that is, not editing this poorly written subhead underscores my point that we really are our own worst proofreaders), so for those reasons, I'm not going to change it. My writer's intuition tells me to leave it alone.

Let's take a look at another writing sample and apply the art/science proofreading technique. Here's the opening paragraph to a press release that describes a film company:

> The Workshop's programs include ten co-productions—overseeing and mentoring the re-creation of programs by television companies in countrys from Australia; and Bolivia to Hungary; and Tibet. The Intaglio Workshop often enters into legal and binding co-mutual partnerships of cooperation with co-production companies on the productions of sets design, editing and on location filming as it guide each localized version and other programs, designed to reflect local languages, customs and educational pre-requirements of local and national government laws. Co-productions required open communication to insure uniformity of the various Intaglio Workshop brands, for example, the Intaglio Workshop logo must appear the same when crossing international borders.

The Art Errors

On the art side, this paragraph needs a lot of work. Some of the problems are so bad that it's impossible to fix them without interviewing the author to find out what she was trying to say. For example, the opening sentence begins in midthought. Because the audience of a press release is an editor or reporter, you should include the who, what, when, where, why, and how of your story in the first paragraph so the reader can quickly determine if the release is newsworthy.

The writer also begins with a low level of detail—an explanation of programs the company makes—instead of opening with a broad, descriptive statement like: "Intaglio Workshop, a leading global video, television, and film production company headquartered in Paris, is one of the major developers of innovative foreign-language programs." In addition, the first sentence has a huge logic problem. People or companies can oversee and mentor, but a television program and co-productions cannot.

The second sentence is almost unreadable. It's fifty-one words long, but that's not the problem. The problem is that the business message gets lost in a tangle of unclear ideas. This is a good example of what the writer's thoughts looked like when they were flying through her head during the planning and first-draft phase, and an even better example of why writing is an integral part of the thinking process: The writer needs to write down these random, unformed thoughts (which she did), then write and rewrite them until they become clear on paper (which she did not do).

A first big step in rewriting sentence two is replacing the phrase "enters into legal and binding co-mutual partnerships of cooperation" with the single word "partners." In addition, my writer's intuition tells me to split the second sentence into two. I'd put a period after the word *filming* and rethink the rest of the sentence and rewrite it like this: "The company also oversees the production of local programming to make sure it conforms to local language, customs, and educational requirements."

The third sentence isn't as bad as the second, but it's still not very clear. One possible rewrite: "Because they carry the Intaglio Workshop brand, all co-productions must comply with the company's branding requirements. For example, the Intaglio Workshop logo must have the same look and feel in every country where the program is viewed."

No reference guide could have helped me make these corrections. I had to rely solely on my writer's intuition to solve these art-based writing problems. As a final reminder, as with most writer-based prose, the entire paragraph is a good first draft, a good brainstorming session, but before sending this press release over the wire, it must be completely revised.

The Mechanical Mistakes

Here's a list of eight science problems I found in the press release.

1. The dash in the first sentence is misused. It's meant to connect a more detailed explanation of co-productions, but what follows could refer to the phrase "Workshop's programs," too.
2. The word *countrys* should be spelled *countries*.
3. The semicolon is misused. No punctuation is needed in the phrase "from Australia and Bolivia to Hungary and Tibet."
4. The phrase "sets design" should be spelled "set designs."
5. "On location" works as a single adjective and should be hyphenated "on-location."
6. The word *guide* after the phrase "on location" is the wrong tense. It should be *guides*. You'll notice that this problem disappeared alto-

gether when I fixed the art problems and rewrote the sentence without using the word *guide.* This is another reason why the art and science proofreading processes should be kept separate.

7. The verb *required* in the last sentence is the wrong tense. It should be *require.*

8. The word *insure,* which means "to guarantee against loss or harm; to issue or procure an insurance policy," is the wrong word. It should be replaced with *ensure.*

If you only fixed the mechanical problems, the paragraph would still be incomprehensible, which is further proof of the importance and dominance of art over science—message over mechanics—in the writing process.

Art/Science and Writing Standards

Doing a good proofreading job in the Edit 1 and Edit 2 steps can sometimes improve your writing one standard or more, from bad to good or good to excellent. Figure 6-3 shows how the writing standards presented in Chapter 1 fit into the art vs. science concept. Documents that

Figure 6-3. Art/Science and Standards.

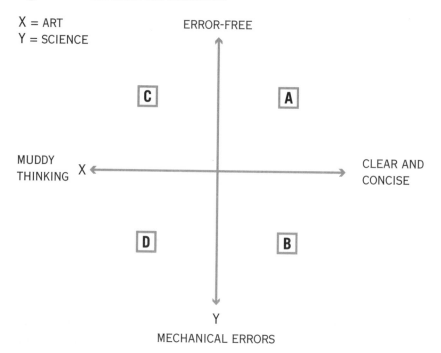

meet the excellent business writing standard fall in quadrant A. Bottom-line bad writing falls in quadrant D; good, borderline, and bad writing fall in quadrants B and C. The art/science proofreading process will help ensure your documents meet the excellent business writing standard so you always look your best on paper.

Organizing Edit 2 Teams

If your group or company does not have access to a professional proof-reader, do the next best thing and organize an in-house editing staff to perform an Edit 2 on all of your public and promotional documents, and private ones if time permits. Survey everyone, from the part-time office messenger to the full-time managing consultant, about his or her writing and proofreading abilities. Regardless of each person's level of expertise, put everyone on the Edit 2 team. List them in order of experience, with the best at the top of the list.

Everyone needs to help out because you can't count on the best proofreaders being available when you need an Edit 2, and any set of fresh eyes is better than none. Also, as noted in Chapter 5, proofreaders do not need to be experts in dangling modifiers to spot one. Teach everyone on the team the art/science editing process, and you will be prepared for any emergency.

CHAPTER 7

HOW TO WRITE ONE-PAGE MEMOS
AND ECONOMICAL E-MAILS

Memos and e-mails are two of the most-used and most-reliable workhorses in business communications. So it's little wonder that companies, government agencies, and organizations around the world promote the use of one-page memos and economical e-mails.

Efficient Thinking

Put yourself in the shoes of decision makers who receive hundreds of memos and e-mails each day. If every memo typically averages two pages, one-page memos would cut their memo-reading work in half. Efficient e-mails that are one to three sentences long instead of several paragraphs reduce their workload significantly more.

Best of all, businesspeople who write brief, content-rich memos and e-mails get noticed because these formats are a sign of well-organized, incisive thinking. Of even more importance is the fact that the skills you develop learning how to create these two concise forms of business correspondence carry over into all other forms, and help you to write clearly and concisely all the time.

When to Use a One-Page Memo

The one-page memo is not the correct format for all business messages. It is most effective when used for:

❑ Summaries
❑ Calls to action
❑ Brief messages
❑ Minutes of meetings
❑ Requests for information

Memos are typically used for internal communications, but there are exceptions based on SAP—subject, audience, and purpose—and company policy. You must decide when it is appropriate to use the memo format in general and the one-page memo in particular.

Also, sometimes a memo is like a résumé. The purpose of a résumé is to include just enough information to land an interview, not the job. The purpose of the interview is to expand on the points in your résumé. Your one-page memo is a success if it piques your boss's interest and generates a request for more details. But whether your boss likes your idea or not, you'll leave a positive impression with a well-written, one-page memo.

When Not to Use a One-Page Memo

You can't stuff 10,000 words into a 300-word format. In other words, you can write a one-page memo summarizing or critiquing an annual report, but you can't include the details of the annual report. That seems obvious, but sometimes when rushing to meet a deadline, people try to save time by choosing a format that is short and easy to write, such as a one-page memo, when the amount of information they must convey can fill a report or white paper.

How to Write a One-Page Memo

As with all writing assignments, you produce a one-page memo by following the Plan Then Write method. But after you produce a final draft, add another step just before Edit 1: a ruthless edit. Here is the step-by-step process:

1. Decide if the material you need to convey is appropriate for a one-page memo.

2. Write out your subject, audience, and purpose (see Chapter 4). Use what you write as an outline for your one-page memo.

3. Write a rough draft without limiting yourself to one page. Let your thoughts flow; don't try and write a draft of a one-page memo in one page. Editing as you write is a bad habit to get into. Producing a two- or even three-page draft is a good start.

4. Write and rewrite your draft until it's as clear and succinct as possible. Put your main point and/or your purpose and call to action in the first or second sentence (or even your subject line), no later. Conclude by telling your readers 1) when you want them to re-

spond, or 2) by what time or date they need to take some action, or 3) what your next step will be.

5. Edit with a vengeance. This is the most important step in the one-page memo process. You can turn almost any other format—a long letter, a report, or a proposal—into a one-page memo with ruthless editing. This is where your writer's intuition really comes into play. Use subheads and bullet points to break your message into readable portions.

6. Perform an Edit 1 and, if necessary, an Edit 2.

Edit with a Vengeance

When editing your memo draft down to one page, what do you take out and what do you leave in? This is a tough call, especially when you feel you've trimmed all the fat and are working on bone and still have more to delete. Again, use SAP, common sense, and your writer's intuition as a guide. First, cut everything that doesn't support your main point or purpose. If you have to delete even more information, prioritize the remaining points by writing a number next to each one, then delete the least important. You'll often agonize over such decisions, but the more you write one-page memos the more proficient you will become.

For example, the following paragraph is the introduction to a long memo. To condense it to a one-page memo, this paragraph must be reduced by at least half, and more, if possible.

To: Sales Team

From: Sales Manager

Subject: Upgrade Client Contact Software

As of April 2, everyone must have the new Time Management Plus client contact software installed on their computers. There will be no exceptions. We are rolling out a new sales campaign on April 23 and will be sending you a new client database on April 3 that will only import into Time Management Plus. On April 2, you will receive an ID and password to load the database. We will conduct a two-day training class on the contact software April 3–4. Attendance is mandatory. I apologize for the last-minute nature of these instructions, but that could not be avoided. After the two-day class, our Help Desk will e-mail you a special phone number that will allow you to reach an expert on Time Management Plus 24-hours a day to help you with any questions you may have. The coming quarter will be crucial to the company, and Time Management Plus will be a key tool to help the sales team meet its goals.

Every sentence in this opening paragraph is important, but you have to cut it to the bone and then some to help the entire memo fit in the one-page format. Which information do you keep and which do you cut? Here is one possible revision. The numbers in parentheses show how I've prioritized the remaining points.

(1) As of April 2, everyone must have the new Time Management Plus client contact software installed on their computers. ~~There will be no exceptions.~~ (2) We are rolling out a new sales campaign on April 23 and will be sending you a new client database on April 3 that will only import into Time Management Plus. (5) On April 2, you will receive an ID and password to load the database. (3) We will conduct a two-day training class on the contact software April 3–4. ~~Attendance is mandatory. I apologize for the last-minute nature of these instructions, but that could not be avoided.~~ (4) After the two-day class, our Help Desk will e-mail you a special phone number that will allow you to reach an expert on Time Management Plus 24-hours a day to help you with any questions you may have. (6) The coming quarter will be crucial to the company, and Time Management Plus will be a key tool to help the sales team meet its goals.

The crossed out information is, in my opinion, completely expendable. Depending on how many words need to be cut to meet the one-page limit, I would delete the remaining points in reverse order, starting with sentence six.

You will often have to make tough decisions when paring down text to fit on one page (and in this example, the decisions become extremely difficult if you have to delete points three or four). However, the benefits of the one-page memo make the challenge worthwhile and greatly improve the productivity of the company's decision makers.

Planning Pays Off

If you don't have a clear-cut, well-developed main point, supporting points, and purpose/call to action, your one-page memo will not be effective. Because they are so brief, one-page memos draw immediate and glaring attention to your subject and purpose, which make up the core of your message. If they are not clear, your one-page memo will be vague and a waste of your reader's time.

Be Abrupt

One-page memos do not have to have the same smooth flow, tone, and transitions that letters, reports, and other formats have. It's okay if they sound abrupt. It's the price you pay for being super-concise. Your readers' time is valuable, and they will consider your abruptness a virtue. You must also become comfortable throwing away whole phrases and sentences. Deleting words that took time, effort, and sweat to produce is something all experienced writers learn to do. In addition, you may sometimes be forced to leave out an important fact or two so your message will fit on one page. Just make sure it's a fact from the bottom of your priority list, not the top. You can include the missing data later in a follow-up report or letter if your reader likes the idea in your one-page memo and asks for more information.

Format Details

The format for a one-page memo is very simple with little room for variation. Here's a generic format.

To:

From:

Subject:

Date:

Attachments:

(Your message)

The attachments line in the header block is optional (if you don't have attachments, don't include it). A thin black line may separate the header information from the message, and the exact order of the other lines may vary from company to company. Otherwise, this format is typical.

Additional format guidelines to consider are:

❑ Typeface and size (12 point Times Roman is popular)
❑ Single or double line spacing
❑ Indented or blocked paragraphs

If your company doesn't specify these finer style points, use your best judgment. Don't cheat the one-page format by using 1/2″ margins, 8 point font, 1/4″ headers and footers, and single spacing without indenting paragraphs or double spacing between them.

Put the Subject Line to Work

Don't write a vague or creative description of your subject in the subject line. Make it work. Consider it a subhead or even your opening sentence. Take a look at the subject line I wrote in the revised "One-Page Memo #2 (additional observations on the space program)" in the example that follows later in this chapter (see page 98). It doubles as the opening line of the memo.

Attachments

If you need to include attachments with your memo—a bibliography, list of Web sites, resources, vendor names, etc.—include the attachment line in your header and use it to clearly and succinctly describe the additional materials. Don't add attachments that are simply an extension of your one-page memo. That defeats the purpose of the format, and your reader will easily see through the deception.

Memo: How to Put a Man on the Moon

In 1961, the United States was behind in the space race with Russia. Just three months after taking office, President John F. Kennedy sent a memo to Vice President Lyndon Johnson asking what our country needed to do to catch up.

Kennedy's one-page memo and Johnson's reply, which has already been edited here from six pages to five to save space, are reprinted on the next few pages (they were declassified in 1974 and are available free online at the John Fitzgerald Kennedy Library at http://www .jfklibrary.org/lbj_space_memo.html). Kennedy's memo is a classic example of a well-written one-page memo. His main point, "where we stand in space," and his purpose/call to action (he asks Johnson to conduct a survey) are clearly stated in his opening sentence. The rest of his memo is extremely brief and to the point, and Kennedy ends by giving Johnson a deadline for submitting his survey. Johnson's reply is also well written, though, out of necessity, much longer.

Rewriting History

Kennedy didn't ask Johnson for a one-page reply to his request for information, but to illustrate my point on one-page memos, I edited Johnson's reply with a vengeance and turned it into two separate one-page memos. I created two because Johnson's letter discusses two distinct topics—separated by the line of asterisks on page three—and therefore it can be rewritten as two separate memos.

Read Johnson's full version, then my one-page revisions to see what I chose to delete. For example, in my revised One-Page Memo #1, I chose to leave out the questions Kennedy asked because I felt the answers gave enough context so that the reader would not be confused. It's more convenient for the reader if I include the questions, but that's a compromise the reader will have to accept in order to receive the greater benefit of the timesaving one-page format.

In One-Page Memo #2, I left out Johnson's original point "g" because it was basically an example of the topic he touched on in point "f". I felt the memo would not suffer by deleting it. But that's just my opinion. Other writers would, no doubt, write different but equally good one-page versions of Johnson's memo. My rewrites are not the only correct solutions.

How would you reduce what I wrote in the two one-page memos even more? How would you have rewritten Johnson's memo to fit one page?

THE WHITE HOUSE

WASHINGTON

April 20, 1961

MEMORANDUM FOR

VICE PRESIDENT

In accordance with our conversation I would like for you as Chairman of the Space Council to be in charge of making an overall survey of where we stand in space.

1. Do we have a chance of beating the Soviets by putting a laboratory in space, or by a trip around the moon, or by a rocket to land on the moon, or by a rocket to go to the moon and back with a man. Is there any other space program which promises dramatic results in which we could win?

2. How much additional would it cost?

3. Are we working 24 hours a day on existing programs. If not, why not? If not, will you make recommendations to me as to how work can be speeded up.

4. In building large boosters should we put our emphasis on nuclear, chemical or liquid fuel, or a combination of these three?

5. Are we making maximum effort? Are we achieving necessary results?

I have asked Jim Webb, Dr. Weisner, Secretary McNamara and other responsible officials to cooperate with you fully. I would appreciate a report on this at the earliest possible moment.

Signed John F. Kennedy

OFFICE OF THE VICE PRESIDENT

WASHINGTON, D.C.

April 28, 1961

MEMORANDUM FOR THE PRESIDENT

Subject: Evaluation of the Space Program.

Reference is to your April 20 memorandum asking certain questions regarding this country's space program.

A detailed survey has not been completed in this time period. The examination will continue. However, what we have obtained so far from knowledgeable and responsible persons makes this summary reply possible.

Among those who have participated in our deliberations have been the Secretary and Deputy Secretary of Defense; General Schriever (AF); Admiral Hayward (Navy); Dr. von Braun (NASA); the Administrator, Deputy Administrator, and other top officials of NASA; the Special Assistant to the President on Science and Technology; representatives of the Director of the Bureau of the Budget; and three outstanding non-Government citizens of the general public: Mr. George Brown (Brown & Root, Houston, Texas); Mr. Donald Cook (American Electric Power Service, New York, N.Y.); and Mr. Frank Stanton (Columbia Broadcasting System, New York, N.Y.).

The following general conclusions can be reported:

     a. Largely due to their concentrated efforts and their earlier emphasis upon the development of large rocket engines, the Soviets are ahead of the United States in world prestige attained through impressive technological accomplishments in space.

     b. The U.S. has greater resources than the USSR for attaining space leadership but has failed to make the necessary hard decisions and to marshal those resources to achieve such leadership.

– 2 –

    c. This country should be realistic and recognize that other nations, regardless of their appreciation of our idealistic values, will tend to align themselves with the country which they believe will be the world leader–the leader in the long run. Dramatic accomplishments in space are being increasingly identified as a major indicator of world leadership.

    d. The U.S. can, if it will, firm up its objectives and employ its resources with a reasonable chance of attaining world leadership in space during this decade. This will be difficult but can be made probable even recognizing the head start of the Soviets and the likelihood that they will continue to move forward with impressive successes. In certain areas, such as communications, navigation, weather, and mapping, the U.S. can and should exploit its existing advanced position.

    e. If we do not make the strong effort now, the time will soon be reached when the margin of control over space and over men's minds through space accomplishments will have swung so far on the Russian side that we will not be able to catch up, let alone assume leadership.

    f. Even in those areas in which the Soviets already have the capability to be first and are likely to improve upon such capability, the United States should make aggressive efforts as the technological gains as well as the international rewards are essential steps in eventually gaining leadership. The danger of long lags or outright omissions by this country is substantial in view of the possibility of great technological breakthroughs obtained from space exploration.

    g. Manned exploration of the moon, for example, is not only an achievement with great propaganda value, but it is essential as an objective whether or not we are first in its accomplishment–and we may be able to be first. We cannot leapfrog such accomplishments, as they are essential sources of knowledge and experience for even greater successes in space. We cannot expect the Russians to transfer the benefits of their experiences or the advantages of their capabilities to us. We must do these things ourselves.

    h. The American public should be given the facts as to how we stand in the space race, told of our determination to lead in that race, and advised of the importance of such leadership to our future.

- 3 -

i. More resources and more effort need to be put into our space program as soon as possible. We should move forward with a bold program, while at the same time taking every practical precaution for the safety of the persons actively participating in space flights.

****

As for specific questions posed in your memorandum, the following brief answers develop from the studies made during the past few days. These conclusions are subject to expansion and more detailed examination as our survey continues.

Q.1 — Do we have a chance of beating the Soviets by putting a laboratory in space, or by a trip around the moon, or by a rocket to land on the moon, or by a rocket to go to the moon and back with a man. Is there any other space program which promises dramatic results in which we could win?

A.1 — The Soviets now have a rocket capability for putting a multi-manned laboratory into space and have already crash-landed a rocket on the moon. They also have the booster capability of making a soft landing on the moon with a payload of instruments, although we do not know how much preparation they have made for such a project. As for a manned trip around the moon or a safe landing and return by a man to the moon, neither the U.S. nor the USSR has such a capability at this time, so far as we know. The Russians have had more experience with large boosters and with flights of dogs and man. Hence they might be conceded a time advantage in circumnavigation of the moon and also in a manned trip to the moon. However, with a strong effort, the United States could conceivably be first in those two accomplishments by 1966 or 1967.

There are a number of programs which the United States could pursue immediately and which promise significant world-wide advantage over the Soviets. Among these are communications satellites, meteorological and weather satellites, and navigation and mapping satellites. These are all areas in which we have already developed some competence. We have such programs and believe that the Soviets do not. Moreover, they are programs which could be made operational and effective within reasonably short periods of time and could, if properly programmed with the interests of other nations, make useful strides toward world leadership.

- 4 -

Q. 2 — How much additional would it cost?

A. 2 — To start upon an accelerated program with the aforementioned objectives clearly in mind, NASA has submitted an analysis indicating that about $500 million would be needed for FY 1962 over and above the amount currently requested of the Congress. A program based upon NASA's analysis would, over a ten-year period, average approximately $1 billion a year above the current estimates of the existing NASA program.

While the Department of Defense plans to make a more detailed submission to me within a few days, the Secretary has taken the position that there is a need for a strong effort to develop a large solid-propellant booster and that his Department is interested in undertaking such a project. It was understood that this would be programmed in accord with the existing arrangement for close cooperation with NASA, which Agency is undertaking some research in this field. He estimated they would need to employ approximately $50 million during FY 1962 for this work but that this could be financed through management of funds already requested in the FY 1962 budget. Future defense budgets would include requests for additional funding for this purpose; a preliminary estimate indicates that about $500 million would be needed in total.

Q. 3 — Are we working 24 hours a day on existing programs. If not, why not? If not, will you make recommendations to me as to how work can be speeded up.

A. 3 — There is not a 24-hour-a-day work schedule on existing NASA space programs except for selected areas in Project Mercury, the Saturn-C-1 booster, the Centaur engines and the final launching phases of most flight missions. They advise that their schedules have been geared to the availability of facilities and financial resources, and that hence their overtime and 3-shift arrangements exist only in those activities in which there are particular bottlenecks or which are holding up operations in other parts of the programs. For example, they have a 3-shift 7-day-week operation in certain work at Cape Canaveral; the contractor for Project Mercury has averaged a 54-hour work week and employs two or three shifts in some areas; Saturn C-1 at Huntsville is working around the clock during critical test periods while the remaining work on this project averages a 47-hour week; the Centaur hydrogen engine is on a 3-shift basis in some portions of the contractor's plants.

- 5 -

This work can be speeded up through firm decisions to go ahead faster if accompanied by additional funds needed for the acceleration.

Q. 4 — In building large boosters should we put our emphasis on nuclear, chemical or liquid fuel, or a combination of these three?

A. 4 — It was the consensus that liquid, solid and nuclear boosters should all be accelerated. This conclusion is based not only upon the necessity for back-up methods, but also because of the advantages of the different types of boosters for different missions. A program of such emphasis would meet both so-called civilian needs and defense requirements.

Q. 5 — Are we making maximum effort? Are we achieving necessary results?

A. 5 — We are neither making maximum effort nor achieving results necessary if this country is to reach a position of leadership.

Signed

Lyndon B. Johnson

My Revision of Johnson: One-Page Memo #1
(reply to JFK's questions)

OFFICE OF THE VICE PRESIDENT

WASHINGTON, D.C.

April 28, 1961

MEMORANDUM FOR THE PRESIDENT

Subject: Answers to your April 20 memorandum re the evaluation of our space program.

A.1 — The Soviets now have a rocket and booster capability for putting a multi-manned laboratory into space and making a soft landing on the moon. Neither the U.S. nor the USSR has a capability for a manned trip around the moon or a safe landing and return by a man to the moon. The Russians might be conceded a time advantage in circumnavigation of the moon and also in a manned trip to the moon. However, with a strong effort, the United States could conceivably be first in those two accomplishments by 1966 or 1967. There are a number of programs which the United States could pursue immediately and which promise significant world-wide advantage over the Soviets. Among these are communications satellites, meteorological and weather satellites, and navigation and mapping satellites.

A.2 — To start an accelerated space program, NASA estimates a cost of $500 million for FY 1962 and approximately $1 billion a year for the next ten years.

A.3 — There is not a 24-hour-a-day work schedule on existing NASA space programs except for areas in Project Mercury, the Saturn-C-1 booster, the Centaur engines and the final launching phases of most flight missions. This work can be speeded up through firm decisions to go ahead faster if accompanied by additional funds.

A.4 — Liquid, solid and nuclear boosters should all be accelerated. This conclusion is based not only upon the necessity for back-up methods, but also because of the advantages of the different types of boosters for different missions.

A.5 — We are neither making maximum effort nor achieving the results necessary if this country is to reach a position of leadership.

Signed

Lyndon B. Johnson

My Revision of Johnson: One-Page Memo #2
(additional observations on the space program)

OFFICE OF THE VICE PRESIDENT

WASHINGTON, D.C.

April 28, 1961

MEMORANDUM FOR THE PRESIDENT

Subject: General conclusions and steps we must take to become the world leader in space.

    a. Largely due to their concentrated efforts and their earlier emphasis upon the development of large rocket engines, the Soviets are ahead of the United States in world prestige attained through impressive technological accomplishments in space.

    b. The U.S. has greater resources than the USSR for attaining space leadership but has failed to make the necessary hard decisions and to marshal those resources.

    c. Other nations will tend to align themselves with the country which they believe will be the world leader. Dramatic accomplishments in space are being increasingly identified as a major indicator of world leadership.

    d. The U.S. can firm up its objectives and employ its resources with a reasonable chance of attaining world leadership in space during this decade.

    e. If we do not make the strong effort now, men's minds will have swung so far on the Russian side that we will not be able to catch up, let alone assume leadership.

    f. The United States should make aggressive efforts as the technological gains and international rewards of a space program are essential in eventually gaining leadership.

    g. The American public should be told how we stand in the space race, our determination to lead that race, and the importance of such leadership to our future.

    h. More resources and effort need to be put into our space program as soon as possible, while at the same time taking every practical safety precaution.

Signed

Lyndon B. Johnson

Memorable Memos

One-page memos are not only easier to read, but because of their brevity they make a more lasting impression than a longer document. Take Lincoln's "Gettysburg Address." This famous speech is actually shorter than a one-page typewritten memo—only 270 words—and was originally intended to be a minor event at the commemoration of the National Cemetery at Gettysburg, which took place on November 19, 1863.

Immediately after the battle (July 1–3, 1863), Pennsylvania governor Andrew Curtin asked a local judge, David Wills, to clean up the battlefield and bury the dead. Wills established a seventeen-acre national cemetery on the site and invited Edward Everett, the most popular speaker in the United States at the time, to give the keynote speech at the dedication ceremony. When Lincoln was invited, he was asked to make a "few appropriate remarks." Everett's speech was 14,285 words long and lasted almost two hours. Lincoln's speech took about three minutes. No one remembers Everett's "Gettysburg Oration," but everyone remembers Lincoln's "Gettysburg Address," which has been translated into twenty-eight languages, from French to Tagalog.[1]

E-Mails

Many businesses today literally run on e-mail. Take it away and the wheels of commerce, in some cases, would grind to a halt. But the verdict on e-mail is mixed. On the one hand, e-mails are an indispensable form of ultra-fast, global communication. On the other, they are abused, misused, and a license to write trivia—and write it badly. Fortunately, this last problem can be fixed by following a few simple guidelines.

Social or Business E-Mail?

Before writing an e-mail, you must first decide if it will be a business or social e-mail. If it's business, keep it all business, even if it's going to your best friend in risk management or your sister-in-law in legal. When writing social e-mails, feel free to test the boundaries of good English usage, but only send social e-mails from your home computer. Assume (because in most companies, it's true) that all e-mails sent from your company computer are archived and available for review at any time by upper management. If you consider your boss the secondary audience for every e-mail you write at work, you will never write an embarrassing or inappropriate one.

And remember, personally revealing and poorly written e-mails, business or social, are sometimes forwarded by friends and colleagues until they find their way into the public domain—along with your name and e-mail address—as humorous spam. That thought alone should be enough incentive to write with care and good taste.

> **"I don't have voice mail on my phone. I gave it up because by the time I get someone's voice message it is probably out of date. But I'll answer e-mail instantly. I make e-mail a priority over everything else. So I think despite the fact that it leads to people being even more careless with the English language, as a means of communication e-mail is the best writing tool we have today."**
>
> Shelagh Lester-Smith, vice president, director of corporate communications and public affairs, Motorola (from her interview in Part III)

When to Use E-Mails

This is a tough call to make because people send everything in the body of e-mails (i.e., not as attachments), from one-line confirmations that a package has arrived to multipage letters and reports. But in general, apply the telephone rule. If you would typically call a person and tell him or her the information over the phone, it qualifies as a bona fide e-mail.

For instance, you would call a colleague to tell her when you would be arriving for a meeting, but you wouldn't call that same person and read her a letter over the phone. Send client lists, reports, white papers, and other large documents as attachments to an economical e-mail. As always, there are exceptions to this rule. For example, many companies want to receive résumés in the body of an e-mail to prevent opening attachments that may contain a virus.

How to Write Economical E-Mails

When writing business e-mails, use the same approach as for writing one-page memos—be ruthlessly brief and to the point. But because e-mails are so short, there is no need in most cases to take a separate sheet of paper and write down your subject, audience, and purpose. You can do that in your head; spend a little time thinking about SAP, then type out your message and edit it with a vengeance. Open with a brief, friendly greeting, then get down to business. Here are five steps for writing an economical e-mail:

1. Determine if a business e-mail (as opposed to a letter or memo) is the appropriate format for your business message.

2. Think about your subject, audience, and purpose (write them out if you think it will be helpful).

3. Write a rough draft of your e-mail in your e-mail software. Don't put a limit on what you write. Let your thoughts flow. Put your main point and/or purpose and call to action in the first or second sentence (or even your subject line), no later. Conclude by telling your reader 1) when you want him or her to respond, or 2) by what time or date he or she needs to take some action, or 3) what your next step will be.

4. Edit with a vengeance. This is the most important step in the economical e-mail process. The editing method described in the one-page memo section (and in the examples that follow) applies here as well.

5. Perform an Edit 1 and, if necessary, an Edit 2.

Subject Lines Will Keep You From Getting Trashed

With all the spam filling up electronic inboxes, many people delete e-mails before they even open them based on whether they recognize the sender from his e-mail address or whether the Subject line describes a familiar topic or something of value to them. To make sure your e-mails get read, write a Subject line that grabs your recipient's attention.

Well-written Subject lines are doubly important because you can't count on someone recognizing your name or e-mail address. For example, if you are sending a follow-up e-mail to someone you recently met, she probably won't know your address, so a Subject line such as "Nice meeting you at the Chamber function" will tell her the e-mail is from a business acquaintance and pique her interest enough to open and read it.

Even if you know the recipient well, an informative Subject line will save your readers time by allowing them to prioritize their e-mails. For example, here are three good Subject lines, in the order they should be read:

"Need your feedback by 5 pm tomorrow"

"Inventory estimates for July that you requested"

"How about lunch Wednesday?"

Subject lines like "Friends," "Hey!" and "Update" are prime candidates for the Delete key.

Too many people appear to think that Subject lines have to be one, two, or three words long, probably because most of the e-mails they receive have short Subject lines and it seems odd to write one that sticks way past the information in the To, From, and Cc lines. Break the habit. Write full, one-sentence lines that touch on your main message and grab your reader's attention. You'll do your recipient a favor by letting him know at a glance that he has an important e-mail waiting for him, and you'll do yourself a favor because your e-mail will get read, not trashed.

Roomy Layout Makes Easy Reading

Blocks of text in e-mails are harder to read than blocks of text in memos, letters, and other documents for several reasons:

❑ The page layout is small and cramped (not the easy-to-read $8\frac{1}{2}$" × 11" space we're used to seeing).

❑ The size of the page area changes from e-mail to e-mail, depending on the size of the message and the e-mail program you use.

❑ The font types and sizes are limited and sometimes bit-mapped, making them difficult to read.

❑ If the writer of the e-mail splices sentences together, doesn't use capital letters, and doesn't spell check, it's a wonder we bother to read the e-mail at all.

To counter these problems:

❑ Write short paragraphs.

❑ Use subheads, bullet points, and numbered sentences to break your message into readable segments.

❑ Put major ideas in separate paragraphs, even if they are one sentence long, so it's easy to reread your e-mail and find these action items.

❑ Put each important message that you want to convey in a separate e-mail (for example, you may have different messages with details about the company Christmas party, a travel itinerary for the conference in Atlanta, editorial comments on a collaborative report, etc.).

❑ Do not write in all capital letters (it's very difficult to read and is the equivalent of shouting), and turn on your e-mail program's spelling and grammar checker if it has one (most do).

Wordy, Vague E-Mails Can Cost Millions

Here are two examples of why e-mails should be edited with a vengeance. The first story was reported in *The Record*.

Workers in companies throughout the country are increasingly inundated with so much e-mail that studies show they lose an average of two hours from each business day. Research by communications consulting firm Rogen International and Goldhaber Research Associates tallied the losses of companies with 100 employees to be about 15,000 work hours, or $420,000 annually, based on average salaries of $50,000. Moreover, poorly written electronic communiqués are adding to inefficiencies on the job, corporate trainer Debra Hamilton said. "E-mail is becoming a burden, not a timesaver," Hamilton said. "There's a lot of waste and it's costing companies money and adding to stress in the workplace."[2]

How much money can a brief but poorly written e-mail cost a company? As much as $622 million, according to this article from *The New York Times*. And no price can be put on the damage to the company's global reputation and brand.

An errant order to sell $4 billion in stocks briefly roiled the market yesterday afternoon, providing another warning of how a clerical error can produce huge risks. The New York Stock Exchange said that Bear, Stearns had intended to place an order to sell $4 million worth of stocks in the Standard & Poor's 500-stock index, but instead asked to sell $4 billion. The order was entered about 3:40 p.m. The orders were canceled within minutes, but not before $622 million in stock had been sold. . . . In the world of program trading, a $4 million order would not be a large one. If it was spread out among the stocks in the S&P 500, it would result in the sale of about 5,200 shares of General Electric, for example. But a $4 billion order would call for selling 5.2 million G.E. shares, along with very large blocks of many other companies. Such large orders would not usually be entered electronically.[3]

Abrupt Is One Thing, Rude Another

As with one-page memos, it's okay to be abrupt when writing e-mails. Your readers will appreciate your brevity. But one danger of being abrupt is that you can sound rude. Here's an example:

> S end me the graphics file by Monday. Report your quarterly results to Edwards in Accounting on Friday at 1pm. Remember to overnight the inventory report to McConnell in Rhode Island.
> P.F.

A well-placed please and thank-you or other kind words will quickly transform this e-mail from frosty to friendly, without adding very much to the word count.

> H ello Bert,
> Please send me the graphics file by Monday and report your quarterly results to Edwards in Accounting on Friday at 1pm.
> Also, remember to overnight the inventory report to McConnell in Rhode Island.
> Thanks for your help.
> Best, Pat

Audience is another factor to consider when determining how much time you should spend making your e-mail sound polite and friendly. How well do you know the recipient? You may be able to send the surly-sounding first example to a close friend who knows you are pressed for time and do not mean to be rude. Another fix is to conclude the aloof e-mail with, "Sorry so abrupt but gotta run." When communicating with a client, upper management, or someone you don't know well, follow the etiquette you would typically use in a formal letter. Begin with "Dear . . ." Use formal and polite language throughout and end with "Sincerely yours." Use SAP and your writer's intuition to determine how formal or informal you should be.

Start Chat/End Chat

One way to write brusque, timesaving e-mails, yet indicate you are not being rude, is by beginning your message with the words Start Chat or simply Chat and concluding the e-mail with End Chat.

I use the word *chat* because of its reference to Internet chat rooms where several people log in and carry on real-time, written conversations with the brisk and abrupt spontaneity of a live telephone conversation. Chat room participants discuss topics ranging from current events to favorite hobbies, and they write in a clipped style that, in an e-mail, would appear rude. But in the fast-paced natural flow of the discussion, no one interprets curt replies or questions as impolite.

Start Chat and End Chat quickly tells your recipient that you are dispensing with e-mail etiquette to reap the greater benefit of dashing off a rapid reply. The person will appreciate the fact that you've also given her the green light to write lightning-fast responses, which will save time and hassles for both of you, because you won't have to struggle over phrasing each reply so it sounds perfectly polite.

Start Chat/End Chat is especially helpful when you begin an e-mail conversation with a colleague, vendor, or customer that will take place over one or more days. For instance, if you are in charge of organizing your company's tradeshow booth and are dealing with a half dozen or more people via e-mail, giving everyone permission to write "just the facts" in the briefest way possible will be a welcome relief to all.

King of Swing

Here's an example of an e-mail that is part business, part social, and all nonsense:

From: Me!

Date: October 1

To: The King of Swing from Wyoming!!

Cc:

Bcc:

Subject: Cocktails and Caribbean Cabanas!!!

hey slugger if you hit this quarters 10% quotas . . . take note we're talking increase here from last quarters home run finish . . . like you did the old rawhide last saturday we'll all be dipping our toes in sundrenched waves of amber hue in the island nations of VERY south miami martinique!! . . . cocktails galore and number crunching on the upside but all that aside . . . sorry have to get serious on you here . . . we have a get together friday with the group to discuss yada yada and its up to YOU to garner that windowroom book it!!! if we have to freeze our tails off we may as well have a lot of sun and snowy peaks . . . and what were your expenses last month i'll need copies by thursday or my butts in the upside of a downside sling . . . and those rockies can't seem to make it into the playoff anytime soon so how much money you losing on those hometown heroes anyway . . . got internet troubles like crazy so you may receive triplicates of this just delete the lot, BONNIES GOT 500 TICKETS!!! scored from human resources so daytona here we come move over kentucky and derby on yourself!! . . . obviously the coming year is coming up roses for lots of reasons not the least is SPRING . . . what say we break some bread after the meet . . . on friday my man . . . PS passing along a few ha ha's I found on the net!!! [eight jokes—not included in this example—are attached to this e-mail]

Rewrite #1: The Business E-Mail

Believe it or not, a business message is hidden inside the "King of Swing" e-mail. Here's what it looks like written as an economical e-mail:

From: John Herbert, National Sales Manager

Date: October 1

To: Ed Patrick, Western Regional Sales Manager

Cc:

Bcc:

Subject: Fourth quarter sales quotas

Hello Ed,

Congratulations on your strong 3rd quarter finish. Yesterday I received our 4th quarter goals and your group's will be 10% over last quarter's.

I'll fly into Denver to meet with your group this Friday to discuss 4th quarter's and next year's goals in detail.

Also, I'll need your September expense report by this Thursday.

Finally, I'll announce this Friday that the top producers for the 4th quarter will receive a trip to Martinique next February. Sounds like a nice incentive. See you Friday.

Regards, John

Rewrite #2: The Social E-Mail

Here's the social e-mail embedded in the "King of Swing":

From: John

Date: October 1

To: Ed

Cc:

Bcc:

Subject: Cocktails and Caribbean Cabanas!!!

Hey, Ed. I heard you were the home run king at your group's picnic last week. Congrats! I'll give you more on this when we

meet Friday, but that trip to Martinique should really spur the
sales teams into action. At least I hope so. When are your Colo-
rado Rockies going to play some October ball? Big news. Bonnie
scored tickets to the Daytona 500 next year. Can't wait. That'll
make my year! What about dinner after the meeting Friday?

See you then, John

When You're Done You're Done

Some people write long, wordy e-mails because they feel that long is
better, that a small e-mail, memo, or letter is the sign of a small mind.
The truth is concise correspondence is the sign of a concise, decisive
mind. If you only have one sentence worth of information, do your
reader a favor and stop after one sentence. People who ramble on after
they've made their point gain reputations for being long-winded and
boring.

What If You Paid a Dollar a Word?

One way to keep e-mails brief is to think of them as the twentieth-
century equivalent of the nineteenth-century telegram (which they
are). When telegrams cost a dollar a word and a dollar was a week's
pay, people quickly learned how to write clearly and concisely. If the
telegram included more words than necessary, you were throwing
away money. But there was danger either way: If the telegram was so
brief that it didn't make sense, you would have to spend more money
to resend it. When writing e-mails at work, pretend you must pay a
dollar for every word you type. You'll use fewer words and save time
on every e-mail you write.

Bcc: Protect Everyone's Privacy

We have all received e-mails with ten, twenty, or more e-mail addresses
in the To: or Cc: lines (Cc: is the abbreviation for carbon copy, a term
leftover from the Typewriter Age when the only way to make a copy of
a letter was to put a piece of carbon paper between two sheets of letter-
head before loading them in the typewriter). The addresses make the
e-mail long and difficult to read. And should the e-mail get routed to a

professional spammer or someone selling a product or service, all of your colleagues and friends could end up on yet another spam list.

The cure: When you broadcast an e-mail to a group in your address book, use the blind carbon copy (Bcc:) feature. Addresses in the Bcc: line will not show up on each receiver's To: line. Only the recipient's address will appear. If you don't know how to use your e-mail program's Bcc: feature, check out the Help menu. It's easy. Bcc: protects your own privacy and the privacy of everyone in your address book, plus it allows you to send e-mails that are less cluttered and easier to read.

Reward Good Writing

If your company has a problem with wordy and confusing e-mails, establish an e-mail standard, distribute several examples of it, and hold a monthly contest for the most clear, concise, and economically written e-mail. Post the winning e-mail on the company intranet and reward the writer with a day off or dinner for two. Make economical e-mails part of your corporate culture. It will save everyone time, so people will actually look forward to checking their e-mail on Monday morning.

CHAPTER 8

HOW TO IMPLEMENT A PERSONAL
WRITING IMPROVEMENT PLAN

Improving any skill takes time and practice. To make sure the concepts in this book take root, it's a good idea to design a customized writing improvement plan.

Where to Begin

An effective writing improvement program begins with an evaluation of your writing skills. It gives you a place to start. The self-evaluation questionnaire that follows may uncover problems that are keeping you from writing well. The three-part questionnaire covers the writing you do on the job and in your leisure time, as well as your reading habits. Reading is key to the development of your writing skills. A friend of mine who teaches a college-level course on composition told me that one of his freshmen students came up after class and asked how he could improve his grammar skills. My friend replied, "Read a lot by the time you're twelve."

He was right. Research shows that reading can improve your writing more than actually writing. Here are the results of two studies in which students were divided into two groups: one that did more writing than reading and one that did more reading than writing.

[I]n one study, the] subjects were high school students, grades nine to twelve. "Writing" classes wrote a theme a week, which was corrected "rigorously" by the teacher, while "reading" classes wrote a theme every third week and spent one period per week reading in class. At the end of the year, both groups showed clear progress, but the "reading" group outperformed the "writing" classes on the

STEP writing test and received higher ratings on content and organization, mechanics, diction and rhetoric.

[A second researcher] did a similar study with fifth graders. One group wrote two themes per week, while a second group did no writing, spending more time reading both in and out of class. Again, both groups gained in writing, with the reading group clearly outperforming the writing group on the post-test essay in all categories (content, mechanics, organization, grammar, wording, and phrasing).[1]

Reading will help improve your writing, which is another good reason—besides simple good business sense—to set aside time to read your industry's magazines and newsletters, as well as general business publications such as *Fortune* and *Business Week*. Your mind maps and remembers the organization, grammar, mechanics, and other good writing skills exhibited in the well-written pieces you read. Now here are five steps to guide you through your personal writing improvement plan.

Step 1: Answer the Self-Evaluation Questionnaire

Type out the following questions and your answers to each on a separate piece of paper.

Part I—Writing at Work

1. Which types of writing do you do most often? (E.g., letters, e-mail, proposals, reports, brochures, articles, etc.)
2. Which type(s) of writing do you like to do? (Briefly explain your answer.)
3. Which type(s) of writing do you not like to do? (Briefly explain your answer.)
4. Do you think writing is easy or hard? (Briefly explain your answer.)
5. Overall, do you like to write? (Briefly explain your answer.)
6. Where do you do most of your writing? (E.g., at a desk on a computer, on a legal pad with a pencil in the park, etc.)

7. Describe how you write. (Start with how you prepare to write and list the steps in your process until you have completed the project. For example, do you procrastinate a lot before sitting down to write? Do you get up and walk around to think while writing? Do you stop writing to look up how to spell words in the dictionary?)

8. What do you feel are your writing strengths? List up to five strengths (e.g., I'm good at grammar; I'm good at outlining what I want to say; I'm very fluent on paper, words come easily; etc.).

9. What do you feel are your writing weaknesses? List up to five weaknesses (e.g., I take a page to say what others can say in two sentences; I'm a poor speller; I get writer's block a lot; etc.).

10. What do you think prevents you from writing well? (E.g., I lack proper training in school; I'm a bad speller; I have great ideas but can't put them down correctly on paper, etc.)

11. On a scale of 1 (least important) to 5 (extremely important), how important are spelling, grammar, and punctuation? (Just write down the number.)

12. What are three writing rules (e.g., "always grab your reader's attention in the opening sentence," "always write a detailed outline," "never use fragments," etc.) that you always try to follow and think are very important?

13. Do you rigidly follow writing rules or consider them helpful guidelines that you can break when you think they should be broken?

14. Which writing reference books do you keep on your desk?

Part II—Writing Outside the Workplace

1. Do you do any writing outside of work?

2. If you answered "yes" to question one, what type(s) of writing do you do? (List all that apply. For example: poetry, newspaper articles, diary entries, children's stories, etc.)

3. Why do you write outside of work? (E.g., for relaxation, for the challenge, etc.)

4. How many hours a week, on average, do you spend writing outside of work?

5. If you attended college, what was your major, and how much and which type(s) of writing did you do in college?

Part III—Reading Habits at Work and Home

1. Which type of materials do you read most often? (E.g., books, magazines, newspapers, business correspondence, etc.)

2. Which type of books do you read? (E.g., mystery, business, horror, classics, etc.)

3. Other than books, which magazines, newspapers, or other reading materials do you read?

4. Why do you read? (E.g., to learn something, to relax, for entertainment, etc.)

5. How often do you read? (E.g., a few minutes a day, a book a week, a book a month, two newspapers a day, etc.)

6. Do you like to read? (Briefly explain your answer.)

"It's easier for managers with good writing skills to have better relationships with their staff and upper management and to perform their jobs better. You can't help but think more highly of people who are good at communicating. Our clients respond better to them, too."

Mitch Bardwell, director/assistant general manager, sales training division, Canon U.S.A. Imaging Systems Group (from his interview in Part III)

Step 2: Ask an Expert

Gather up your questionnaire and three to six writing samples (that have not been edited by someone else), then ask a qualified writer—a friend whose work has been published, a teacher at a local college, a colleague whose writing ability is beyond question—to review your packet. The questionnaire will give this person invaluable background on your writing history. Ask the expert to write a list, based on your writing samples, of your art and science writing strengths and your art and science weaknesses. This person's list is often very different from the strengths and weaknesses you write in your questionnaire.

A quick read of Chapters 5 and 6 will bring your writing expert up to speed on the art and science of writing. Use the list of weaknesses as the starting point of your personal writing improvement program. Use the list of strengths as a source of pride and confidence in your writing ability.

The Importance of Knowing Your Strengths

No one I've asked has ever been given a list of his or her writing strengths. Not in grade school, high school, college, or a commercial workshop. That's a shame because everyone has writing strengths, and if you're only told what you do wrong, you assume you have no strengths and therefore do everything wrong.

I remember attending a writing seminar in which the instructor critiqued a writing sample from each participant. I read all the samples before the criticism session began. I was impressed with one letter in particular because it was so well written, and wondered what the instructor would say about it. When we came to that piece, the teacher listed a dozen different ways the letter could be improved without once congratulating the writer for doing an excellent job to begin with.

War and Peace can be improved. That's not the point. Criticism is helpful and unavoidable in a writing class, but a little praise is a more powerful learning tool than reproach, which is how most inexperienced writers take criticism. A simple statement like, "This letter is well written. We can discuss many different ways to say it just as well, but let's not. Excellent writing, Participant X," can do more to increase the confidence and writing skills of a student than a year's worth of workshops.

Steps 3 and 4: Plan Then Write, and Work on One Weakness Each Week

Step 3, learn and apply the Plan Then Write method, is thoroughly covered in the preceding chapters of this book, so I'll move to step 4. Everyone has writing weaknesses, even the very best writers. The difference is that experienced writers are usually well aware of their weaknesses and keep a sharp eye out for them when rewriting their drafts. That's what inexperienced writers should do, too. Copy the list of strengths and weaknesses your writing expert gave you into your Edit 1 Notebook. Add weaknesses and strengths as you discover more.

Choose the first writing weakness on your list and turn it into a weeklong mini-workshop. If it's a mechanical problem, look up the solution in the appropriate reference guide, write the solution down in your notebook, and study it until you know how to fix the problem without looking up the answer. If it's a style problem—for example, you routinely write long, wordy sentences—write down the solution, even if it's as simple as "Use my writer's intuition to edit long, wordy sentences." Proofread everything you write that week, from one-sentence e-mails to five-page letters, for the problem. At least once a day for five business days in a row, write a sentence or paragraph with the problem in it and then correct it.

The writing problem may not go away in a week. In fact, it will probably pop up from time to time in future assignments (you spent years developing this habit; it will take time to disappear). But you will know how to recognize and fix it, and the bad habit will eventually vanish over time.

Don't forget to read your list of writing strengths at least once a week, too. Business writing is lonely work. When no one is around to give you encouragement, you have to be your own coach and cheerleader.

> **"Hiring employees who write well gives us a tremendous business advantage. Their presentations are more sophisticated, and successful presentations mean more business for the company. Also, good writing promotes personal growth, so we both win: The company benefits from employees with excellent writing skills, and certainly the individuals benefit, personally and financially."**
>
> Paul Carlucci, chairman and CEO,
> News America Marketing
> (from his interview in Part III)

Weaknesses Become Strengths

As you cross a weakness off your list, ask yourself if the solution to that problem is now a strength. The "I write long, wordy sentences" problem may become a "I write strong, crisp logical sentences" strength that you can write in that section of your Edit 1 Notebook. What was once a source of frustration has been turned into a source of confidence.

Step 5: Measure Improvement Over Time and ROI

Use your writing weaknesses list to track improvement over time. Mark the date that you feel you mastered the problem, then check it off your list. Also, if you or your company paid for anything associated with your custom writing improvement plan—your writing samples evaluation, books, a professional proofreader, etc.—you can also use your Edit 1 Notebook to measure the return on investment (ROI). As your weaknesses disappear and your writing improves, you can calculate whether the money was well spent.

The Benefits of a Custom Plan

A custom writing improvement plan that begins with an evaluation pinpointing your strengths and weaknesses is the fastest road to improving your writing. It's also good motivation. You are more apt to study and work hard to eliminate errors you know are preventing you from writing well than you are to study a list of top-ten writing problems that you may or may not have. For example, why study active/passive voice if you don't have that problem? Granted, studying anything about writing can be beneficial, but precious workshop time is best spent working on known weaknesses. The results will be significant and measurable.

Experienced vs. Inexperienced Writers

In Chapter 2, I explained the difference between experienced and inexperienced writers. I'd like to expand on those differences now that I've covered all of the concepts in the Plan Then Write process. A primary difference between the two types of writers is attitude, not the number of years each has written. For example, the experienced and inexperienced freshman composition writers in Mike Rose's study were in the same age group, so they had been writing about the same number of years. What set them apart was their approach to writing. The experienced freshmen rely on their writer's intuition and have a more pragmatic, trial-and-error, process-based approach.

Inexperienced writers try to pound round pegs in square holes. They have a sense from previous writing instruction that there is one, correct, formulaic way to write. This rules-based approach causes them nothing but trouble.

Two more differences: First, because experienced writers have a more developed writer's intuition, they are faster problem solvers and hit on a correct solution to a writing problem sooner than inexperienced writers. Second, experienced writers are comfortable with the chaos of the trial-and-error, problem-solving approach and understand there are no shortcuts.

Writers at any level can make a great leap forward in their development by adopting the attitude of experienced writers: There are no rules, only rules of thumb. Writing is the process of moving from one problem to another using your writer's intuition to solve them. Plan then write and proofread twice, and try to have a little fun while you're at it.

PART

II

HOW THEY DO IT

Q&A'S WITH SUCCESSFUL BUSINESS AUTHORS

Part II features interviews with professional writers and best-selling authors who talk about how they write. This behind-the-scenes look at the composing process of successful, contemporary business writers will not only give you helpful tips that can improve your writing, but an inside look at the composing process these writers employ to produce good writing time after time. The techniques they use to write articles and books apply directly to everyday business correspondence. You'll notice that I often ask each author the same key questions. I do this so you can compare the consistency of their answers to crucial areas of the writing process.

One way to learn a skill is to imitate the actions of others who have mastered it. The problem with applying this method to writing is that it's not feasible for a group of people to look over the shoulder of a published writer while she composes a magazine article, business book, or newsletter. While not a substitute for that experience, these interviews do provide the next best thing to pouring a cup of coffee, pulling up a chair next to these authors, and watching them work.

Also, pay attention to the "writing lifestyle" tips revealed in these interviews. They're as helpful as the rules of thumb these authors relate. For example, I remember reading that Ernest Hemingway stopped writing at the end of each day in the middle of a paragraph or idea that was flowing well. That way it was easier, mentally, to pick up his pen and start writing the next day.

In a more contemporary example, Stephen King was attending a Mets baseball game when a rain delay stopped play. King pulled a raincoat over his head, whipped out his laptop, and knocked out a few pages of horror. I used to think the setting had to be "just right" to write: noise-free, notes lined up, and a fresh cup of Barry's Gold Irish tea at my elbow. It was very liberating to learn that a pro like King could whack out a few pages anytime, anyplace, under any conditions.

Finally, George Bernard Shaw's wife once picked up a first draft of one of his plays and said something to this effect: "George, this is pure crap." He responded, "Ah, but wait until the seventh draft." If a Nobel Prize winner can write drivel for the first few versions of award-winning plays, it's okay for me to write an embarrassingly lousy first draft of a business letter.

These are very helpful lessons, and the reason why I asked the authors such questions as where they write, if they use a computer, when they knew they were good writers, etc. Not always, but sometimes, their answers reveal a tip or insight that will help make you a better writer.

When working on writing assignments that are especially tough, take time out to browse and reread bits and pieces of these interviews. They'll boost your confidence and help jump-start your writing process. There's nothing more comforting or encouraging than hearing professional writers talk about the same problems you're facing, and discovering that the problem-solving process associated with writing is as hard for published writers with years of experience under their belts as it is for you.

RHONDA ABRAMS
THE SUCCESSFUL BUSINESS PLAN: SECRETS & STRATEGIES

Rhonda Abrams writes the nation's most widely read column on entrepreneurship and small business. With 20 million readers, her weekly columns appear in more than 100 newspapers as well as USA Today.com and Inc.com. Abrams is also the author of the best-selling, step-by-step business plan guide, *The Successful Business Plan: Secrets & Strategies*. Her second book, *Wear Clean Underwear: Business Wisdom from Mom,* was named a Book-of-the-Month Club selection and was reviewed in *The New York Times, People* magazine, and *Inc.* magazine. Her most recent book, *The Successful Business Organizer,* includes the information and tools an entrepreneur needs to get a business up and running. You can read her columns and get more information at www.RhondaOnline.com.

Q: Do you think that writing rules complicate the writing process more than they help?

R.A.: Many people are confused because there are so many different outlets for writing these days, and the same rules don't necessarily apply across the board. The way you write an e-mail is much different from the way you write a proposal. That's why the context of everything you write is so important. Why are you writing? Who are you writing it for? How much time do you have to write it? What is your purpose? And that's really where I'd start: What is the purpose of the piece you are writing? How you write a book is very different from how you write a newspaper column. One of the problems with businesspeople who have been around for a while or who work for large, formal corporations is that their main purpose for writing any type of assignment is simply to get it done. The idea is to impress the boss by having done it rather than to communicate an important idea. That's obviously the wrong purpose.

Q: What other writing problems do you see in the business world?

R.A.: Jargon. Too many writers hide behind industry jargon. For example, I met someone who told me about his new company. It sounded very interesting, so later I visited his Web site. Now, I have a fairly good understanding of technology, but after reading the information on his Web site, I couldn't tell if his company sold hardware or software or who its customers were. They assumed their audience understood all the high-tech language, but that's always a mistake. You'd be surprised at how many people in an industry don't understand all the jargon. Writers have to be careful with terminology. If you can say it without jargon, do it. If you can't, then explain your terms.

Another problem I see a lot is that writers are afraid to be informal. People usually write informal e-mails, but the minute they have to write a letter or report, they get stiff. I write very much the way I talk. My goal is to have my readers hear my voice—as if I were speaking to them—when they read my work. That's really effective writing.

Q: What personal writing rules have you developed?

R.A.: I use a lot of conjunctions, and I like to write in the first person. I'm also a big believer in bullet points. People don't read—that's one of Rhonda's Rules—so I make it easy for them to find out what they need to know without reading full sentences.

Also, as any professional writer will tell you, writing is not important, rewriting is important. Good writing is the result of looking at and revising a draft two, three, or four times. I'm shocked at the number of people who think, "Okay, I've written this and therefore none of it can be touched." One rule that is incredibly liberating for anybody who has a fear of writing and just wants to get started is to write a crummy first draft—just get it down. Use a first draft to teach yourself what you want to say. Typically, it's not until I finally finish my first draft that I figure out what I want to say. Invariably, the end of my first draft is the beginning of what will later be my final draft. You have to have the guts to throw away the words that were simply helping you to think things through.

Another big mistake I see a lot of writers make, and it's a really tempting trap to fall into, is doing all the work for the reader. Some writers document every step of the thinking they used to arrive at a conclusion. You end up leaving nothing to the readers' imagination, nothing for them to figure out. When that happens, the reader is going to get bored. People think faster than they read, so it's all right to leave some steps out.

A writing tip that I got from one of my very first editors turned out to be incredibly helpful over the years: Watch your verbs. Verbs hold up a sentence, and nothing is more dreadful to the written language than a document that is completely written with "to be" verbs. We use that verb form a lot in spoken language, so it's easy to slip into that style when we write. But it can make writing very deadly if every sentence includes "I was, he was, she was, and they were." So write your first draft down and edit it for context and content, and then go back and change the "to be" verbs into strong active verbs.

Q: What is the first step in your writing process?

R.A.: The first step is trying to figure out what I want to say. I usually do that during my morning walk. So writing doesn't necessarily start at the computer. While walking, I don't try to think of the exact words I want to write, just the ideas. Now, when I write my columns, I'm not worried about using what I write to get a promotion or secure a client. I've done that before; but for my own writing, I'm in the enviable position of deciding my purpose and what I want to say. I finally got to the point in my career that many writers dream about, which is getting paid to write about topics that I choose.

One way to view the writing process is to divide it into two parts: art and craft. The art of writing is figuring out what you want to say that's unique and important, creating a phrase that's memorable or an approach that's different. Art also encompasses learning new things before writing about them. People forget that writing is a wonderful tool for learning about yourself and the world around you. Most people have to research something about their subject before they can write about it.

Then there's the craft of writing, which is making sure your verbs are lively and your prepositions don't dangle. It's easy enough while writing your first draft to forget to put a verb in a sentence. Part of the craft of writing is noticing those types of mistakes while proofreading and fixing them. I think too many businesspeople approach writing from the craft side first, rather than the art side. They don't allow enough time to think about what they want to say; they just dive right in and edit as they write their first draft and, once they finish it, they think they're done.

Q: Often, professional writers never think they're done with a draft; they never want to put it down. Do you think that's true of the average business writer?

R.A.: Unfortunately, no. An interesting point about professional writers is how hard it can be for them to recognize that what they've written is good. I heard the author Jane Smiley being interviewed on the radio. She wrote the novel *A Thousand Acres*. It's a fabulous book. But she hates it! She said she won't read it and that she didn't enjoy writing it. Yet it won a Pulitzer Prize and the National Book Critics Circle Award.

Q: What role does audience play while you're writing? Do you envision them sitting across the desk, talking to you?

R.A.: No, I don't, but it's very important to have a good sense of who your audience is, and I think we all do that naturally when we write. Being very clear about who your audience is will help you tremendously. I have a staff of people doing writing projects for me, and the first thing we talk about is our readers. Who are they? We define that before writing anything. Some people do not, and I think it shows in their writing. If you don't know who your audience is, it's easy to talk down to them, or assume they know more than they do, or confuse them in many other ways. For example, I have written business plans, proposals, Web site copy, and other projects for clients. The audience for these projects was not my clients, but their clients, so I had to be very careful while writing to keep the correct audience in mind. The question of audience shapes the way I write and the point of view I take, and it brings a certain kind of response to my writing. That's very important to me, very important.

Q: Who edits and proofreads your work?

R.A.: It depends on whom I'm writing for and what I'm writing. If I'm writing an article for a newspaper, an editor at the paper will read and edit the piece before it goes out on the wire. When I write books, the publishing house assigns an editor to the book. When I published a book through Random House, I had an editor, copyeditor, and lawyer look at my manuscript. In addition, I hire my own editor to check the manuscript before I send it to my publisher.

Q: If a group of business writers asked you to give them tips on how to improve their writing, what would you tell them?

R.A.: Tip number one: Rewrite. It's not about writing, it's about rewriting. That's the most important thing I can say. Two, use good, strong verbs. Verbs make your sentence. Three, lighten up! And four is write a lot. To become a good writer you have to write a lot. I wrote a newspaper column for five years before I really found my voice. Writing takes time, just like any other skill.

Q: Do the writing rules taught in school play a role in the writing process?

R.A.: I think the most important writing foundation I have is an innate sense of outlining what I want to say. An outline or structure is a critical component of any good writing. I disregard other rules frequently. I'll begin sentences with a conjunction; I'll end sentences with a preposition. I know what the rules are, but I'll choose to ignore them. I've fought with editors over grammar. But I write to be lively, so I'm willing to break the rules. I know the rules because I use them so often, but I break them when I feel it's appropriate.

Q: When did you realize that you wanted to be a writer and how did you know?

R.A.: I realized it in the eighth grade. I had a very good eighth-grade English teacher who had us write stories. We wrote little serial stories, and I remember we had to create a mythological figure. We also did sentence diagramming, which I hated at the time, but it turns out to have been a very useful exercise. I was always a very good writer in school and college. I was on the staff of my high school newspaper, and I thought I wanted to be a lawyer, but I got distracted in pursuit of that goal and now I'm a professional writer.

Q: At what point in your writing career did you finally realize you were a good writer?

R.A.: I don't know. It gradually came over me that writing was something I was good at. I started writing professionally as a hobby, doing film reviews for a monthly newspaper in San Francisco. I took a lot of pride in writing good, clear film reviews. And it was fun! I was doing it totally for fun. I wasn't getting paid to write the reviews, but when people told me how much they enjoyed my writing, that was enough payment for me. I worked hard to make my first book, *The Successful Business Plan,* a readable book. It paid off because it sold well. Someone even told me that you could read my book at the beach. In fact, about a year after it came out, I met someone at a wedding who said, "I've just come back from trekking in Nepal. I was allowed to take one book, and I took yours with me." I said, "You're out of your mind!" But she really enjoyed it. There's probably nothing I take more pride in than trying to write well.

Q: What types of writing do you do most often?

R.A.: I write my column every week and e-mails every day. I have to admit, though, that I hate writing e-mails, but not as much as I hate writing business letters. One of the great developments of the last few years is the demise of the business letter. When I was younger, working at a company, I had to write business letters all the time. I'd look at the blank paper and say, "What do I have to say to fill this page up?" Those were really hard. Today, I don't have to write business letters, memos, reports, or any of the typical daily business correspondence most people have to write. I am free at last!

Q: Do you use a computer to write?

R.A.: I use a computer 99 percent of the time, although you'll never catch me without paper and pen so I can jot down notes when I'm away from my computer. I'll write notes while I'm at a meeting or anywhere. I like using a word processor. It's the great liberator for writers because you can sit down and just start writing and rearrange all the pieces into a coherent whole. The hardest thing about writing is the opening: How are you going to open your column, chapter, or letter? With a word processor, you don't have to start at the beginning. Forget it! Just write the rest and come back to it. You'll usually discover your opening sentence toward the end of your writing process, anyway.

Q: In your opinion, what shape is business writing in today?

R.A.: Unfortunately, most people who write about business don't write very well. They don't write very clearly. On the other hand, I actually think most e-mails I get are great, basically because the writers say what they need to say and aren't as stressed out about writing e-mails as they are when writing a report or a proposal. I get e-mails that are one or two words long that communicate everything that needs to be said.

Q: How important is writing in the business world today?

R.A.: Let me answer that by telling you about a venture capitalist I met at a conference. We were talking about how hard it is to find good employees. He said when he's looking to either hire a new person or invest in a training program for a current employee, the two skills he looks for are the ability to think critically and to write clearly. That's more important than anything else. And I just thought, "How interesting. Here's a high-finance person who is oriented to making millions and millions of dollars and these are the two skills he values most; and they have nothing to do with finance." Regardless of all the computers and televisions in our culture, we're still a very verbal society. Words are really important.

KEN BLANCHARD
THE ONE MINUTE MANAGER

Ken Blanchard is the chief spiritual officer of The Ken Blanchard Companies, Inc., a full-service, global management training and consulting company that he and his wife, Dr. Marjorie Blanchard, founded in 1979 in San Diego, California. His best-selling book, *The One Minute Manager,* coauthored with Spencer Johnson, has sold more than 10 million copies worldwide. It is still on best-seller lists and has been translated into more than twenty-five languages. Blanchard's more recent books that appear on the *Business Week* best-seller list include *Whale Done!, Raving Fans, Gung Ho!,* and *High Five!* For more information, visit the company's Web site at www.kenblanchard.com.

Q: How do you approach your writing projects?

K.B.: I learned my philosophy of writing from Spencer Johnson when we wrote *The One Minute Manager* together. He knows as much as there is to know about writing. The philosophy that he developed is that you should only write the first draft and then give it to a sampling of your reading audience and let them write the other drafts. All of my books go through six or seven drafts based on feedback from potential readers, customers, before they are ready for publication. It works wonderfully. We have a form we use that asks people what they like best about the book, what they would change to make it the best book they ever read on the subject, what they would title the book, and who they would share it with.

I have a funny story about using this method. I wrote a book with Norman Vincent Peale called *The Power of Ethical Management*. I invited Norman and his wife, Ruth, to attend a feedback dinner I organized at the Skaneateles Country Club near our summer cottage in upstate New York. Since Norman had begun his ministry in nearby Syracuse, 300 people attended. We got into some heated discussions about what worked and didn't work in the draft of the book. After we finished this process, I asked Norman to speak to the group. He was about eighty-eight at the time. He stood up and said, "I've never been to a free-for-all like this in my life. I've written thirty books, and when I finish one, Ruth and I pray. But Ken doesn't trust that process."

Q: Did anybody ever say you were a bad writer?

K.B.: Yes, everybody. However, I had one teacher in high school, Miss Sims, who I wrote about in my book *Everyone's a Coach,* which I coauthored with legendary football coach Don Shula. Miss Sims inspired me to keep writing. She gave me an F on the first paper I wrote for her and wrote more in red ink in the margins than I had originally typed. But she included a note that said, "I am doing this because I think you can be a good writer. And this paper falls way short of your potential." She kept on my back all year. The last paper I turned in received an A, and she gave me an A for the course. She said all the terrible writing I turned in at the beginning of the year was stuff I needed to get out of my system. She was a great teacher.

When I was in graduate school, most of my professors told me I could never be a college professor because I couldn't write. Later I learned that the problem with my writing from their point of view was that you could understand it, which meant it wasn't academic enough. But, because of their feedback, I decided to become a college administrator.

My first job, after receiving my Ph.D., was administrative assistant to the dean of the business school at Ohio University. Not long after, the chairman of the department, Paul Hersey, who was a great teacher—I decided to take his course the second semester I was there—comes into my office and says, "Ken, I'm looking for somebody to write a textbook with me. I know what needs to be in it, but I just can't write. I'm a nervous wreck. Would you be willing to write it with me?" I said, "Let's do it! You can't write and I'm not supposed to be able to, so we should be a great team!" So we wrote a book called *Management of Organizational Behavior* that was published in 1969. The eighth edition recently came out. It has sold well over a million copies. The students love it because they can understand it. They understand it because Hersey and I didn't know any big words.

Shortly after the book was released, I quit my administrative position—which I was lousy at—and became a full-time faculty member. Then I left Ohio University and went to the University of Massachusetts. In six years I became a full professor with tenure and then went on a sabbatical leave to California. Paul and I were planning to write a book on raising children, which we later did, called *The Family Game*.

It was in San Diego that I ran into Spencer Johnson at a cocktail party. My wife, Margie, met him first and introduced us. He was a children's book writer and Margie said, "You two should write a children's book for managers. They won't read anything else!" Spencer was working on a book about one-minute parenting with a psychiatrist. I invited him to a seminar that I was doing the next week. He came, sat in the back, and laughed all day. Afterward he came up and said, "The hell with parenting. Let's go for *The One Minute Manager*."

That was in November 1980. We had a first draft completed by the end of December, and we self-published it the following May. It sold 20,000 copies with no advertising before we went to New York to sell it to a publishing company. William Morrow published *The One Minute Manager* nationally in September 1982. In February 2002, it was number nine on the *Business Week* best-seller list in paperback and number fifteen in hardback. Not bad for a book that was almost twenty years old.

Q: What would you say to a person who thinks professional writers know a secret writing formula?

K.B.: Well, I'd tell them they're misinformed. What they need to do is get their ideas down on paper. Get their "diarrhea" version out first; don't worry about editing and punctuation until later. There are plenty of professional editors you can hire. It's a rare writer who is good at both writing and proofreading, so don't let that discourage you. You want to get your ideas out. In fact, I recommend to some people, if they're auditory, to dictate the book. Don't even write it. Get it typed up and edit from there and make sure it makes sense. But get the first version out so you can get it to people for feedback. All you need to know is a message that needs to be out there.

Q: So anybody can write nonfiction with practice?

K.B.: Yes. With fiction, I think, you need a certain kind of talent. But anybody can master nonfiction if they work at it. It's just communication of good ideas that can help others.

Q: At what point in your life did you consider yourself a writer?

K.B.: Well, probably when I started working on my first book, *Management of Organizational Behavior.* That's when I realized that I could write.

Q: When did you realize that you were a good writer?

K.B.: When I showed my books to people and they said, "That's good." I never judge my books on what I think. Always judge your writing by what your potential audience thinks. Feedback is the "breakfast of champions."

Q: What process do you follow when you write?

K.B.: The first thing I ask myself is: What do I want to focus on, what do I want to teach? I always try to break my subject into three or four main points, the most teachable concepts, because I don't think most people can grasp more than that.

The second question I ask is: How do I want to teach it? Do I want to write it like a regular book, a parable, a quotation book? I get too many ideas to do all my writing by myself, so I work with other writers. When I got the idea to do my most recent book, *Whale Done!*—which is about how they train whales—I worked with two trainers, Thad Lacinak and Chuck Tompkins, who have worked with whales for over twenty-five years. When I learned their techniques, I then said okay, how do we make this content simple? What's the story line? We decided to write a parable because that seemed to fit the content best.

The book is about a businessperson attending a conference in Orlando. He's worried about problems at work and also concerned about his relationships with his kids and his wife. He decides to take a day off instead of worrying about everything and goes to SeaWorld. The Shamu show really affected him—the performance and the cooperation the trainers got from the whales was amazing. The businessperson says to himself, "I'm not getting that kind of cooperation from my people and my kids." So he races down the stairs and talks to one of the trainers. That begins a story that eventually changes his life and the lives of those he touches.

Q: Do you write an outline or just start writing?

K.B.: My coauthors and I make an outline of the contents and then an outline of the story line. Then our task is to connect the two! After that, we start writing.

Q: Does your approach to book writing transfer to business writing?

K.B.: Whether it's a book or a business letter, you need to continually get feedback until people say, "That's fabulous." When they say that, you know you're fine and that you're done writing.

Q: Who edits your work?

K.B.: You always get a final edit from your publisher, but the writers I've worked with are pretty good at that, too.

Q: What about you personally? Is proofreading a strong point?

K.B.: No. I took the college SATs four times and I finally got 502 in English and 465 in math. My mind is not a typical scholar's mind. My wife says I invent words. She did very well on the SATs because she had English teachers who made her read the classics and underline any word she didn't understand and then look it up. I never had any of that.

Q: People who are poor proofreaders of their own work are usually quick to pounce on a typo in a letter they receive. That mind-set causes lots of anxiety in some business writers.

K.B.: The one thing that's saved a lot of us now is e-mail, because people's expectations about e-mail are so much lower. You're just communicating. But for some reason when we receive regular business correspondence—letters, memos, and such—people want to get their red pens out. It helps that I have a good secretary who checks what I write. But you shouldn't worry if you don't have good proofreading skills; just make sure you hire someone who does. It's like the guys who wrote *Now, Discover Your Strengths* [Marcus Buckingham and Donald O. Clifton]. Everyone should find out what their writing strengths are, and then get others to fill in their weaknesses.

Q: Do you ever get writer's block?

K.B.: Ten years ago I did, but not much anymore. If I do, I just get up from the desk and walk away. Whenever I sit down to write, I first pray and ask the Lord to get my ego out of the way. That really helps a lot. Too many writers get writer's block because they listen to their egos telling them everything they write has to be perfect. They forget that their goal is to communicate and just share their ideas.

Q: Have you developed any writing rules over the years?

K.B.: My biggest writing rule is: Just get started! That's the hardest thing for people. It's easy to come up with excuses not to write. Get started and be open for feedback. Look upon writing as a journey. You'll get better the more you write. You also have to know the best time of day to write. I'm a morning person. When I get up, I often take a walk and think about what I'm going to write that day and psyche myself up.

Q: Is there a difference between how you learned to write in school and how you write today?

K.B.: I think school teaches more theory than practice. You get lots of practice in the real world, but schools should be doing that, too. They should make you write a lot and give you feedback. And your grade should be based on how well you're writing at the end of the course, not an average of your work throughout the semester. I really love that approach. It's more realistic.

Q: Do you think of academic writing rules when you write?

K.B.: Sometimes. Strunk and White's *The Elements of Style* is an excellent guide. If I ever have any concerns, I look at that, but I don't let rules get in the way of my writing.

Q: Do you edit as you write?

K.B.: No. I write first and edit later. If not, you can spend months on one chapter. I'm always more interested in knocking out a first draft, warts and all.

Q: What do you feel are the main reasons for poor writing in the world today?

K.B.: People don't open themselves to feedback and help from others. It makes sense to have someone else look at the letter you wrote before sending it out. That's how you learn. Other people will spot your mistakes before you will. It's just common sense.

Q: How important is business writing today?

K.B.: A lot less than it was a decade ago. People are using other media: voice mail, e-mail, videoconferencing. I think it could end up being a mistake.

Q: Do you wait for inspiration to strike before starting a project?

K.B.: I wait for a good idea. I meet lots of people who give me great ideas. I have a strategy a friend taught me that I call "ping or thud." A ping is, Whoa! That's a really interesting idea. A thud is, Forget it. I wait for pings. My problem is, I get too many pings!

RICHARD BOLLES
WHAT COLOR IS YOUR PARACHUTE?

Richard Bolles is the author of *What Color Is Your Parachute?* This practical manual for job hunters and career changers is revised annually. Seven million copies are in print, in ten languages. Twenty thousand people buy it each month, and it is often called the Job Hunters' Bible. Bolles runs a companion Web site at www.JobHuntersBible.com.

Q: When did you start to write?

R.B.: The first thing that you should know about me is that I'm an Episcopalian minister. I started writing as soon as I was ordained—back in 1953—because I had to give a sermon every Sunday and I was not an extemporaneous speaker. I always wrote out every single word of my sermon. I would start on Saturday night about four or five in the afternoon and write well into the night, sometimes until four in the morning. Then I would take it over to the church at the crack of dawn and read the manuscript two or three times from the pulpit to be sure that it was firmly in my mind. When I actually preached the sermon, I would only use the manuscript as a guide, not read it word for word. I used it as a springboard into the pool of my thoughts. One of the lessons I learned early on—after writing sermons nearly every Sunday for sixteen years—was that writing and speaking go hand in hand. In those days I typed everything on an IBM Selectric. I threw away many drafts. I would write two or three paragraphs then realize that wasn't the route I wanted to take with my thoughts, and then throw away the paper. I had a wonderful woman in my parish who wanted all of the drafts that I threw away. She said I threw away more good ideas than most writers ever write, so I gave her my discards every Sunday. That's another lesson: You often have to throw away work, good ideas to boot, that you spent hours writing. It's just part of the process of distilling the best from all that goes through your mind.

Q: Have you developed any personal writing rules?

R.B.: I have several rules that I use to govern my writing, and the first rule is: Never look for the perfect sentence. I have a Snoopy cartoon in my office that says, "Your new book has a great beginning. Good luck with the second sentence." I believe that lots of writers kill their ability to write well by trying to begin with a perfect sentence and trying to polish each sentence they write, as they go. I'm a stream-of-consciousness writer. I put down on paper all the thoughts that go through my mind. And I mean that literally. If I think, "I'm having trouble thinking how to start this article," then that's what I write down on paper or on the computer. My rule is, "If I think it, I must write it." Later one can go back, of course, and polish that. A good analogy is brainstorming. The first rule in brainstorming is never to criticize an idea that somebody else proposes because that kills creativity. The same is true for individual writers. If you censor or edit what you write while you're writing it, you'll short-circuit the creative process. You should welcome any idea that spills out onto your paper, and critique it later.

Q: When did you make the move into business writing?

R.B.: I don't call myself a business writer. I have never used that designation. I refer to myself as a career writer. I write about careers, and careers only. I started writing about that subject in 1970. I was supervising a group of campus ministers in nine western states, from ten denominations. Part of my job was to travel to their campuses, and that included Alaska and Hawaii, and find out what problems or issues they had. One issue stood out from the rest—budgets. After World War II, the men and women came back from the battlefield and gave generously to their churches. The old saying is that there are no atheists in foxholes. The budgets grew and the parishes expanded dramatically during the 1960s. Then the retrenchment came and church budgets declined. One of the first line items to go was minister salaries. As the church budgets in the late 1960s started to decline, eliminating campus ministers looked like an easy way to balance the budget. Hence they were being fired, in the majority.

So these men came to me and said, "What do we do?" and I said, "I don't know, but I'll try to find out." I traveled 68,000 miles that year and researched the problem. Afterward, I put together a tiny manual for them, summarizing my research, and self-published it in December 1970. It was about 168 pages long and I called it *What Color Is Your Parachute?* Two years later, after the self-published version sold out, a commercial publisher, Ten Speed Press in Berkeley, California, stepped into the picture and published *Parachute*'s first commercial edition in November 1972. By 1974, it was on best-seller lists. It's still the most popular job-hunting book in the world. Since 1975, I have revised and updated the book every year. So I'm not resting on my laurels. I rewrite the book every year. The most dramatic rewriting occurred for the 2002 edition. I rewrote the whole book "from scratch." I have been doing this annual rewriting for over thirty years now, and it is a very interesting exercise to take a completed work that's hugely popular—it has sold 7 million copies and 20,000 people purchase it every month—and try to see how I can reframe it, rewrite it, and make it more lucid. Each year I look at the book and say, "Where did I go wrong? How can I improve this? What new ideas do I need to put in here? What old ideas do I need to explain better?" That's a fascinating task, to have a chance to go back and take your original work and continually improve it for thirty years.

Q: Do you find writing hard or easy?

R.B.: That depends on what I'm writing. For example, I was once asked to write a column for the *San Francisco Chronicle* and the *San Francisco Examiner* every Sunday. It was an interesting exercise for me because each article had to be exactly 800 words. People used to write and tell me my column was the very best in the newspaper, that they always looked forward to it, and so on. They complimented me on how effortless my writing was. I wrote back and said, "It's not that effortless. I sweat bullets writing it." So for eight months I had that discipline in my life, and I learned a lot from it. But after eight months, I gave up the columnist assignment—I couldn't stand the time it took to write the piece down to 800 words; I can't even say "hello" in 800 words. It took me two whole days to write the article. I suppose if I lived in a cave and didn't have any distractions, I could have written it faster, but it's astonishing how long it can take to write an article that has strict limits. I have no such constraint with *Parachute*.

Q: Why do you think people find writing difficult?

R.B.: What makes writing such an arduous task in the minds of most people is the fact that our culture tends to teach—in university, high school, and elsewhere—that you should do two processes at the same time: You should create or brainstorm, and you should edit. It's only when people separate those two processes and say, "No, the brainstorming is one thing and the editing is another process entirely" that they will learn how to write well. You really need to separate those two tasks if you are to write at your best. If you don't separate them and try to do both at the same time, that kills the creative impulse. So that's my guiding principle for how I write, and that's what I tell anybody who asks me for writing advice. When they take my advice, they come back and say, "Oh, this is so helpful. I wish somebody would have told me this ages ago."

Q: Who edits your work?

R.B.: I do. I have people who read my copy for stupid mistakes, but I never have an editor proofread—which often means "rewrite"—my work. Because my book is such a long project, I usually stop and edit what I've done about halfway through. I need to polish it so I can see where I need to go next. I compare writing a book to a walk in the woods. You go down a path and you're not sure where it's taking you. Suddenly you come to a fork in the path, and you can't figure out which one you should take. So you turn around and look back to see where you've come from, to get your bearings and help you decide which fork to take. Stopping to edit halfway through a book is like turning around and looking back to see where you started, so you can get a better idea of where to go next. I think it's very important that the writer do that, not an editor.

Q: At what point in your writing career did you know that you were a good writer?

R.B.: Early on, but only because I had an advantage that most writers don't have: When I wrote something, I got feedback within an hour. In my parish priest days, every Sunday, after church was over, people would tell me what they liked and didn't like about my sermon. Instant feedback! Lucky me! I learned a lot from that constant weekly feedback. One of the difficulties business writers face is that they don't get feedback on everything they write, and they don't get feedback from a wide variety of people—unless of course they write for a magazine, newspaper, or Web site. I recommend instant feedback to everyone; it sure helped me become a better writer, fast.

Q: What physical routines do you have when you write? Do you use a computer, a pen and paper?

R.B.: Sometimes I'll jot down ideas on a piece of paper. Sometimes I'll use an outlining software program that nobody's ever heard of. I work solely on a Macintosh, and the program I'm talking about was invented by Noah and if not, certainly by Moses. It's a wonderful outlining program; you can expand or collapse it like an accordion. The trouble is, I don't have a set method. I sometimes work in certain ways, and sometimes I just sit down and start spewing. I just start writing and see where it goes. It's very interesting sometimes to have no framework and no outline.

Q: What motivates you to sit down and write?

R.B.: I sit down to write when I'm passionate about a topic. I have to be convinced that there's something worth arguing about, on behalf of the reader. For example, when the Internet first hit the scene, people liked to take online psychology tests to determine their IQ or the vocation they should have. I looked at these tests and thought, "Some people are going to be steered in the wrong direction by taking these tests too seriously, so I must write an article about that."

I was passionate about the subject and I was determined to save people from letting an Internet test take them down a wrong path in life. So I wrote. I do believe that there's no sense in writing an article if your goal is nothing more specific than, "What am I going to rhapsodize about today?" You have to have a set purpose. You must have something important to say. Without that energy—and it is energy—I think the writing is often listless and the writer comes across as being bored and/or boring. Let me tell you a story about a "boring" conversation I once had. I was talking to an acquaintance over dinner one evening, telling her about an event in my life that I thought was really interesting. But she suddenly interrupted me and said, "You know, I'm really bored by what you're telling me." I was stunned! Then she continued with this astute observation: "Because I can't find anything in my own life that I can relate it to." I thought what she said was genius. And so, I think that when people write, they need to constantly ask themselves, "How does this relate to my audience, the lives of my readers?" Finding the answer to that question will help a writer translate his passion, his energy, into an article, sermon, or letter that his audience will read with passionate interest.

MARCUS BUCKINGHAM
FIRST, BREAK ALL THE RULES

Marcus Buckingham is a global practice leader at the Gallup Organization and the author of *First, Break All the Rules,* with coauthor Curt Coffman, and *Now, Discover Your Strengths,* with coauthor Donald O. Clifton. Both books have been named to *The New York Times* bestselling list.

Q: What would you say to someone who thinks published writers know a secret writing formula?

M.B.: That it's true, but I'm afraid I can't share it with you. All kidding aside, the truth is there is no secret formula. You discover how to write as you write. I simply write the way that I would want to be written to. That's the only formula I have. First and foremost, I want to write things that I would want to read. Another thing that helped me tremendously is that I wrote both of my books with a specific person in mind. I wrote *First, Break All the Rules* to a particular manager that I know and *Now, Discover Your Strengths* to a person I wanted to help. I wasn't trying to write out a theoretical case in either book, or persuade a mass of people on a particular point. I was just trying to write to an individual. A book is a very, very intimate experience. I thought it would be helpful if I imagined myself sitting in a room just talking with one person.

Q: Does that approach make writing easier?

M.B.: There's a great quote, though I can't remember who said it, that goes: "Writing is easy. I just slit my veins and let the words flow onto the page." Allan Bennett, the English playwright, refers to writing as wooing words. Writing is hard. People call it a grind, but it's less of a grind than it is a search. I don't know of any writer who takes dictation from God. Everyone is trying to find out a way to say something so that people will be interested in it and won't lose their train of thought. So whatever type of writer you are, you're always trying to keep people's attention. When it came to writing discipline, I was very straightforward with myself. I wrote a thousand words a day. Some days I wouldn't hit a thousand, and my wife would always tell me it's not the day, it's the week. It's five thousand a week. A trick that I and other writers use is to stop writing each day in mid-sentence. It enables me to sit down the next day and start writing again immediately.

Q: What is your writing background? Were you a writer before you wrote your first book?

M.B.: I wrote reports for companies. I was a managing consultant at the Gallup Organization and I would write reports on individuals and companies. I did a lot of analysis: How engaged are your employees? How engaged are you? Where are your company's strengths? Do I see you fitting into this company? I would write about management, leadership, organizational development, organizational effectiveness. That kind of thing. I had never written a book before, however. But I had a very good agent who told me that I had some good ideas and should write a book proposal. She said if you can't write a book proposal, you can't write a book. I wrote nineteen drafts of the proposal before she would let it go off her desk.

Q: So you basically made the leap from work-a-day business writer to published book author?

M.B.: Yes, I mean I always had this love of words and writing and got a kick out of finding good word combinations. You have to know a good word combination from a bad one when you see it. I don't know how much of that you can teach, but you can't teach the love of writing. You can, however, get better at writing no matter what level you're starting from. I had a good writing background from attending college and my work at Gallup and other jobs, plus enough ideas to write a book, but I had no experience at all in taking an idea and turning it into eighty thousand words!

Q: Do you have any personal writing habits?

M.B.: A very good friend who is also a good writer, a TV writer and producer, told me that one of the secrets to good writing is to read in between sessions of working on your draft. Read a lot. Read somebody good. It doesn't have to be in your style, just read somebody good so you can see what good writing is like while you're writing. So I bought Hemingway's short stories. Whenever I got stuck, I would just read his stories. He writes such short, clear declarative sentences, it enabled me to remember what good writing was like and continue on.

Q: At what point did you consider yourself a writer and why?

M.B.: I don't know that I do think of myself as a writer. I try and write, but I don't sit around and call myself a writer. But I like the idea of that. It sounds glamorous to say you're a writer, but I think of myself more as an explainer. Martin Amis is a writer, someone who takes massive joy in experimenting and playing with narrative and prose. I don't do that. Now, there are passages in both of my books where I thought, hey, that's pretty good. But those are the ones your editor tells you to delete anyway! They say editing is like killing your children. There are times when I thought I was a writer and then my wife would come in and say, "This is crap!" And when you've been properly humbled, you go back and start writing again with the correct perspective.

Q: I was once told every writer needs an editor, someone to keep you on track.

M.B.: It's like the old cliché about Einstein. Someone who didn't recognize him once sat next to him at dinner and asked him what he did. Einstein said, I study physics. His whole point was you keep learning, you keep studying, you're never done. So as a writer, I'm constantly thinking about getting better. And of course, by the way, I rewrite everything a lot. You have to do that. You have to constantly write, which is why I think e-mail is so good. It forces you to write and discover new ways to express yourself. E-mailing has been a really good addition to my daily routine. One of the other things that writing is really good for, and it took me a long time to realize this, is that it forces you to think everything through. If you're giving a speech or giving a presentation, you can gloss over certain things that you don't want your audience to dig into too deeply, but when you're writing you can't. You have to think it all the way through, and that is very helpful for businesspeople, authors, everyone.

Q: That's what businesses want, anyway—clear thinking, good ideas.

M.B.: Exactly. The act of writing is the process of clarifying thought. Not just for the reader, but for the writer. Whenever I get depressed about writing and I sit down with a blank sheet of paper and think I'm ready to slit my veins, I think about just getting something down on paper. The other thing I find helpful when writing is remembering to write a story. And I don't mean, here's an anecdote with a plot and characters, I mean everything from a business report to a book has to have a beginning, a middle, and an end. Both of my books have a beginning, a middle, and an end. There is a trajectory to them. People like to read parables and stories. If you're writing a business book or letter, your readers have to have a reason to turn the page, and the power of your prose won't do it. There needs to be momentum, and you have to create that; you have to set up the questions at the beginning. That's actually one of the more fun things to think about, How am I going to get the reader to turn the page? Now we're on quest together!

Q: When it comes to business writing, though, it doesn't have to be the same kind of quest that, let's say, Oliver Twist took. It can be something as simple as why are sales down 20 percent?

M.B.: Correct. You start with that question and suddenly everyone's on a quest to get the answer. One of the reasons for the success of my first book, and why it's still on the best-seller list everywhere, is that it has nothing to do with good writing. The key is that the book asks the right questions right at the start. What do the world's best managers do to be successful? Do you want to know? Okay, read on. That's one of the reasons why *Good to Great* [Jim Collins] and *Built to Last* [James C.

Collins and Jerry I. Porras] are good books. How can companies go from good to great? See, I'll read that book. How are companies built to last? I'll read that book, too. An editor I ran into once told me that the secret to a great business book is that it should have only one idea. Just one. If you can't describe what your book's about in one sentence, you probably don't have a clear book. Now, I don't know if that's true of a report, but I thought it was a very helpful piece of advice from somebody who knew his stuff.

Q: When did you consider yourself a good writer and how did you know you were?

M.B.: The only time I knew I was writing well was when people in the know, editors and other writers, said it was good writing. It goes back to when I was writing reports. I never wrote boringly, and people wanted to actually read my reports and said that I should write a book. I always enjoyed writing. I quite like the process and I love reading my own stuff. But I learned to never fall in love with what I wrote. Someone once said to me, the reader wins. So if a reader doesn't understand something I write, I don't get defensive, I change it. If they didn't get it, I didn't write it correctly.

Q: What is your writing process?

M.B.: First, I have to figure out what my book's about. I have to have that one-liner, that one idea. Secondly, I have to figure out the trajectory. And this is all planning. I must figure out where I'm going to start, what's the middle, and what's the end. Why would you turn the page? Which ideas flow first? What comes next? That might take a month, but I'll just sit with a pad and paper and I'll try and imagine how I'm going get from here to there and why a reader would want to come with me. Prior to that, however, I will have gathered a ton of stuff: stories, ideas, images, data. I'll do interviews, which not only give me content but inspiration. I'll take my notes and play with them, rearrange and reorganize them until they gradually take some sort of shape. I'll make file folders—chapter one, chapter two, etc. I can't start writing until I know what goes in each chapter. I'll wait until I have several file folders filled with information then dive in and begin writing. I'll start at 9:30 A.M. and stop at 4:30 P.M. and end in the middle of a sentence. When I get to the end of a big section, I'll rewrite it. I'll sit down in a big coffee shop somewhere and go through the whole chapter. I'll imagine I'm reading it like the reader, for the first time.

Q: How does that process apply to writing business reports?

M.B.: It's the same process, just not as long. I start by gathering information, then I figure out what my flow is, my beginning, my middle, and end. This approach, by the way, isn't how I was taught to write.

Q: That's my next question: Does your professional writing process differ from how you were taught to write in school?

M.B.: I don't know about the United States, but in the United Kingdom—I'm an English citizen—you're taught to write by making your case block by block by block, until you get to a point that your argument is so self-evident no one can believe anything differently. Then you write your conclusion. I went to Cambridge University and received an excellent education, but the unfortunate thing is that if you write like that, no one wants to read what you have written. You have to start by defining your quest or your readers won't follow you. It's so terribly obvious, but it's really hard to do when you're trained to write another way. You have to do the same in your business reports. You've got to start by saying, "This is all I'm going to tell you at first, but follow me and the trip will be exciting, challenging. Let's go!"

Q: Do you think of writing rules as you write?

M.B.: Only two. One is don't use passive voice if I can help it. I know that's silly, but it makes for more aggressive writing. The other is never use an adjective. When you've finished writing, cut out every adjective! Now I break that rule all the time. I've got lots of adjectives in everything I write. But my point is adjectives are lazy.

Q: So all the rest of the rules they teach you in school . . .

M.B.: I don't think about rules at all. Split infinitives and so forth? I split infinitives all the time. I don't care much about that stuff. I try and write aggressively, with purpose. I try and write so that you want to read it. And the rules don't fit into that. Use the active not passive voice is probably pretty good advice. So is avoid adjectives, but I break those rules, too. My goal is to do whatever I must to make my writing more clear and concise.

Q: What about grammar, spelling, and punctuation? What role do they play in your process?

M.B.: None. Grammar is simply the result of somebody trying to put an underlying rule to good writing. Grammar is derived from good writing, not the other way around. You can't write well by making everything you write grammatically correct. Grammar is a by-product of good writing; it's not a creator of good writing. So I don't think about it at all. I try to write clearly. The grammar will be there.

Q: Having said that, in the business world, as you know, mechanics mean a lot. You can look awfully unprofessional on paper if you have a lot of errors. What is your advice to businesspeople who aren't good proofreaders and can't give their letter to someone to proofread because it's due in half an hour?

M.B.: Run spell check. Grammar? Forget it. Do the best job you can in the time given and turn it in. Write clearly and concisely. Get your flow right, get your facts right.

Q: Did you ever have writer's block?

M.B.: No, but I suffer from idea block. It's frustrating and can sometimes be hopeless. I think, "I'm never going to do this. I'm never going to be able to express this."

Q: How do you work through that?

M.B.: Alcohol. No, I'm kidding! I just write it out, write through it.

Q: If you feel business writing needs improvement, what are the main reasons for poor writing in the business world today?

M.B.: Poor thinking and jargon come to mind right away. It seems some companies feel they have to create a new language to express themselves. Coopetition? What is that? Well, it's competition and cooperation. Oh, please. Save me from that. Peter Drucker writes well because he doesn't allow that stuff. He thinks clearly. Drucker is a classic because he's a good thinker.

HUMBERTO CRUZ
TRIBUNE MEDIA SERVICES SYNDICATED FINANCIAL COLUMNIST

Humberto Cruz is a long-time financial journalist who has been syndicated by Tribune Media Services of Chicago since 1992 and whose columns now appear in more than sixty publications nationwide. In addition, he and his wife, Georgina, started "Retire Smart," a column nationally syndicated by Tribune Media Services. Georgina and Humberto, who came to the United States from their native Havana, Cuba, in 1960 and settled in Florida, have been featured in *Money* magazine, *Kiplinger's Personal Finance* magazine, and the *Reader's Digest*. Both hold degrees in mass communications from the University of Miami.

Q: When did you start writing?

H.C.: I became a journalist in 1968, but the road to becoming a journalist begins a few years earlier. I was born in Cuba and came to the United States in 1960 at the age of fifteen. At the time, I knew little English. I attended Westport High School in Kansas City, and because I didn't know English well, I struggled to understand what people were telling me. My English class teacher suggested that I join the student newspaper. That seemed preposterous because of my language skills, but to make a long story short, I started to write for the paper. I learned from the very beginning to keep things simple when writing, and to use simple language. That lesson always stayed with me. Keep it simple and try to use words that are not very long. Pretend that you are talking with the reader and use words that are easily understood. Why use a long word when a short one will do?

Q: What personal writing rules have you developed over the years?

H.C.: One of the things that I do when I have finished writing a piece is to put it aside for a few days. I write a weekly column and I try to be diligent and have it completed several days before it is due. I put it aside and go back a day later and read it again and say, "What can I cut out of this? What can I lose? Can I condense it? How many words are more than three syllables?" Deleting long words is not always an easy decision. Some long words are appropriate at times, but I do read everything I write to make sure it's simple enough.

Q: Could you please describe your writing process?

H.C.: First and most important of all, I consider my readers' point of view: How much do they know about the topic? How technical should I be? For example, I recently wrote a review of a software program developed by an online finance company that explains how to invest money. It was a rather involved process. I had to sign up as a monthly subscriber, answer questions about my personal finances, interview other people who used the software, and follow my own investments for a few weeks to see the results. My information-gathering process alone took about six weeks, and all of that had to be condensed into an article of no more than twenty column inches. It was a difficult story to do because I could literally have written a very large magazine article on the program. In addition, my audience was not a financial audience, so I couldn't assume they had a sophisticated knowledge about investing.

So I thought long and hard about how I could approach the topic in a simple yet interesting way. I remembered that the program forecasts the success of your investments by displaying icons. If it feels that you have a very good chance of reaching your goals, it shows a small picture of a bright, shiny sun. If it thinks that you have very little success of reaching your goals, it displays dark clouds. So I finally hit upon a lead that said, "I saw the sun shining brightly on my computer screen and I knew life was good." I wanted to grab my readers' interest and have them ask, "What is he talking about?" so they would want to read more. Then I wrote, "The odds that I would have the income that I wanted when I retired were greater than 95 percent now, the best odds that the computer program that I was using gives." I was trying to establish right away that I was using a software program and that I was using it for projecting future retirement income. But it was written in such a way that a nonfinancial audience would understand. That was my goal.

In addition, I try to use parallels or similarities or comparisons to common everyday things when I write, so people have a point of reference.

In addition, the body of the piece must support the point that I am making, and if there is a contrary point of view I insert it fairly soon—no later than the fifth paragraph—for balance and fairness. But if I'm arguing against that contrary viewpoint, I proceed to argue against it strongly so that my position is clear to the reader. Finally, I very consciously close the piece in a manner that connects back to the beginning and reinforces my main point so that the article goes full circle.

Q: What's the first thing you do after completing a first draft?

H.C.: I go back and see how many sentences I can break down into two or three sentences. A sentence should have a subject, a verb, and an object, but if it has twenty-five modifiers, then it's too long. So the first thing I do is look for the subject/verb/object combination, and then determine if the sentence needs fixing. I'm also very conscious about varying the length of sentences, sometimes for emphasis. For example, when I'm explaining a complicated process, I purposely begin with a long paragraph to show by the length of the paragraph itself as well as its content that the process is complicated.

Q: How much do you think about writing rules while you write—rules such as, "Don't end a sentence with a preposition"?

H.C.: Frankly, I never think about the rules. You cannot ignore the rules; they're there for a purpose, which is to make it easier for people to understand the written word. But rules are a means to an end, not an end themselves. When I write, I focus on what I want to say, not rules. A big part of my writing process is that I live with a project for a while. Often, ideas for starting an article come to me when I'm falling asleep or just waking up in the morning, when I'm totally away from my notes, which I have all over the place. I simply sit down and write, not from memory, but after having thought about my topic for a long time. I sit down and write what I know. If I come to a part I don't know or haven't thought about much, I'll leave a place marker. For instance, if I want to start an article with a quotation, I may simply type the word *quote* at the top of the page and continue writing because I can go back and find the quotation in my notes and add it later. I don't want anything to interrupt the flow of writing down what I do know about my subject. I don't stop to capitalize words or fix other errors. I write what I want to say and then I go back and fill in the details later. I don't want to slow down or stop my thought process in any way while writing a first draft.

Q: How do you know what level of language to use?

H.C.: I always assume that my readers do not know sophisticated financial terms. I avoid insulting them by implying that they do know. When I can, I weave the definition of a term into the context of the article instead of just defining the term in a dictionary-like way. That way, the meaning of the term becomes obvious while reading the article.

Q: What types of writing do you do most often?

H.C.: I do three newspaper columns a week, which are nationally syndicated. I recently started a fourth one, so that's mostly what I do: column writing.

Q: Who edits and proofreads your work?

H.C.: The business editors at each newspaper read everything I write, as well as several copyeditors.

Q: If a group of business writers asked you to give them one or two writing tips that would improve their writing, what would you tell them?

H.C.: Check, double-check, and triple-check any numbers or calculations you include in your reports or letters to make sure they are correct. Do the same to each sentence and comparison that you use. I deal with a lot of numbers, and I am pretty proud of the fact that since I started writing my column, I can recall only one time that I have had to publish a correction. And that was one too many. I am extremely proud of that detail. A second tip would be if your subject matter is complex, make sure you understand it completely before trying to write about it. I don't know how many times I have heard other writers say, "This is hard to explain. I'm not sure I understand this myself." How can you possibly explain something if you don't understand it? Often, writing is a tremendous test of what you truly know and what you only think you know.

Q: Where do you write and what equipment do you use?

H.C.: I write on an IBM-compatible computer at home, using Microsoft Word. I am a morning person, so I try to do my heaviest, most complex writing in the morning and leave the afternoon for fact gathering. Typically, I get a second wind in the late afternoon and write more then, if necessary. In short, I try to write when I am at my best. But I do most of my thinking while I'm away from the computer. Often, the actual writing is the least effort in the process. The real effort takes place long before I sit down to write. I think, "How am I going to structure this? How am I going to say this?" while I am showering, shaving, or listening to the radio. The thinking is the hard and most crucial part.

Q: Any parting thoughts?

H.C.: A few points bear repeating: Keep your audience in mind. Understand what you want to say before you start to write. Make your point, back it up, and then summarize at the end, so there's no doubt in your reader's mind what you're trying to say. And always approach every writing project by asking yourself, "What am I trying to say and to whom?" and "How can I say it in the simplest possible way?"

GAIL EVANS
PLAY LIKE A MAN,
WIN LIKE A WOMAN

Gail Evans is the best-selling author of *Play Like a Man, Win Like a Woman: What Men Know About Success That Women Need to Learn.* Her book made the *New York Times, Business Week,* and the *Wall Street Journal* best-seller lists. A pioneer in broadcast journalism, Evans joined CNN at its inception in 1980. She went on to create the first television talk show to feature women discussing major news issues, and in 2000 became executive vice president of Domestic Networks for the CNN Newsgroup. The recipient of many awards and Emmy nominations, she now serves as a consultant to CNN, is a member of the International Women's Forum, and sits on the boards of several universities and not-for-profit organizations.

Q: What types of business writing did you do at CNN?

G.E.: Reports, memos, and proposals in which I created ideas for new programs. I've written a lot of those over the years. Most don't run more than a couple of pages because one of the things that I learned in business from Ted Turner is that if you really know what you're talking about, you can say almost anything in a few pages. Usually, the longer the presentation, the more confused the presenter is.

Q: Did you write those program proposals in a formal style?

G.E.: No. When I'm working on a project that I feel great passion and excitement about, my spoken word comes through. When I write in a formal style, it's contrived to achieve a specific result.

Q: What's the difference between the approach you took to writing your book and writing program proposals?

G.E.: I transcribed a lot of my book. I taped myself talking, transcribed it, then cleaned it up. One of the most important things I did while working on my book was to make sure that what I was writing was in my voice. I think that had a great deal to do with why the book became a best-seller. People constantly tell me that when they read my book, they feel as if I'm in the room talking to them. That's why they found the book easy to understand and use.

Q: At what point in your life did you consider yourself a writer?

G.E.: I don't consider myself a writer. I think writers are those who create beautiful literature. I'm a very good communicator, but I don't think I'm a very good writer.

Q: You're defining writing as literature, not business correspondence?

G.E.: Right. Business writing is about making your point and making it as concisely and abruptly as possible, so that your reader "gets it."

Q: Do you see your book as an extension of the type of business writing you do for CNN?

G.E.: I think my book is an extension of me. It isn't an extension of my business writing. I find that over the years—and because of e-mail— my business writing actually gets more and more unacceptable. The people who taught me how to write, I think, would be horrified by how the written word is used in the modern day. The written word has become more of a translation of the spoken word. Terrible punctuation, terrible grammar, and the only reason spelling isn't terrible is because everybody spell checks it!

Q: You just said that e-mails are poorly written because people write the way they speak. But a moment ago you said the reason your book sold so well is because you wrote it the way you speak. What's the difference?

G.E.: Today's e-mails don't sound important. They sound like a direct translation of speech instead of a more formal mode of speech. E-mails sound more like a kitchen conversation than a cabinet meeting in the Oval Office.

Q: What's the cure for poor e-mail writing?

G.E.: E-mails have eliminated a huge amount of the time spent on pretentious writing and wasteful telephone conversations, so we certainly don't want to get rid of e-mail. However, I think we all need to become a little more vigilant about what we say in e-mails. If we keep in mind that e-mails never disappear and that our personal names and a record of what we write are sitting on a computer somewhere, we all might write with more care.

Q: When did you know you were a good writer, and how did you know?

G.E.: I don't know that I am a good writer. All I know is that I can communicate. When I think about writing as a creative endeavor, I don't think I'm very good. But when I think about writing as a simple form of communication, a way to show somebody something or let somebody know what I want or need, then I think I'm very effective. I'm a good salesperson, but it's taken a lot of years for me to be comfortable thinking my spoken word is good enough to be my written word.

Q: How do you know when to stop writing? For example, how did you know when your book was well written and finally finished?

G.E.: When I realized that I was beginning to beleaguer the point. One of the things that I felt was very important and focused on all the time was, Could I communicate my messages in a clear, concise, fast, easy way? Because one of the problems I've seen over the years with many business books is they keep beleaguering the point; they keep trying to prove it over and over again. I focused on saying what I felt was right, my opinion, and people would either accept it or reject it. I wanted a book that people could digest in one sitting. If it was daunting and difficult and huge, people wouldn't read it.

Q: Could you describe the process you follow when you write?

G.E.: When I get an idea, I sit down and write about it. I just let it flow. I put words down as fast as I can—whatever I'm thinking about goes on the page. I don't worry about spelling, I don't worry about grammar, I just type. As long as I keep myself excited and interested about what I'm saying, I'm not really thinking about who I'm writing to as much as I'm thinking about what I have to say. After I've said everything that I can possibly think of saying on the subject, I start to rewrite it. At this stage, when I was writing my book, I started working very heavily with an editor. When working on a big writing project, it's very important to work with somebody who can stop you from going too far in one direction or getting lost. But once I get into a subject, it's all-involving to me. I never have to say to myself, I'll work on it from ten to twelve today. Once I start, I want to find every minute I can to write more and more and more. That's never been an issue for me. Getting started is difficult, but once I get started, I find it hard to stop.

Q: You say getting started is hard. What do you do until you get to a point where you can start to write?

G.E.: I do a lot of thinking about what I want to say and take notes.

Q: Do writing rules play a role in your process?

G.E.: They really don't. I let somebody else think about those. I keep going back to my main focus: communication. All I think about while writing is, How do I write what I want to say in a way that people can clearly understand it? I don't think about the formal aspects of writing when I write. So the answer is no, never.

Q: What about, grammar, spelling, and punctuation rules?

G.E.: Same thing. I pass that to somebody who knows how to do them correctly. I'm the world's worst speller, and I don't want to claim I've got an A in any of that. My book draft was proofread by editors, copyeditors, and then I hired another proofreader myself because I didn't want any mistakes, because grammar and punctuation are important. But I depend on copyeditors for that because those people know their craft. I'm a communicator.

Q: What's a business writer to do when she has to turn in a long report but doesn't have access to a professional proofreader?

G.E.: That's very complicated. While I think that my grammar is mediocre and my spelling is terrible, I won't interview somebody who applies for a job with a typo on her résumé. You don't have to be an expert in the formal aspects of writing; there's no way to master it all. But you can find someone who is an expert. That shows me you pay attention to details. You don't have to be a good speller, but you should know where good spelling is available and make sure you get it.

Q: Inexperienced writers think that professionals know a secret formula for writing. What would you say to a person who holds that view?

G.E.: I don't think there's any secret to writing that you aren't taught. I think by and large most people don't understand the real secret to writing, which is to learn how to write the way you speak. It makes your writing authentic and genuine. It's always a struggle for me because when I write, I'm much more pretentious than I am when I speak. When I write a business letter, I tend to formalize what I have to say to conform to some convention that I'm not sure is actually there, which is the wrong approach, but I find myself doing it anyway. However, when I have a business communication that doesn't have formal quotes around it, I write exactly the way I speak.

Q: And do you think that comes off better than the other?

G.E.: Absolutely. One of the things that comes through in any kind of writing is your personality. And your personality is an important business tool. The person you're dealing with must get a sense that you're genuine, that there's integrity in what you have to say. People look for that, and it shows in your writing.

Q: What differences do you notice in the way you were taught to write in school and how you write as a professional?

G.E.: I was taught to write much more formally, much more manipulatively and verbosely. But I quickly learned in business that straightforward and clear writing is best. As a matter of fact, a lawyer recently told me that he knew we were going to get along well when I sent him an e-mail that outlined in two sentences exactly what I needed from him. He told me later, "I didn't know you and you didn't know me, but when I got this totally understandable communication, I said, 'This is somebody who just wants to solve a problem.'" He went on to say the e-mail didn't have all of the complexities we learned in school. I just said what I needed to say, and he was able to send back what I needed, and we solved the problem very quickly. That's how business should be done, and that's the role writing should play in business.

Q: So the writing training you received in school was a mixture of good and bad. It taught you positive things, like how to put your thoughts down logically, but also negative things, like being too formal and verbose.

G.E.: Right, but I think it's good to go through all of that training. In school, you cover all of the areas of writing. Once you get out, you can begin eliminating the things that don't work for you and keep those that do. That's how you develop your own style. The more powerful you are in business, the more your writing becomes you—the more your own style shows through. My bet is that the Jack Welches of this world do not write formal memos. They cut right to the chase.

Q: What personal writing rules have you developed over the years?

G.E.: The main one is try not to be pretentious. Write directly to the reader. Understand whom you're writing to, then write simply—the way you speak—and get your point across as quickly and clearly as possible.

Q: If you feel business writing needs improvement, what are the main reasons for poor writing in companies today?

G.E.: People are not completely confident about what they want to say. They're trying to make what they have to say look better by writing around it, rather than writing to the point.

Q: Instead of being confident in their own voice and just saying what they want to say?

G.E.: Yes. Finding your voice is the most important thing you can do in both written and spoken communications. It's a huge struggle for people to find their own voice. They spend too much time trying to reinvent themselves into somebody else's voice because they think somebody else knows how to do it better. What they don't understand is that they will always be more powerful in their own voice.

Q: Does good business writing give a business a competitive advantage?

G.E.: Yes! That's what is missing most in the business world today—good writing. The greatest trouble we have is finding good writers.

Q: Where do you find good writers?

G.E.: The best way to become a good writer is to become a good liberal arts major.

Q: I read about one businessperson who said he could teach a Cub Scout to do financial portfolios. He wants to hire people who can write and communicate.

G.E.: That's right. We need people who know how to write and speak clearly, so clients sit up and listen and stay involved in what the company has to say. Everything else I can teach you. If you come to me and you can write and speak well, then I can teach you to do anything.

Q: So if you can't write and speak well, no matter what the job is, you'll fall behind?

G.E.: That's right.

Q: What's your advice to beginning business writers?

G.E.: Whenever you write or speak, you always take a risk that somebody is not going to like what you have to say. You're constantly putting yourself on the firing line, but that's good, that's how you learn. You're the only person that really has to judge you. If you get caught up in everybody else's opinion of you, you'll never advance.

GREG FARRELL
USA TODAY MONEY
JOURNALIST

Greg Farrell writes for the Money section of *USA Today*. He won a Jesse Neal Award from the American Business Media for investigative reporting in 1995. Farrell received an MBA from Columbia Business School in 1998.

Q: Is there a difference between the way you were taught to write in school and how you write as a professional?

G.F.: I took a writing class in college, but I didn't get much out of it. What I've learned professionally is the importance of the question, Who's your audience? You're not writing to a vast, nondescript mass of people. It's impossible to succeed at writing if you think that. In my case, it's an audience of 3 million people who have picked up *USA Today* in the hopes of learning something interesting and relevant about their world. But sometimes I'm writing for an audience of one or two people: the editors who will decide whether or not I should proceed to report a story. No matter what you write, you want to answer your audience's questions. That's a key part of communicating succinctly, clearly, and persuasively.

Q: What personal writing rules have you developed over the years?

G.F.: I used to write long, clunky sentences with lots of dependent clauses. Instead of trying to break a thought down into bits and pieces, I'd try to communicate one long, flowing thought. That's extremely difficult to do with clarity, and it's easy to lose readers. So one rule I've developed is to write short sentences that make a clear point and then move on to the next point in my argument.

Q: Has anyone ever told you that you were a bad writer?

G.F.: Not in so many words, but when I first started in this business, I had an experience that made me feel that way. I had never felt more discouraged in my life. Within a month or two of joining a weekly community newspaper, I got taken to the woodshed by my editor. He pointed out numerous weaknesses in my stories that week. Not weaknesses in the reporting, but weaknesses in the writing. I remember that night clearly: where I was sitting and where he was sitting. It was devastating. That's how you learn, of course. Since then, I've had to deliver that kind of bad news to young reporters, but I begin by telling them about the time it happened to me. The point is not to give up, but to learn from criticism.

Q: Do you think about writing rules while you write?

G.F.: Yes and no. I don't think about them consciously. In that sense, writing is like driving on a road. Experienced drivers don't think of every sign that they see, yet after awhile you develop these automatic reflexive mechanisms that make you aware that a stop sign is approaching or that Exit 10 is coming up. You don't actually read all of the signs as you did when you first started driving. While writing, you develop a dual level of consciousness. I don't ignore the rules, but I don't follow them slavishly, either.

Q: Do you spend a lot of time polishing and revising your drafts?

G.F.: One goal of the writing process is to get all of your thoughts out on paper and worry about rephrasing and polishing them afterward. As a reporter, I usually don't have that luxury. I have to hit it right the first or second time through, because the article's due in a half hour. Reporters learn how to write 300- to 400-word stories very quickly, or they don't stay reporters for long.

Q: At what point in your career did you consider yourself a writer?

G.F.: When I was in high school and college, I thought I was a writer. But the more I wrote for a living, the less I thought of myself as a writer. I think of myself as a reporter in the literal sense: one who reports or communicates information. In my mind, fiction writers are true writers. They have incredible imaginative powers that enable them to create interesting stories. The type of thinking that I do is much less imaginative and more linear. I try to figure out why something happened, or tell readers why a particular event is important.

Q: At what point did you know you were a good writer?

G.F.: Early on in my career, I wrote a long profile of a business executive who was changing jobs. The story required me to dig deeper than I normally would, and I had the space to spin the yarn out—to describe this man's past, how it led to the present, and the importance of the move he was making. I remember vividly the satisfaction I got out of that piece, and the positive feedback from readers who were not used to that level of reporting and writing at the trade magazine where I worked. I realized then that I had a knack for doing in-depth profiles.

Q: Inexperienced writers think published writers know a secret formula for writing that allows them to write a final draft first time around. What would you say to a person who holds this view?

G.F.: Many people believe that there is a secret formula, some magic involved in writing, and that only a chosen few are born with the talent to be good writers. That's a dangerous misconception, and it can lead to bad decision making: Instead of selecting the simplest, most accurate word, you reach for an expensive word; instead of describing your proposal in straightforward terms, you begin layering it with complex clauses that draw the reader's attention away from your point. Keep it simple!

Q: Some professional writers can look back and pinpoint the moment when writing finally "clicked" for them, when they knew what they wrote was good, bad, or mediocre and why. Did you ever have such a moment?

G.F.: That "clicking" moment occurred after a sabbatical from journalism—when I dropped out to attend business school for a year. I was interviewing with the head of human resources at a newspaper—not *USA Today*—and the subject turned to writing. It suddenly occurred to me that the most important element about writing had nothing to do with craft: It was all about the thinking behind the writing. If your idea was strong, and was borne out by reporting, your writing would be strong because it accurately translated strong thinking.

Q: Whether you're a business writer or a journalist, keeping your audience's needs in mind is important: constantly putting yourself in their shoes. How do you deal with that?

G.F.: I'm constantly rereading my leads from my audience's point of view and saying things like, "That lead is flat, this one is too clever." I've written leads that are too clever by half, and my editors wisely suggest that I rethink them because they don't communicate or tell the story effectively. It's tempting to show your readers how clever you are, how smart you are. But in the long run, you're impeding your ability to communicate your message.

Q: After your editor looks at the story, where does it go?

G.F.: It goes to copy to make sure that all of the t's are crossed, the i's are dotted, and the spelling is correct. It's my job to make sure the story is ready for publication, but the copy department is a safety net in case the editors or I miss something. It always helps to have a fresh set of eyes read your work.

Q: There's a general impression among novice writers that if you master grammar, spelling, and punctuation, you've pretty much mastered writing.

G.F.: Following the rules doesn't guarantee success. One of the best reporters at *USA Today*, a terrific writer, will write sentences that don't have a subject or a predicate. His writing is very conversational. He'll write the way he speaks. One of the reasons he's so good is that he's developed a style that's not shackled to the rules that we grew up with. His style communicates extremely well. The point or argument he's trying to make is never in doubt, it's always clear to the reader. Grammar, punctuation, and spelling do aid effective communication, but keep in mind the ultimate goal is to clearly communicate a thought, an idea—not to write an article or letter that has zero errors.

Q: In your opinion, what shape is business writing in today?

G.F.: I see lots of press releases, story pitches, etc., and I rarely notice which ones are well written and which ones are not. What I do notice are the public relations people who have done their thinking ahead of time and those who haven't. I get too many pitches for stories that are of no interest to me or *USA Today* because the writer didn't stop to think and do his or her homework. I get the impression these people are pitching a story to *USA Today* because their boss told them to, not because it's right for us. Figuring out your audience is far more important than how well a press release is written.

Q: Does that approach carry over into all business writing?

G.F.: Sure, the same rule applies to an executive writing a memo: The important thing is to know your audience and know what you're trying to communicate to that audience. Don't write for length; write for results.

MICHAEL LEWIS
THE NEW NEW THING

Michael Lewis is author of several national best-sellers including *NEXT: The Future Just Happened,* an insightful analysis of how the Internet affects how we live and work, *The New New Thing*, which focuses on Jim Clark, a new capitalist adventurer in Silicon Valley, and *Liar's Poker,* which is based in part on his own experience working as an investment banker for Salomon Brothers. Lewis is currently a contributing writer to *The New York Times Magazine,* and he has served as editor and columnist for the British weekly *The Spectator* and as senior editor and campaign correspondent for *The New Republic.* Lewis holds a B.A. from Princeton and an MSc in Economics from the London School of Economics.

Q: At what point in your life did you consider yourself a writer?

M.L.: When I started to make my living as a writer. I felt uncomfortable telling people I was a writer when I was doing it on the side. I was working at a Wall Street investment bank and publishing articles in magazines in my spare time. It felt dilettantish to claim I was a writer when I wasn't really making my living as a writer. This was before my first book, *Liar's Poker.* About the middle of 1988, I quit my job at the bank and started to give it a go as a writer. That's when I felt perfectly comfortable telling people I was a writer. I was living off the advance from *Liar's Poker,* plus magazine income.

Q: When did you know you were a good writer?

M.L.: I think I had an aptitude for it when I was pretty young, maybe fifteen or sixteen, simply from the response I got to some of the things I wrote for school. I prided myself on my abilities as a writer even then. But it never occurred to me that I would make a living doing it, because I didn't know anybody who did. That was an alien thought. To graduate from college, I had to write a senior thesis. I remember thinking it was beautifully written and begged my adviser for a compliment. He finally said, "Well, let's put it this way, never try to make a living as a writer." He didn't think much of it. So even though I thought I had some aptitude for writing at an early age, I never had a sense that I could make a living doing it until I actually was.

Q: When did you start freelancing?

M.L.: When I lived in London. I went there for graduate school. Afterward, while working for Salomon Brothers in London, I became a professional writer. That was great because London really is the capital of the written word. It was a challenge to try and assimilate into British literary culture, to write for British magazines. It's not uncommon for the editor of a British magazine to call you up at four in the afternoon and say, "Can you give me a piece on X by tomorrow morning?" because they themselves are so facile at writing. The English approach the written word like an engineer approaches a problem. There's no romance to it with them, especially in journalism. Their educational system teaches them to think in perfectly formed paragraphs, and they think the act of writing is as matter-of-fact as sitting in a chair.

Compared to the average writer in America, professional English writers believe writing is easy. There's much less nonsense about producing a piece of writing. That's a very healthy approach to take because a lot of writers work themselves into a state where they freeze up and get writer's block because they create expectations they can never meet. The English never get to that point because they never stop and think about what the hell they're doing; they just do it.

Q: That's a good trick to play on yourself, just to get started.

M.L.: That's right. It gets you going. And it is true. As someone once said, writing is rewriting. You have to get something down on the page to work with. Whenever I have problems getting something out, I'll often turn the music on loud, drink three cups of coffee, and write something just to get it started. Once I get something on the page, all of a sudden—it's amazing—the ideas start to flow. It's rare that I have a completely formed idea about what I'm going to write before I sit down and write. The ideas come out of necessity, out of having to sit there and being forced to put words on the page. If I get myself in the state of mind where I'm not ready to write because I don't know exactly what I'm going to say, I'll procrastinate. So I often tell myself that writing is putting your butt in the chair.

Q: That's another good approach: lowering your expectations just to get the ball rolling.

M.L.: It really works. I'll give you an example of how demand can produce supply writing. I used to be the American editor for *The Spectator* magazine in London. One Sunday evening, while I was on a book tour in the United States, I was about to go to bed because I had to get up at six to do a television show. I get a call from London. It's an editor at *The Spectator* saying, "Where's my cover story?" I said what do you mean? He said I had agreed to write the cover story at a lunch meeting we'd had a few days earlier. I disagreed. He said, "Michael, this is serious. I've got a cover that needs a story." I said, What's the cover? And he said it's a picture of Goofy, the Disney character, dressed up as a banker. He faxed me the picture, and I sat down and wrote a 2,000-word article. I had no choice. My friend wouldn't have a magazine issue if I didn't fill the vacant space. So that's just one illustration of the amazing things you can do when you have to put words on the page. In the movies, writer's block is the guy sitting staring at the screen for hours and hours. I think the real writer's block is the guy refusing to sit down and stare at the screen.

Q: Inexperienced writers think that professional writers know a secret formula for writing. Many also assume professional writers are experts at

grammar, spelling, and punctuation. What would you say to a person who holds this view?

M.L.: It's not true. There are a lot of professional writers who don't write very well to start with. But the secret to good writing, if in fact there is a secret, is to have something compelling to say so people will read it no matter how badly punctuated it is or what the grammar is like. That's the starting point. If you have nothing to say, no matter how pretty your grammar and punctuation is, you're going to be lost. After that, I think most people get themselves in trouble trying to make a writing project more complicated than it is. My advice to new writers is to look at what you've written and see if it would be better at half or a third of its current length. There is a tendency to pretty things up. Spare, simple, clean is the key to getting across a message.

Q: Some people equate spare and simple writing with elementary-school writing.

M.L.: That's wrong. I would recommend George Orwell to anyone who wants to see the power of a simple style. He's the best example of how powerful a simple style can be. He's also someone who had very important things to say, good ideas. That's what drives good writing.

Q: You write a lot about financial topics. Do you have a background in finances?

M.L.: My undergraduate degree is art history. I first thought I wanted to be an art historian, but the same man who told me that I shouldn't be a writer told me that I shouldn't plan to be an art historian, either.

Q: How did you get into finance?

M.L.: I drifted into it. I walked into an introductory economics course in my senior year and took it pass-fail. I was riveted and regretted not doing a lot more in economics. So I enrolled in a master's program in economics at the London School of Economics. They offered this un-usual program where people who majored in other subjects could come in and essentially do their entire undergraduate curriculum in one year, and then do the master's in a year. I spent two years at the London School of Economics and was hired by Salomon Brothers in London. They shipped me back to New York for a while and then back to London, where I settled for another six years.

Q: How do you write? What process do you follow?

M.L.: That depends on what I'm writing. I basically have three lengths: column length, which is 750 to 2,000 words; a really long piece of magazine journalism of 7,000 to 10,000 words; and the third is book form. I also write movie scripts, but that's a different animal. In the case of shorter pieces of writing, which is probably what you are focusing on because of the interest of your audience, what I normally do is sit down and bash out ideas, not worrying about how it all fits together. I'll write paragraphs on a subject and when I've depleted my mind of the subject, I'll put it away. I'll close the file and go do something else. I'll come back to it a couple of hours later, print it out, and look at it. Actually, let me back up. If it's a column, I'll first do some research by browsing the Web, visiting people, or just looking for things that are related to my subject. Then I'll take a lot of notes and turn those into paragraphs and turn those into an article.

For me, the trick is finding out how to start it. I'll typically write most of the piece before I've written the beginning. It's a very messy process. Usually I write the guts of the thing first and then go back and write the beginning. A huge part of writing is tone. Tone of voice distinguishes good writers from people who just have words. When you read a piece of writing by Mark Twain or George Orwell or Tom Wolfe, you're with a distinct character. A unique tone of voice comes off the page. Each time I sit down I have to find my voice; I have to hear the voice. It has to feel right for the piece. We all modulate our voice, and I just try to find the right tone for whatever it is I'm writing.

Q: What writing habits have you developed?

M.L.: One of the little tricks I play on myself is, I try to get myself into different states of mind when approaching a subject. I try to come at the topic at different angles or in different moods. [Pulitzer Prize winner] Teddy White said that he wrote on caffeine and edited on alcohol. If I'm living with a long piece of writing for days, or in the case of a book for months or a year, I'll have a glass of wine or something when I edit, or I'll take a walk with one of my subjects. Once I've got something in my head, I'll go for a long walk and think about it. Once I've got a key to an idea or a story, the more I turn it over in my mind, the more mature it gets. I think not being satisfied with easy answers or explanations about things is a big benefit to any writer. So if I write a column from one point of view, I'll try to look at it from another point of view and argue with myself to see what comes out of that. A lot of writing is anticipating the objections of the reader before the reader even has them. You're seducing the reader, so if the reader is put off by a sentence or two, you lose them for good. I try to consider all of the possibilities before I put a piece of writing in print. You never succeed, but it's a healthy process.

Q: What would you tell writers who edit as they write?

M.L.: I think it would be paralyzing to edit as you write. It's two separate processes for me. I'll write something, print it out, go through it with a pencil, and then plug in the changes. I will edit a piece of writing several times. And usually what I'm doing is getting rid of the excess. The purpose of the editing process is to make the draft simpler and more straightforward. The things that I thought were cute or funny or elegant the first time through look unnecessary or ridiculous the second or third time through.

Q: Do you think about school-taught writing rules while you're writing?

M.L.: Not at all. Never. I try to make the printed word sound like the spoken word, and the spoken word tends to be direct, active voice, declarative sentences. I go in that direction when I'm editing. It isn't so much a rule, it's more of a feel. And that feeling comes from developing a taste for writing and from reading a lot. One thing that's very healthy to do from time to time is to read something you wrote ten years ago to see if it can stand the test of time. It's amazing how a person can think something they wrote yesterday was so good, and then when they see it five years later they're embarrassed by it. But to answer your question, I don't follow any academic rules. The truth is, I'm a half-educated man. I never studied English literature, and I was a mediocre student during that period of life when one learns the rules of grammar. So I don't know English grammar all that well.

Q: How would you compare business writing—letters, memos, reports—to writing magazine articles and books?

M.L.: Business writing is a different thing altogether. If you're writing a business letter, you get yourself in all sorts of trouble by being colorful. The goal of business writers is different from the goal I have when I sit down to write for my audience. I try to make a noise. If I did that in a business letter or when writing something about a product, I'd be fired for sure. The business writer is a suppressed creature. He really is! I remember having to write letters for various enterprises that I was associated with. My bosses said if I expressed my personality in what I wrote, the piece would be too entertaining and not lead to business, but to something "bad." I never learned what the bad thing was, but the point is, business writing simply delivers a message and that's it, you're through. It's not a magazine article.

Q: Many business writers think they should be colorful and have killer opening sentences that grab a reader, like the opening to Moby Dick, "Call me Ishmael!"

M.L.: If they think that they're in trouble. They should write, "Call me tomorrow!" For a business writer, that's better than "Call me Ishmael!"

Q: What about grammar, spelling, and punctuation rules? Do you think about those as you write?

M.L.: Well, I don't misspell things intentionally, and punctuation is all about taking a breath. It's all about where you want your pauses in the piece of writing, which helps create your voice and tone. I'm very finicky with punctuation because of that. Usually when I write something for the first time I have a tendency to use too many semicolons. When I edit, I'll go back and pull a lot of those out. If you use terrible grammar, people will think you're uneducated, but grammar is not a law. Grammar is an evolved tradition and you can deal with it as you want to deal with it. Some rules of grammar are better founded in reason than others. I think it's useful when subjects and verbs agree, but I don't think rules like "never end a sentence with a preposition" are terribly useful. It's rare that I catch a grammar error that I didn't intend to make. Usually I don't care all that much about grammar, and if I break the rules it's because it made it easier for me to say the things I wanted to say. I simply don't pay that much attention to it.

Q: What's your physical writing process? Do you always use a computer?

M.L.: I started out my life by writing longhand and then moved to a typewriter when I was twenty-four and a computer when I was twenty-six. I've used a computer since then. I prefer a quiet place where there aren't a lot of people, but I've been forced to write in all kinds of horrible situations.

Q: Is there a difference between how you were taught to write in school and how you write as a professional?

M.L.: School writing is very formulaic and you're not encouraged to have any kind of voice, to express any kind of view. You're actually not encouraged to say anything. Everything you write is some variation of a cheesy book report. You don't even know it's bad. Writing is regarded as something distinctly different from speaking, which is a myth taught to you in school. I had to unlearn that in order to write effectively. You have to write it as you would say it. You want to create a proximity between yourself and the reader, make the reader feel like you're sitting right next to him telling him the story. But your professor or your teacher, on the other hand, wants to feel distance, but that's not good writing. This is why. When I worked for *The New Republic,* there was a general understanding among the editors that two kinds of people couldn't write, and we would have to rewrite what they sent us. The first was the university professor. Some of the most famous university professors in the world would write us articles and they were completely unreadable. The second was daily newspaper reporters. They had a different problem. They were great at writing up a newspaper report, but when they wrote a public piece that had an opinion in it, they got very confused. These two groups are almost institutionally incapable of writing well in that kind of forum. There's a reason for it. There's an inherent pomposity that's encouraged in schools, and that's something that really should be unlearned. Pomposity is not a useful trait in a writer.

Q: Have you developed any personal writing rules over the years?

M.L.: No, I don't have hard-and-fast rules, but I can tell you this: The more ruthless I am with my writing, the better it is. It's a cruel process.

Q: If you agree that business writing needs improvement, what do you feel is the main reason for poor business writing in the world today?

M.L.: The first problem with most business writing is that the writer is scared of the person he is writing to. I mean, he's afraid that he's going to be misinterpreted, that he's going to get in trouble if what he writes is misread. That's a horrible starting point for a piece of correspondence. Fear leads to all kinds of trouble. You don't say what you mean, because you think you are going to get into trouble if you don't make it clear. The second reason is pomposity; it's a huge problem, like thinking it's best to use ten words when three will do. Using official-sounding words is another form of pomposity. Some people think it's a sign of intelligence, but it's really dishonesty. In many cases, business-people feel a need to disguise their motives. Most business writing is, in one way or another, sales literature. You're crippled at the outset if what you think you're writing is not absolutely true. What makes a piece of business writing exciting is when you feel the piece is worth taking a risk, but most business writing is calculated to minimize risk.

SUZE ORMAN
THE 9 STEPS TO
FINANCIAL FREEDOM

Suze Orman is the author of three consecutive *New York Times* best-sellers—*The Road to Wealth, The Courage to Be Rich,* and *The 9 Steps to Financial Freedom*—and the national best-seller *You've Earned It, Don't Lose It.* Her latest book is *The Laws of Money, The Lessons of Life.* She is the personal finance editor for CNBC, and she has written, coproduced, and hosted three PBS pledge shows based on her books, which are among the most successful in the network's history. A Certified Financial Planner professional, she directed the Suze Orman Financial Group from 1987–1997, served as vice president of investments for Prudential Bache Securities from 1983–1987, and from 1980–1983 was an account executive at Merrill Lynch.

Q: What would you say to a person who thinks there's a magical formula to writing well?

S.O.: I would tell him or her that it's a false view and will lead to serious disappointment. Writing is hard work, not magic. It begins with deciding why are you writing and whom you are writing for. What is your intent? What do you want the reader to get out of it? What do you want to get out of it? It's also about making a serious time commitment and getting the project done. Here's what I mean. When I was writing *The 9 Steps to Financial Freedom* and *The Courage to Be Rich,* I worked from 6 A.M. to 2 A.M., every single day, with no break, until they were finished. This kind of sustained effort helps you to maintain a clear train of thought, which is crucial to the process. I once wrote 30,000 words and then my writing time got interrupted for three weeks. I did a million things before I got back to that project. As a result, I had to reread the 30,000 words and try to reconstruct the exact intention and emotion that I had when I left off. So much had happened that, in the end, those 30,000 words took on a different tone when I rewrote them. The key to writing is sticking with it until the project is complete. No magic there.

Q: Like any other job, writing is just hard work.

S.O.: Right. You have to focus on what you are doing. When I write, that's all I do. When I am on television or on the radio, that's all I do. Compared to writing, TV is easy because it is over in a matter of minutes, tops, an hour. My radio shows can take up to two hours. Writing, however, represents a more serious time commitment. I used to have the luxury of writing twelve to fourteen hours a day because I didn't have to go to another job. That's no longer true. That also wasn't the case when I was writing my first book, *You've Earned It, Don't Lose It.* It took longer to write than my other books because I was also working in my financial planning practice. Still, it never would have gotten done if I hadn't taken two weeks off and secluded myself in order to finish it. If you are writing a book and you want to finish it, then take a vacation from your job and spend every second of your time working on it.

Q: What would you say to a business writer who's knocking out letters and e-mails every day?

S.O.: Apply the same approach, just scale it down. Lock your office door, switch the phone to voice mail, and focus on the letter until it's done. You have to know how to organize your time and delegate responsibility to others. I've learned how to do that with my company. It's streamlined to three people: two assistants, one on each coast, and myself. The three of us handle everything, from the books to the public appearances to all the minutiae that keep the company running smoothly. Everything funnels through me, from artwork to Web site design, and people wonder how anyone can accomplish all of that. It's simply a matter of being focused, of doing one thing at a time and doing it well, and of sticking with a project until it's completed. Nothing gets put off until tomorrow that can be done today.

Q: So dedication is the key?

S.O.: It's certainly one key. A clear sense of purpose is another. It's important to remember that people buy or recommend a book because they can understand and make use of its message, not necessarily because it's stylishly written. Do the writer's words bring the truth behind her words to life? Does the writer have a passion for her subject? Sometimes a writer can have an impeccable vocabulary and an elegant grammatical style but nobody can relate to what he or she writes because there's no passion there. In today's world, people are overloaded with information, and writers need to keep their message simple and clear. I want people to understand both my words and the spirit and meaning behind them. That's what I aim for.

Q: At what point in your life did you consider yourself a writer?

S.O.: Certainly I didn't imagine that I had the ability to write a book before I wrote *You've Earned It, Don't Lose It.* As I was working on it, I kept asking myself, Who are you to write a book? But I got past that by telling myself that I was somebody who was just trying to convey her thoughts. I kept it simple and never looked back. Even now, I'm not sure that I would identify myself as a writer. I think it's dangerous to define yourself by what you do, as opposed to who you are. I'm Suze Orman, who has the ability to write books, give talks and seminars, be seen on TV, and host a radio show. I do not get caught up in labels, because if any of those labels ever went away, then who am I? I want to define my success by how I feel about what I've created, and I want to create the clearest, most useful things possible in all the mediums I work in.

Q: So it goes back to clarity of expression?

S.O.: Yes. When I was writing *The 9 Steps to Financial Freedom,* I reread the first three chapters every day. Each time, I loved them more, which told me that I was on the right track. I asked friends to read them in front of me. I could tell by looking at their faces if their concentration was wandering or if the text had captured them. I paid careful attention to every word I wrote to make sure that it was absolutely clear.

Q: How do you write? What process do you follow?

S.O.: I'm currently making notes on a new book idea that's very different from what I've written before. Every time I think of a concept and I'm not at my computer, I jot it down. It's important to write down every little thought, because the same good idea rarely comes to you twice. I may never use all my notes, but I have them just in case.

Q: Do you plan a lot before you write?

S.O.: No. When I started to write *The 9 Steps to Financial Freedom,* I only knew the titles of each chapter. So I wrote the book according to how I taught the topics in seminars or talked to my clients about them. I decided not to read any other financial books while I was writing, because I didn't want other people's ideas in my head. I wanted to make sure that I was expressing my own thoughts and concepts.

Q: Do you ever suffer from writer's block?

S.O.: No. My problem is that I have too much to say. I can go on about an idea that I'm excited about.

Q: Do you think about the rules you learned in school while you're writing?

S.O.: No. I grew up on the south side of Chicago and the schools I went to didn't teach or encourage writing. I also had a speech impediment. Because I couldn't speak up, I didn't learn to read at the usual time. Because I couldn't read, I did very badly on my tests and always thought that I was dumb. I never tried to read, and I never tried to write. Luckily, I was brilliant in math. I could do anything when it came to numbers.

Q: When did that change?

S.O.: It started as a fluke. I was a financial adviser at the time and decided to write a book to give to my clients. When a publishing company expressed an interest in it, I thought it was incredible that a publisher was willing to pay me to write a book that I was planning to give away!

Q: Who edits your work?

S.O.: I usually write with Cheryl Merser, who is my personal editor. She does not work for a publisher. I'll write something and she'll edit it. We send it back and forth until it's just the way I want it. Then it goes to the editor at the publishing house. I always have a personal editor working for me because I don't want to worry about punctuation and grammar. With me, it's about the message.

Q: Have you developed any personal writing rules?

S.O.: No. I write exactly what I think. If I'm thinking it, I'm writing it.

Q: What do you see as a weakness in financial/business writing today?

S.O.: Many business and financial authors write words, not truths. They're writing from a detached point of view. They haven't sat across a desk from a client and experienced that person's pain, worry, fear, or sorrow about his or her financial situation. Unless you have experienced what you are writing about, to me you are a reporter, not a writer.

Q: Do you do a lot of business writing for your own company?

S.O.: Yes. Everything comes from me: e-mails, letters, memos, you name it.

Q: Does everything that you've talked about regarding writing your books apply to your business writing?

S.O.: Yes, it does. For instance, I was recently offered an honorary doctorate and a teaching position at Wesleyan College in Georgia. I wanted to write a personal letter to the president of the college, declining its wonderful offer, because I was fully committed for the year. Rather than worrying about whether what I was writing was letter-perfect, I focused on choosing the words that would convey my heartfelt regret at having to decline what I knew was an honor. Now, did I spell check the letter and try my best to make sure that the commas and periods were in the right places? Yes. Did I obsess about it? No.

ROY WILLIAMS
THE WIZARD OF ADS

Roy H. Williams is the author of *The Wizard of Ads* (named the 1998 Business Book of the Year), *Secret Formulas of the Wizard of Ads* (a *New York Times* best-seller), and *Magical Worlds of the Wizard of Ads* (a *Wall Street Journal* best-seller). Williams teaches creative thinking and human persuasion in a three-day Wizard Academy that is attended by advertising agencies, college professors, CEOs, broadcasters, and journalists from around the world. His books have been translated for international distribution in China, Brazil, and Israel. A lifelong student of the human race, Williams is forever seeking to answer the question, "What makes people do the things they do?" Many of his insightful answers are posted at www.WizardofAds.com and www.Wizard Academy.com.

Q: How did you break into the writing business?

R.W.: I actually bridged into writing as a profession when I was nineteen years old. My wife and I needed money, literally, to buy groceries. And so I got a second job working in the middle of the night on weekends changing tapes at an automated radio station. I didn't get to talk into the microphone, I just worked the tape machine. When one tape ran out, I just hit the button on the next tape machine. And that was my job. I got $3.35 an hour. While doing that, I noticed there were a lot of truly bad commercials on the air. So I said to the manager, "How about, while I'm sitting there all night with nothing to do except press a button every thirty minutes, I try writing some ads for you?"

I wrote a number of ads, and it wasn't long before advertisers began requesting me to write theirs. Pretty soon I was hired full-time at the radio station, and I was invited to become a salesperson. I moved up to sales manager, and at the age of twenty-six I became general manager with a staff of thirty-two people, all of whom had college degrees and all of whom were older than me. I was able to turn an opportunity to write radio ads, initially for no pay, into a successful career.

Q: What types of writing do you do most often?

R.W.: I write everything, from sixty-second radio ads and direct-mail letters to magazine columns and chapters in my books. I also write in a short format. I believe that no matter how complex something is, you can communicate the foundational truths of any subject in one 8½" × 11" sheet of paper in 12-point type.

Q: Many people think that published writers know a secret writing formula that allows them to produce final drafts the first time around. What would you say to someone who holds that view?

R.W.: That it's a counterproductive view of the writing process. Every writer that I admire writes very slowly, painstakingly slow. My average column is between 500 and 600 words. Yet it takes me anywhere from twelve to twenty hours to write because of all the rewriting. And every time I look at a draft I say, "Now how much of that will get edited and revised?" My wife Penny recently read something I wrote and immediately said it was two totally separate stories. She told me where to divide it and suggested a new ending for the second one. She whacked about 120 words and made it enormously better. That type of editing, that kind of give and take, happens very often when I write. You can always spot beginner writers because they have too much emotional attachment to what they have written and never want to delete anything. A good editor who really cares about you usually cuts your favorite passages! Writing is a painstaking process, even if you're a gifted and talented writer. In my experience, it's the level of commitment and dedication that separates the published from the unpublished.

Q: What do you do during the twelve to twenty hours it takes to write your 500-word articles?

R.W.: Half of that time is spent doing research. You have to gather data and check your facts so you know what you're talking about. Specifics are always more believable than generalities, and specifics come from research. So half the time is spent gathering information, and the other half is spent arranging the information. I usually start with a 2,500-word document. Then I begin cutting. All of the things that do not support my point get whacked. I keep cutting and cutting and cutting. When you cut it down to the bare minimum, the essence, and you've said what you want to say as cleanly and as powerfully as you can, you're done.

Q: What about grammar, spelling, and punctuation skills? Are you good at all of those?

R.W.: Absolutely not. I only attended college for two days and didn't pay much attention. The only grammar, punctuation, and spelling that I know is what I learned in my junior and senior years of high school in Broken Arrow, Oklahoma. I had a competent English teacher who loved her job and did her best, but I thank God for the spell checker in my word processing software! So I have little to no competency in the technicalities of spelling and grammar. I depend on others to help me proofread my work. In my estimation, the people who overestimate the value of spelling, grammar, and punctuation become editors.

Q: Many business writers think that if they master the mechanics of writing—grammar, spelling, and punctuation—they will be good writers. What's your response?

R.W.: When people get too focused on the mechanical process of writing, anything from sentence structure to punctuation usage, it's apparent they're looking for a formula or a set of rules to abide by. That's a trap. And anytime that you think you're going to write everything according to some formula, you're setting yourself up to be incredibly average at best, a failed writer at worst. It reminds me of an old quote, a writer's quote: "Most editors are failed writers, but then so are most writers." Good writers don't follow a set, standardized formula. Everybody has a different methodology, one they discover over time that works for them.

Q: Then how important are the mechanics in the writing process?

R.W.: I compare grammar, spelling, and punctuation to business attire. What is correct business attire? The answer is anything that does not distract from you and what you're trying to say. Therefore, what you wear when doing business should, effectively, be invisible. It should not distract from the person that is you. Likewise, if your mechanics do not distract the reader, then they are effectively invisible and are therefore perfect.

Q: Has anyone ever said that you were a bad writer?

R.W.: Yes, as a matter of fact. I once showed a coworker an ad that I knew was very good, and he made a big production out of wadding it up and throwing it in the trash can. He then started writing from scratch to show me how it was "supposed" to be done.

Q: Can you walk me through the mental process that you follow when you write?

R.W.: There are three steps to writing well in my opinion, regardless of what you are writing. Step one: how to end. Step two: where to begin. Step three: what to leave out. Also, I only write one draft that I keep changing and changing until I don't believe it needs to be changed anymore. When I'm finished, there may not be a word left of what I originally wrote down.

Q: How do you write? What is the first thing you do when you sit down in front of a blank piece of paper?

R.W.: I never sit down with a blank piece of paper. If I have an interesting thought, I'm one of those guys who scribble it down—twenty-four hours a day, 365 days a year, whether I'm falling asleep or talking to someone. It might be just a half sentence scribbled on the back of a receipt or the back of my hand, but I need to write it down before it evaporates. After a while, when you have enough interesting thoughts, you'll begin to realize that you can connect these thoughts together. That's why I say that I never sit down with a blank piece of paper, because anytime I sit down to write about a topic, I instantly realize that I've thought about the topic before.

That's what I call the benefit of the disorganized mind. Here's what I mean by that. Most people put ideas into compartments. For instance, while listening to an advertisement, they will put the information into a mental compartment that's marked Advertising Knowledge. Later, whenever the topic of advertising comes up, they will draw from that compartment. At best, people who do that can only regurgitate what they have learned and never create new things. That is an example of an organized mind: a place for everything and everything in its place.

I have a totally different filter. Anytime that I see or hear something that is the least bit interesting, I write it down and throw it onto the pile of interesting facts that I keep stored in my mind. It's this great, big, heaping pile of disorganized stuff. But before I throw it on the pile, I will examine the thought carefully. I will imagine looking at the shape, the color, the texture—that is, the components of the idea. So anytime somebody says, "I need an answer. I need a solution to X," I say, "Okay, what are you trying to accomplish? What are you trying to communicate? What would the answer look like? What would be its texture and color, its smell and taste?" And then once we have identified what an answer would look like—for example, we determine that it would look like a book—I'd say, "Wait a minute, I've seen parts of that before." And I would go digging through my pile of facts and images, and say, "There it is, there's the thing you're looking for."

If you want to be creative, if you want to come up with new stuff, gather interesting information—anything that catches your attention. Write it down, study it, and don't worry about how you're going to use it. It will pop into your head at the appropriate moment. If you follow this process, you'll never run out of things to say.

Q: How would you apply that advice to writing a sales report?

R.W.: The first thing everyone should do when writing a report is say, "What are the non-negotiables? Is there a certain style in which this report must be presented? How much leeway do I have when writing this report?" You want to make sure that you know what's expected of you. Once you understand the format, try to make things as glowingly simple as you possibly can.

In addition, if your report will include new information, you must be able to relate the new data to things that they already know. In other words, people cannot truly understand new information until they relate it to something they've all experienced before. It's an old adage, but there's nothing new under the sun. What appears to be a new truth is usually something that has been true and around forever, but presented in a new light, with new packaging.

For example, Henry Ford did not start the first car company in the United States, and he didn't invent the assembly line. Most people think he did both. There were 2,000 automobile manufacturers in the country before Henry Ford made his first car. Also, Ford was in a Chicago meat-packing plant when he noticed that a series of butchers, each performing one highly specialized function on the carcass, could process the meat faster and with a much higher degree of precision than if one butcher tried to do all of the different steps alone. Henry Ford had the wisdom to connect, in his disorganized mind, the meat-packing assembly-line process with an automobile assembly-line process. If you connect new information with known information, people will grasp the new information instantly.

Q: What personal writing rules have you developed over the years?

R.W.: One rule is to write every day. I spend all day, every day, scribbling myself little notes that are useful or interesting. Then I type them into my computer so I can find them when I need them. Most of my writing is done in the early morning hours. I will get up anywhere between 3:30 and 5:30 in the morning, and I will write anywhere from two hours to as many as eighteen hours. On a typical morning, I'll write two to four hours, and do it before the rest of the world is even awake. That's when I do all of my best writing. I do my information gathering in my off-peak writing time. I could open a file and show you a couple of hundred works in progress, some of which will become very valuable and useful resources some day, while others will end up nothing more than a weird tangential adventure. That's another rule, if you want to call it that: You have to get used to the fact that not everything you write will see the light of day.

Another rule I try to follow is, tell the punch line first, open with the conclusion. Most people build up to their point. But you're better off to open with the point that you want to make and then fill in the supporting evidence. Attention spans are incredibly short, so it's best to let people know where you're going with a summary up front and then add the interesting details to support your opening argument. This works best for me, and I think most people today want writers to take this approach. We're all inundated with information, and one way to wade through it all is to read the main point right away and then decide if you want to read the rest of the piece. That applies to everything, even newspaper articles. If I don't see a journalist's point in the first three paragraphs, I move on.

Q: Who edits your work?

R.W.: I have a whole building full of people who edit my work. The woman who answers our telephones is a retired professor of English from the University of Oklahoma, and two other associates have a master's degree in English. Everything I write I set aside for a while and come back to with fresh eyes—when I no longer have it memorized, and it is no longer fresh on my lips. At that point, awkwardly written sentences will jump out at me. So in one sense you can say I edit my own stuff, even though many other "me's" with fresh sets of eyes edit it, too. By the time I send a piece of writing to someone in-house for editing, there's usually very little that needs to be changed. I don't let anybody see a draft until I have been working on it for a long period of time. If someone needs something turned around quickly, it won't be as good as something that I have messed with for an extended period of time.

Q: Many business writers are more interested in editing their piece while writing it, rather than using that time and brainpower to communicate their message clearly and . . .

R.W.: . . . concisely. I know what you mean. They are hesitant to move their argument forward, to do the writing, because they lack confidence in their writing abilities. The most valuable tip that I can give anybody is: If you want to be a brilliant writer, truly a brilliant writer, then you need to read books of poetry. Poets are the most confident group of writers I know. Let me explain. The simple truth is that a poet is the only writer whose goal is to persuade, to truly persuade and cause you to see things with different eyes, and to communicate that new perspective in a very brief, tight economy of words. Poets use unusual combinations of words in a very unpredictable way. Poets have the freedom to put together sentences and utterly break the rules of communication. One of my favorite examples is from Edwin Arlington Robinson's poem "Richard Cory." One line says that Richard Cory "glittered when he walked." Now nobody actually glitters when he walks, but the line communicates a wealth of facts about how people felt about this man. Most people don't have the courage or the confidence to write "and he glittered when he walked." Your average businessperson doesn't have to write like that, but to have the confidence to write like that is important.

Q: When did you know that you were a good writer?

R.W.: The moment for me was in fourth grade. We were asked to write a short story, and I wrote this thing that I thought was hysterically funny. When I read it to the class, they thought it was hysterically funny; it brought the house down. The funniest line—and I remember it like it happened this morning—was "and the dog was arrested for disturbing a roadside bush." When you're in the fourth grade, a dog peeing on a bush is hysterical. I said to myself, Gee, I'm pretty good at this. From that day forward I pursued storytelling.

THE IMPORTANCE OF WRITING ON THE JOB

Views from Corporate America

How important is writing in today's tech-fueled business world? I asked executives at leading global and Fortune 500 corporations, and you can read what they have to say in the interviews that follow. But here's a sneak preview. Remember the platitudes about good writing skills that your high school and college English teachers repeated ad nauseam: Good writing skills help you present your ideas more professionally; they make you a valued employee who stands out from the crowd; they save your company time and money; they improve your problem-solving and critical-thinking skills; they help you get a job, keep a job, and climb the corporate ladder.

They're true.

When I taught college writing courses, I met many students working on business degrees who felt learning how to write well was not important (some even arranged their class schedules so they never took a course that required writing) because they were going into finance, accounting, programming, management, and other business specialties that didn't require any writing. Or so they thought. These interviews offer solid proof that teachers can pass on to their students that learning to write clearly and concisely is not only important, in some cases it's crucial to advancing in a career.

Years ago when I boarded a plane and someone asked what I did for a living and I said freelance writing, it didn't elicit more than a polite, "Oh." When asked that question after I started my business-writing training company, without fail the person would start telling me about the writing problems in his company. It seems one of the hottest unspoken topics in business today is the need for improved writing skills. Because companies operate at warp speed, businesspeople must write just as fast, which is causing problems. For example, e-mail is often viewed as a double-edged sword: While a valuable communications tool because it's fast and friendly, e-mail is also a license to write quickly and badly, according to some businesspeople.

One of the many helpful ideas in these interviews is the fact that corporations equate clear writing with clear thinking, which is key to being promoted in any company. The interviews offer candid opinions and advice, and show how careers can be affected depending on how well you communicate with your colleagues and clients.

AT&T
WILLIAM OLIVER, PUBLIC
RELATIONS VICE
PRESIDENT

AT&T is among the premier voice, video, and data communications companies in the world. The company runs the largest, most sophisticated communications network in the United States, backed by the research and development capabilities of AT&T Labs. A leading supplier of data, Internet, and managed services for the public and private sectors, AT&T offers outsourcing and consulting to large businesses and government. With approximately $37 billion of revenues, AT&T has relationships with about 50 million consumers and 4 million business customers.

Q: How much weight does your group give to good business-writing skills when it comes to reviews and promotions?

W.O.: In our public relations organization, we give a lot of weight to writing skills. In fact, for years we've used a career-development appraisal process that's based on two fundamental skills: writing and relationship building. While we look at other skills further up the appraisal pyramid, writing and relationships skills are our two foundation blocks. We give a pretty thorough writing test to any candidate for employment in this department, and some people actually do wash out every year. Sometimes candidates with superb relationship skills, people who can do wonderful things for us in communities around the country, don't pass the writing test. But we decided a while ago that we wanted to build an organization where writing is an equally strong skill across the organization. No one-trick ponies here, we hope.

Q: How is the writing test evaluated?

W.O.: It's blind in terms of scoring. A group of peers from the organization looks at the material submitted by a candidate. The judges don't know who the person is or what position she's applying for. They evaluate the material based on several criteria: news writing, editorial writing, speech writing, advertising copywriting, and more. We value good writing, and we value a wide variety of writing. Maybe we're different. The public relations department has historically been an integral part of the company's business. Back in the 1920s, a gentleman by the name of Arthur Page was the first corporate vice president of public relations of any major corporation in the U.S., and he worked at AT&T. The Arthur W. Page Society—a professional organization of the top 250 corporate communications officers in the country—was named after him. So AT&T's PR department has been an integral part of the decision-making process of our business since the 1920s. I've worked at several other companies, so I have some basis for comparison. Because writing is such an important part of the public relations organization, and because public relations is such an integral part of the decision-making process at AT&T, writing perhaps has a higher value in our culture than it does at comparable corporations.

Q: If you notice that someone's skills are deteriorating, what do you do to improve them?

W.O.: We suggest they take a refresher course at PRU, the internal Public Relations University we instituted a number of years ago. We're very proud of it. PRU has a variety of intermediate and advanced writing courses. Based on a performance evaluation, for instance, an employee might be encouraged to sign up for a specific class. But we also have a lot of folks who take courses voluntarily to improve their skills.

Q: Does AT&T provide writing training for non-PR employees?

W.O.: Yes. There's an AT&T School of Business that offers writing courses.

Q: Outside the PR organization, how important is writing at AT&T?

W.O.: It depends on the organization. In some groups, writing is one of the major criteria by which people are advanced. For instance, my good friend John Zeglis, the CEO of AT&T Wireless Services, constantly emphasizes that "good writing simply reflects good thinking." There's an expectation, particularly as you go up the hierarchy of his organization, that you're going to need to *think* clearly, and one way to understand if a person can really think clearly is to see if he can write clearly.

Q: Most PR assignments are written for an outside audience. How do you ensure that everything is error-free?

W.O.: We've developed a number of internal processes that try to emulate manufacturing processes when it comes to editing and proofreading. When we write news releases, opinion pieces, annual reports, speeches, or any other PR project, there are several quick editorial checkpoints each piece must pass through to ensure the final product is the way we want it. While we don't have the luxury of having a big proofreading staff, like a newspaper or magazine, we try to be thorough.

Q: How do you define good writing? Zero errors?

W.O.: That's a good question. Ultimately, the final proof of writing quality is its effect. Was the message clearly received by its intended target audience? That performance standard is the same whether we're talking about a memorandum sent to 130,000 employees or a page from the annual report sent to our 3 million shareholders. We do periodic research to determine how well the messages we're sending out are being received and understood by individuals. So the test of good writing is the results it gets.

Q: What business advantages do employees who write well give AT&T?

W.O.: I'll go back to the clear thinking, clear writing equation. People who can quickly communicate the essence of their message, say in an e-mail, save the company time and money. Those who can effectively communicate the gist of what they're trying to say give us a business advantage, whether it's a sales call or some other business negotiation. Besides timesaving and efficiency, good, concise writing helps the organization achieve its strategic objectives. One thing we know from experience is that when we set a clear objective that is well defined and unambiguous, we have an excellent chance of success. Vague objectives lead to vague results. We see it time and time again. Clear writing reflects clear thinking, and clear thinking by everyone in an organization gives it a strategic advantage.

Q: What overall shape is business writing in today?

W.O.: I can't speak for all companies, of course, but you certainly see pockets of problems. Take the legal profession, for example. I work with a lot of lawyers. Some are probably the clearest thinkers and writers I know. John Zeglis, for example, was AT&T's general counsel before becoming a CEO. But for others, their legal training seems to guide them toward hedging and obfuscation, which often leads to a level of writing that may be superb from a strict legal standpoint, but appears to all the rest of us to be silly. Not all legal writing is like this; it just seems that for some reason, too many lawyers have a hard time rising above their legal training to communicate effectively with real people about real ideas.

Q: Is it fair to say that your company runs on writing?

W.O.: I'll put it this way: It certainly runs on thinking. And to the extent that there's an association between thinking and writing, then that's true.

Q: Do different areas within AT&T communicate in different ways?

W.O.: I'm sure they do, but what I notice more is a difference in the way different generations communicate. A dear friend of mine who recently passed away, Pat Jackson, was a public relations consultant who enjoyed saying that for people under the age of forty, the concept of the paragraph died several years ago. Senior managers, many in their fifties and forties, grew up and became successful learning how to read and write formal—some might say ponderous—paragraphs. That's how they were taught to communicate. But Pat used to say that younger people learned to comprehend information orally, on television or the radio, or graphically, in bullet points, etc. Pat was firm in the belief that writing in "traditional" paragraphs was not the most effective way to communicate with people under forty. That was a strange thought inside AT&T, a large, conservative 100-year-old corporation. But we've tried to understand what he was saying and incorporate that thinking into how our PR organization operates. The Internet and e-mail have actually facilitated that approach because they lend themselves to a less formalized style of writing. Anyway, I think there's a lot to be done in the area of making companies more effective communicators internally and externally, and it's useful to bear in mind that for a large and growing number of people, the paragraph is dead.

Q: All successful people have two traits in common: They write well and speak well. Does that saying hold true at AT&T?

W.O.: We can all think of exceptions, but I think by and large that's true. People who don't write and speak well have to have exceptional abilities in other areas, like finance and technology, to get ahead in the organizations. Those who are "communications challenged" often have to jump a higher hurdle; they have a greater burden of proof, if you will, to demonstrate the quality of their intellect compared to someone with reasonably well developed writing or speaking skills.

Q: Can you think of any employees who were recognized or advanced their careers because of their writing skills?

W.O.: That's certainly true in the public relations profession. I can think of good general writers who have gone on to become, say, a speechwriter for the chairman of the board and have been promoted into executive positions in which they have a policy creation role, all because they know how to write and think well. They advanced almost exclusively as a result of their ability to listen well, think well, and translate it into effective writing.

Q: Do communication and leadership skills go hand in hand?

W.O.: I think so. When someone from the cadre of CEOs-in-waiting—executive vice presidents, senior vice presidents, etc.—finally takes on the mantle of leadership for the entire company, writing and speaking skills become paramount. If a person is selected CEO because of abilities other than communication skills, the first thing she must do is quickly develop those talents in order to survive. It's hard to be an effective leader without the ability to write and speak well.

CANON U.S.A., INC.
MITCH BARDWELL, DIRECTOR/ASSISTANT GENERAL MANAGER, SALES TRAINING DIVISION, IMAGING SYSTEMS GROUP

Headquartered in Lake Success, New York, Canon U.S.A., Inc. is an industry leader in professional and consumer imaging equipment and information systems. Canon's extensive product line enables businesses and consumers worldwide to capture, store, and distribute visual information. Canon U.S.A. employs more than 11,000 people throughout North, Central, and South America, and the Caribbean. In 2001, total Canon sales in the Americas reached over $8 billion. The personal opinions expressed in this interview are not necessarily representative of the policies or opinions of Canon U.S.A., Inc., its parent, subsidiary, and affiliate companies.

Q: What business advantages do employees who write well give your company?

M.B.: They make the company more effective and enhance our reputation. Good writing skills are a positive reflection of the quality people we hire. Clients see the difference, too. They feel more comfortable and confident working with a Canon salesperson who is a good communicator.

Q: What value does your sales group place on good writing and why?

M.B.: A high value. Writing is a fundamental skill that is important to every professional in every industry. There's also a constant need to communicate better. Add to that the new communication channels—the Internet, e-mail, and instant messaging—and you can see why mastering the basics in writing is essential. The value is on writing with clarity, precision, and conciseness. Then there's speed. Every business puts a high value on speed and turnaround. When you are strug-

Mitch Bardwell interview courtesy of Canon U.S.A., Inc.

gling with writing skills, it slows down the process. That delay is a disadvantage—for both the individual and the company.

Q: What's the relationship between being a success and writing and speaking well?

M.B.: It's a direct relationship. Some people, especially those fresh out of college, think all they have to do to get promoted is increase their sales numbers, not realizing that the further they rise in the company, the more writing they will have to do. I know several people who openly admit they have poor writing skills and that this deficiency impacts their job performance. We train our people in nine core skills, and one of them is communication, written and verbal. If they score low in communication, the test score itself is not going to hurt their career, but their weak writing and speaking skills could. If they can't effectively communicate with their peers, our customers, and me, sooner or later that will catch up to them.

Q: How much weight does your sales group give to good business-writing skills when it comes to annual reviews, promotions, and bonuses?

M.B.: Depending on the job, it can be quite a bit. We're a sales organization that relies more on presentations and one-on-one meetings than writing, but we also create a lot of training materials that require excellent writing skills. We develop two-day, instructor-led courses that include a participation guide, support media, course descriptions, course proposals, and other publications. So in that area of our business, writing skills are very important.

Q: What does your company do to evaluate and improve the writing of its employees?

M.B.: At Canon, we're encouraged to improve all our business skills—writing included. This can be through internal or external course opportunities. We offer, for example, writing courses, like our Successful Writing for Business class.

Q: Does Canon provide online writing courses?

M.B.: No. We're starting to develop an e-learning site for our salespeople, but as of now, we don't offer an online business-writing course.

Q: So you see a difference in job performance between those who write and speak well and those who don't?

M.B.: Sure. It's easier for managers with good writing skills to have better relationships with their staff and upper management and to perform their jobs better. You can't help but think more highly of people who are good at communicating. Our clients respond better to them, too.

Q: Is it fair to say that your company runs on writing?

M.B.: Yes, it is. We rely on e-mails, reports, memos, and other correspondence to do our business.

Q: Does poor writing cost your company time and/or money?

M.B.: Clearly, good, direct, well-prepared writing makes projects run more smoothly, makes meetings more effective, and makes presentations more productive.

Q: In your opinion, what shape is business writing in today and why?

M.B.: I think it's fair to poor. Tom Brokaw has a follow-up book to his best-seller, *The Greatest Generation,* called *The Greatest Generation Speaks: Letters and Reflections.* One thing Brokaw points out is that the nineteen- and twenty-year-old soldiers who fought in World War II had a real command of the English language. They were able to clearly and beautifully articulate their feelings. I doubt if the average twenty-year-old today could do the same. Writing skills seem to have deteriorated from one generation to the next, and it may be partly due to insufficient emphasis in our schools.

Lack of confidence is also a problem. For example, people almost always say they don't look good on videotape. They are very critical of themselves because watching the video is like looking in a mirror. I think writing is a paper-based mirror. When people read what they write, they don't like it and think they're bad writers. One cure is to get positive feedback, to be told what you do well as a business writer. The only problem is that lots of businesspeople don't know how to talk about someone else's writing. It's hard for them to distinguish good writing from mediocre or weak writing, so therefore it's difficult for one businessperson to critique another businessperson's writing.

Q: Any other reasons?

M.B.: Yes, people need some motivation to improve their writing skills. They have to believe that writing does make a difference on the job, that it's effective in some way. I remember a story about a fourteen-year-old boy who bragged to his teacher that he could talk his way out of anything and therefore didn't need to know how to write. It turns out this same kid had a pair of sunglasses that broke the day after he bought them. The teacher told him, "If you knew how to write well, you could write the sunglasses company and get a free pair to replace the one that broke." As an exercise, she had this boy call the company to complain, and had another boy in class write to the company.

The kid who wrote a complaint letter got something like ten pairs of free sunglasses, and the other boy couldn't even get through to customer service on the phone. It was a great example, especially for kids, of the power of writing. But whether you're a child or an adult, you have to see how a skill is going to help you before you will be motivated to work at the skill. Business writing is like that, too. Good writers have a definite career advantage that poor writers do not. The problem is that some businesspeople don't believe it. They either don't want to take the time to fix their writing or they blame their lack of success on other things.

Q: Did good writing skills help get you where you are today?

M.B.: Yes. I know from feedback over the years that my writing skills are pretty good. I communicate often with management and staff, so I'm always using and sharpening my writing. I started in this organization as a field instructor thirteen years ago, and I'm a director now. I know my writing skills were part of the reason I moved up the ladder. I didn't pay as much attention as I should have in seventh-grade English, but I work on my communications skills all the time.

CISCO SYSTEMS, INC.
JERE BROOKS KING, VICE PRESIDENT OF WORLDWIDE MARKETING COMMUNICATIONS

Jere Brooks King, when interviewed for this book, was vice president of worldwide marketing communications for Cisco Systems, the worldwide leader in networking for the Internet. More information on the company is available at www.cisco.com.

Q: In your opinion, what shape is business writing in today?

J.K.: Business writing is at that stage where it would receive a passing grade, but not much better. I think that, unfortunately, most people can't tell the difference between average writing and superb writing. So superb writing often goes unrewarded and unnoticed. Businesspeople fall into the journalist syndrome and try to keep their writing on an eighth-grade level, the lowest common denominator, and simply follow the basic rules of grammar and use a reasonable vocabulary. There are very few people—few and far between—who write in an articulate, well-crafted fashion.

Q: What percentage of business runs on writing?

J.K.: That's a hard question to answer. In today's world, I would guess that more attention is starting to be paid to the written word because of the prevalence of e-mail and Web pages. In other words, you are no longer calling someone to get an explanation of, let's say, how a product works. You're going to a Web site and reading information about it. Also, instead of placing a phone call to someone, you're sending her an e-mail. The Internet is putting increasing importance on strong writing.

Q: How important are good business-writing skills?

J.K.: They're extremely important. You will be more successful as a businessperson if you can communicate well. Good writing skills are a crucial part of that. In a technological world, if you can rise above the acronyms and state something in a clear and persuasive manner, verbally or in written form, you will be that much more ahead of your colleagues. You just will. It's a bonus.

Q: What's one of the biggest business-writing challenges at Cisco?

J.K.: In technology-oriented companies like Cisco, the challenge is to take a complicated topic and make it simple and understandable. This is true for technology companies across the board. Also, there are different audiences who read our material. What we say to a CEO about the Internet and how a network operates is far different from what we would say to a network administrator. In the same way, an average consumer looking to buy a new car will read the glossy brochure, but if a designer of car engines is in the market for a new car, he or she will want a whole different level of communication about the automobile and its complexity. So, in a company like Cisco, we have to make sure we match the style and level of complexity of the writing to the audience. In all cases, however, it's a matter of taking complicated subject matter and making it relevant to the reader.

Q: What are some of the different types of writing assignments at Cisco?

J.K.: Writing assignments and formats vary a great deal. We don't require one person to write a broad range of material. The person who writes the end-of-the-month report doesn't write a product brochure. That's typically handled by someone with marketing skills. The person who writes the user manual, which requires a greater depth of detail, doesn't write the patents submission, because that requires yet again a far more detailed level of explanation. Each of these examples goes to further and further depth in terms of knowledge of the subject, product knowledge, technical ability, and the communications skills needed to be articulated at each level.

Q: How do general writing skills fit with the need to have specialists who are trained to write specific assignments?

J.K.: I manage the Marketing and Communication organization, so I hire writers for various jobs. With that background, it's clear to me that good writing skills help you regardless of what position you hold in the company. Success is often dependent on persuasively presenting yourself and your ideas: The better idea will win. And you can do that verbally, but oftentimes it requires a written plan or a written presentation. Writing is a key component of success for everyone. So I'm a strong believer that everyone should have good writing skills.

Q: What value does Cisco place on good writing skills, and does the company provide incentives of any kind to encourage people to improve their writing?

J.K.: Many of the job descriptions within my organization require good communication skills, so the combination of written and verbal skills is required to be successful on the job. As far as incentives, every quarter within the marketing organization we hand out awards to teams who create a marketing program that we think effectively communicates the Cisco message in an effective manner. It obviously must be well written, have a compelling idea, and be persuasive, clear, and articulate.

Q: Does Cisco have any checks in place to ensure high-quality communications with its customers?

J.K.: We proactively monitor customer satisfaction on a daily basis around the world. One way we do that is with an online survey mechanism, so if a customer is unhappy due to a miscommunication of some sort, we find out about it quickly and solve the problem.

Q: How does Cisco help employees who need to improve their communication skills?

J.K.: We assess any possible weaknesses and then recommend courses of action. The action varies with each case, of course. We don't have a set program but, for instance, if someone needs to polish their writing skills, we would recommend he take a course at a local college. We don't have an internal writing-training program in place.

Q: How do you know when someone needs help?

J.K.: If an employee's writing is bad enough to affect his on-the-job communications, his manager will tell him. But I think more typically—and this happens at all companies—a person will be asked to write a general piece of correspondence, an e-mail or Word document, for instance, and send it to someone else. If it's not well written, the recipient will say, "I don't get what you're trying to tell me. I don't understand this." You don't usually hear people say, "This is not written well." The complaint is more along the lines of, "What do you mean by this?" On the flip side, if you've done a really good job writing the piece of correspondence, the recipient will say, "I'm going to forward this person's e-mail because they said it so well, why should I repeat it?" That's the ultimate compliment.

Q: Do you have an opinion as to why some people with college or post-graduate degrees write at a basic level?

J.K.: I'm sure that it is because they're not required to write at any higher level. As long as what they write meets the basic requirements, they've done their job. These people have usually been hired to build or reengineer a product, invent a new technology, sell or install products, talk to customers—not once did I mention the word *writing* in any of those job descriptions, right? Writing is not their primary job.

Q: Did good writing skills help you get where you are today?

J.K.: They certainly did. I wouldn't be in the communications field if I didn't have that skill set. But then I enjoy writing. I always have.

CITIGROUP
NICK BALAMACI, DIRECTOR OF INTERNAL COMMUNICATIONS

Citigroup is the preeminent global financial services company with 280,000 employees and some 200 million customer accounts in more than 102 countries. Citigroup provides consumers, corporations, governments, and institutions with a broad range of financial products and services, including consumer banking and credit, corporate and investment banking, insurance, securities brokerage, and asset management. Major brand names under Citigroup's trademark red umbrella include Citibank, CitiFinancial, Primerica, Smith Barney, Banamex, and Travelers. Additional information may be found at www.citigroup.com.

Q: What business advantages do employees who write well give your company?

N.B.: The clarity of communication is what ultimately gets a customer to buy your product or service, or a colleague to buy into your ideas. Good writers are a precious commodity because they can get a message across in the most economical way. Good business writing also helps clarify a company's identity. Whether focusing your identity in the marketplace or your position on the issues, clear, concise writing gives you a competitive advantage. You can't achieve it solely through oral communications.

Q: How much weight does your business give to good business-writing skills when it comes to promotions?

N.B.: Communications—writing and speaking—are among the core competencies managers look at when it comes time for promotions and raises. Of the two, writing is probably the best way to develop and showcase your communications expertise. Writing requires you to take thoughts that are not fully formed and shape, condense, and clarify them into a sharp message.

Permission of Nick Balamaci, Director of Internal Communications at Citigroup.

Q: What resources are available for employees who need to sharpen their skills?

N.B.: Citigroup offers its employees training in writing, presentations, and other areas, both online and in the classroom. If communications comes up as an issue during an annual review, there are a number of options to recommend.

Q: Has Citigroup established any writing standards?

N.B.: No. We have graphic and design standards but no writing standards beyond those we all learned in college English.

Q: What types of business writing are primarily done at Citigroup?

N.B.: Every kind you could possibly imagine. It's the world's largest diversified financial services company. We have 280,000 employees in 102 countries, and our component businesses range from brokerage houses and investment banking to insurance and personal banking. Every one of these businesses has its own needs in terms of communicating with clients, crafting messages to the public, and keeping in touch with employees.

Q: Do Citigroup executives write more or less as they climb the corporate ladder?

N.B.: There's no hard and fast rule. I see some instances where they do more and others where they do less. However, writing will always be required in any executive-level position. The rise of e-mail has really emphasized that need. At one time, if your writing skills were not that great, you could get away with letting your assistant clean up your drafts or dictated memos. But e-mail is instantaneous. It represents a very basic, revolutionary change in the way we do business. Now everyone from an intern to the CEO must be able to sit down and compose an e-mail message and have it be coherent, sharp, and not a waste of time. E-mail has put a premium on writing skills. It's brought them back under the spotlight in a way that few would have predicted a dozen years ago.

Q: Do you think e-mails are viewed as a burden or a blessing at Citigroup?

N.B.: I think e-mail is considered a blessing. From what I can see, it's not abused. People take it seriously. After all, it's a great tool. E-mail is a big reason for the productivity increases in the last five to ten years. The efficiency it creates and the way you can get work done and keep track of things, manage projects, articulate ideas—it's just extraordinary.

Q: Is it fair to say corporations run on writing, in the sense that if you forbid all written communication, from e-mails to ads, business would slow to a crawl?

N.B.: It goes without saying that companies would be crippled without writing. You can't function today without it. A mom-and-pop operation could probably get along without writing, but not a company the size and scale of Citigroup.

Q: What value does Citigroup place on good writing?

N.B.: I don't think writing in and of itself is what is valued, but rather the results it achieves. The ability to craft a message and achieve a desired result is valued highly. Writing is the key to getting good ideas out of your brain and into the world.

Q: Can poor writing cost your company time and/or money?

N.B.: Absolutely. Say a corporation sends out a memo announcing a new employee benefit with a sign-up deadline. If the memo is poorly worded, it can cause enough confusion that the deadline has to be extended. Then the process must start over again, which costs time and money. No company can tolerate too much of this.

Q: What types of writing do you do on a daily basis?

N.B.: These days I primarily write e-mails. I used to write a lot of speeches, articles, presentations, and so on—now I most often edit them.

Q: What is your writing process?

N.B.: I sketch out some key words or thoughts on a piece of paper and then I sit down at the computer and start to hash it out. Once the piece is on the page, I spend a significant amount of time revising it and then polishing it and putting the finishing touches on it.

Q: Do you think of the writing rules that you learned in high school and college while you're writing?

N.B.: Absolutely. And I break every one of them!

Q: When it comes to grammar, spelling, and punctuation, do you have someone check your work?

N.B.: No. I'm fairly good at that.

Q: Did good writing skills help you get you where you are today?

N.B.: Without a doubt. The trajectory of my own career is based on writing. I studied history in school, not business. But I always loved words and writing, so I did freelance writing while I was in school, and after school I took a writing job because I had those freelance credentials. Writing is a very marketable skill. I could sit across the table from a client and say, Hey, look, I can create a sentence, a paragraph, an article, or whatever you need to convey your idea or message. That's a valuable commodity.

Q: What shape is business writing in today?

N.B.: I would say it's fair. One of the reasons is the rise of video and the graphics-intensive World Wide Web as cultural mainstays. They were not as big, obviously, a generation ago. The Web didn't exist and video touched a limited number of households. So that's one thing. Another reason is the isolation of business from humanities studies. The more years I spend in business, the stranger it is to me that business majors focus so little on the humanities, which are such a leavening agent. Courses in literature and philosophy touch on the essence of the human experience, and business is all about people. The reverse is true, too. Humanities studies are too isolated from business courses. I learned very little about business in my undergraduate years and graduate school. And yet, economic issues have always been of vital importance in world affairs. I think we would gain a lot if more business subjects were taught to humanities majors and more humanities taught to business majors.

Q: Are writing and speaking key characteristics of corporate leaders?

N.B.: Absolutely. There's no leadership without clear communication. In order to rise in an organization like Citigroup you must be able to convey your ideas to large numbers of people in an understandable, concise, and appealing way. Leaders must be persuasive communicators in order to inspire others to help them achieve their goals. That's accomplished, in most instances, through a combination of writing and speaking.

Q: All successful people have two traits in common: They write well and speak well. Does that saying hold true for Citigroup?

N.B.: Writing in and of itself is no guarantee of success in the business world. Action and good thinking and leadership are the keys to success. However, writing is a means to achieve action and good thinking and leadership. You can be a terrific writer and sit in your cubicle and send lovely messages, but if you don't pick up the phone and talk to people and have meetings and inspire people to share your vision and exchange ideas, you're not going to go very far. You could be a highly gifted writer, but you will only be called upon to do episodic communications like articles and speeches. I don't think you'll do much more.

Q: Can you explain in more detail how writing is a means to clear thinking and becoming a leader?

N.B.: An amazing thing happens as you mature as a business writer, as you progress and get better and better. We all start out writing on a basic or tactical level: pumping out e-mails and reports and speeches and articles. Then slowly and naturally you ratchet up your writing, which ratchets up your thinking. You start to think at a higher level about strategy: What are the key messages my company must convey to the outside world? Now writing has taken you from the content-creator level to the strategic-thinker level. That's how writing kicks you up the corporate ladder. It's a maturing process. At some point, you make that transition from being able to write a great speech to being able to go beyond what was asked of you and develop or sharpen key messages to build into the speech. All of a sudden the light bulb comes on and you have the ability to identify and clarify a vision and purpose. Good writing skills foster good thinking. So now you not only have improved your critical thinking ability, but because you're a good writer, you can convey your ideas quickly and concisely to others. That's what leaders do.

DELOITTE CONSULTING
VICTOR NAU, PARTNER

Victor Nau, when interviewed for this book, was a partner at Deloitte Consulting, one of the consulting arms of Deloitte Touche Tohmatsu, which is one of the world's leading professional services firms. With nearly 90,000 employees in over 130 countries, Deloitte Touche Tohmatsu provides world-class consulting, assurance and advisory, and tax services to nearly one-fifth of the world's largest companies, public institutions, and successful fast-growing companies.

Q: What type of work do your consultants do?

V.N.: It's a combination of business and information technology consulting, so we do a lot of writing and presenting. We have a worldwide staff of nearly 7,000+ consultants in Deloitte Consulting. We prepare proposals and presentations for new client businesses, and once we have their business we develop deliverables, which includes more writing. We write up progress reports, detailed charters of what each one of our work areas will entail, everyone's roles and responsibilities, etc. We refer to it as a stream of work because we deliver a stream of ongoing reports and presentations to our clients. We have to have good communication skills at the lowest structural level of a project, but we also need to be able to sit down and, in a short fifteen- or twenty-minute meeting, explain the benefits of our project to the client company's CEO and get approval to go forward with further funding.

Q: So writing and speaking skills are . . .

V.N.: . . . extremely, extremely important. We present to CEOs and senior management of global companies all the time. These executives always want to know, first and foremost, the intrinsic value of our services. We have to be able to communicate that value in written and spoken form. So our consultants must excel at writing, speaking, and knowledge content.

Q: What weight does your company give to good business-writing skills during annual reviews, promotions, and pay raises?

V.N.: Writing is weighted very heavily across the board, especially in annual reviews and promotions. For our annual reviews, we ask employees to write a list of the contributions they've made to the firm that year. The list must be succinct, just two- or three-sentence statements that highlight their accomplishments at Deloitte Consulting. When it comes to promotions, we dig a lot deeper into their communications skills. We not only look into what they've done for the firm, but how well they communicate with colleagues and clients. We're a consulting firm, so communication is our business. If our employees write and speak well, we will be successful. Compensation increases are based on the annual reviews and promotion reviews, so good communication skills factor into both.

Q: Do your job descriptions for new hires focus on writing and speaking skills? Is that a prerequisite?

V.N.: Definitely. Whether the candidate is fresh out of college, graduate school, or a seasoned consultant, he must have superior writing and speaking skills. As I said earlier, communication is our business.

Q: How do you evaluate the writing skills of new hires?

V.N.: We give them a set of questions during the interview, plus ask them to respond to a case study. They have to answer the questions then write a solution for the case study. After reading their brief answers to the questions and the longer solution to the case study, we have an excellent feel for how well they communicate on paper.

Q: If a consultant's writing skills start to deteriorate, what do you do?

V.N.: If need be, we send them to a professional writing course. But first, we have them review the archive of written materials we've built up over the years—case studies, proposals, magazine articles, etc. The clients' names have been deleted to maintain confidentiality. By reading these documents, a consultant can get a feel for the structure and cadence of how something should be written. It's an educational review of what good writing looks like.

Q: Is it fair to say that your company runs on writing?

V.N.: It runs on writing, presentation skills, and content knowledge. Those three items. Our experience and knowledge differentiates us from the competition. How we communicate that content is what sells us. If our people don't have good writing and presentation skills, they won't be able to sell our services.

Q: What business advantages do employees who write well give your company?

V.N.: They clearly give us a competitive advantage. Confidence is a persuasive trait, and people who write and speak well exude confidence. Our clients look for that. They feel very comfortable working with consultants who write well. It's proof that they think well, too. When you're giving a presentation to a prospective client who will be spending millions of dollars on your services, you must be articulate and the presentation must be well written, succinct, and easy to read and understand.

Q: What shape is business writing in today?

V.N.: Somewhere between fair and good. Based on how I learned to write, the teaching of writing skills seems to have deteriorated over the years. I think attitudes toward writing have become blasé. A lot of the business writing I see needs a good proofreading. I read too many sentences that don't have a logical structure, which reflects poor thinking.

Q: Does poor writing cost your company time and money?

V.N.: More than that. Poor communication skills could cost us our complete livelihood. If we don't communicate effectively, we may as well just walk away from the business because we're not going to be able to relate to what our clients need. The most important thing we can do is listen to our clients, put together a solution for their problems, then communicate that solution to them. Writing and speaking are the lifeblood of our organization.

Q: All successful people have two traits in common: They write well and speak well. Does this saying hold true for your company?

V.N.: Without a doubt. Here's an example. A large manufacturing company asked us to bid on a project that involved evaluating its financial systems. During our presentation—which took hours of research and writing to create a concise, persuasive pitch—I explained the approach we would take in just a few minutes. That turned out to be our biggest selling point, the fact that we were able to quickly and clearly articulate our solution using words and pictures. We did that successfully and as a result, we won the job unanimously. Clear communication was our biggest differentiator. Our competition had some of the same skill sets we did, but we communicated better and won the bid.

Q: How do you recognize and reward good writing and presentation skills?

V.N.: On one hand, the reward is becoming a good consultant, which is emotionally rewarding to the individual, knowing that you are successful at what you do. On the other hand, writing and speaking well converts into money for us as an organization, and we recognize a consultant's contribution with a pay raise, promotion, or bonus.

Q: Did good writing skills help you get where you are today?

V.N.: Yes, they did. I did not acquire really good writing skills until undergraduate school. I went to an excellent high school, but it wasn't until college, when a professor took the time to sit down and show me the logical way to write and organize my thoughts, that I really understood how to write. Some of my high school teachers told me that I would never be a good communicator. I'd love them to see what I'm doing today! What my college professor taught me was a real breakthrough for me personally. That bit of writing instruction made my entrance into the business world a lot easier. I went from college to the information technology business, so the ability to structure my thoughts logically gave me a huge advantage. That skill allowed me to communicate to the average businessperson, and it has helped me though the rest of my business career. I work at it all the time, even today. Continuous improvement of communication skills is the mark of a good consultant or any other successful businessperson.

MARRIOTT INTERNATIONAL, INC.
ROGER CONNER, VICE PRESIDENT OF COMMUNICATIONS

Marriott International is a leading worldwide hospitality company with operations in the United States and sixty-five other countries and territories. Its operations include three major businesses: Marriott Lodging, which operates or franchises more than 2,500 hotels and resorts totaling approximately 450,000 rooms worldwide; Marriott Senior Living Services, which operates senior living communities throughout the United States; and Marriott Distribution Services, which provides food and related products to Marriott's operations and external clients across the United States. Marriott International, headquartered in Washington, D.C., reported systemwide sales in 2001 of $20 billion and has approximately 150,000 associates worldwide. More information about the company is available at www.marriott.com.

Q: What value does Marriott place on good writing?

R.C.: A high value because we have a very strong culture in our company that encourages candor. Bill Marriott wants employees to say what's on their minds. He learns more from his employees every day than any other source. And in that kind of culture, good writing and verbal communication are highly valued.

Q: Do employees who write well give your company a business advantage?

R.C.: If you take two people who have equal talents in most areas, the one with the superior writing skills will always have a leg up on the other. Superior writing represents an ability to think more clearly. The thought process occurs first, and writing is a result. But in turn, the ability to write well also impacts the thought process. They work in tandem. That's why strong writing skills are very important in all positions. I look at it in terms of presentation and preparation. If you're making a request or seeking a decision on an idea, the likelihood of receiving a positive reply improves if you can clearly explain what you are seeking. The ability to get what you want has a direct correlation to strong written and verbal communications.

Q: Can poor writing cost your company time or money?

R.C.: Yes, it can. We generate a vast amount of written communications every day, from hotel reservations and customer letters, to advertisements and internal correspondence. We produce so much that if it's not done well, it's a huge waste of money and time. The penalty for poor written communications is much greater than just having your hand slapped for a grammatical error. If poor writing causes a program that costs hundreds of thousands of dollars to not be successful, or not be as successful as it could be, the penalty to the company is exponentially greater than the writing error itself.

Q: How much weight does Marriott give to good writing skills when it comes to raises and promotions?

R.C.: Communication—the ability to say things well both verbally and in written form—is a major part of the communication rating in our performance review. There are eight or nine different subjects under the Communication section of the review. A manager will sit down with each employee and talk about each subject, then rate the employee on each specific area. A "1" rating is the highest performance level and a "4" rating is the lowest. So yes, written communication is a part of our annual performance review, which not only helps individuals develop their career to the fullest potential, but also helps determine their annual salary increase.

Q: Are writing and speaking skills only evaluated in the communications part of the review?

R.C.: Some elements under the Leadership section involve communication. Overall, our review process is weighted fairly heavily in terms of communication. That's because there are many different kinds of writing in a business environment, from letters and strategic plans to memos, news releases, and internal publications. We feel it's very important here at Marriott to be equally adept at all of them.

Q: What does Marriott do to improve the writing skills of employees who need help?

R.C.: Marriott is famous for its training across the board, which includes programs to improve writing and speaking skills. If a manager felt someone in his or her group needed help with communications skills, or if an individual was seeking help, courses are available internally, or there might be a course offered outside the company that the employee would have a chance to attend.

Q: Does Marriott have a corporate university?

R.C.: Not per se. We do have a virtual university with a broad array of courses and subject matter. Our hotels are the best places for learning so they are our laboratories, our universities, every day.

Q: Do you offer online writing courses?

R.C.: It's done in person with a live instructor.

Q: Does Marriott have an established writing standard that spells out what good writing looks like?

R.C.: No, but I wish we did. Marriott is known for its standard operating procedures (SOPs). In fact, *Fortune* magazine ran a profile of the Marriott organization, and the article says something to the effect that next to the U.S. government, there's no one with more standards that it follows day in and day out than Marriott. But we don't have an SOP on writing that I'm aware of. I guess it's too broad an area for an SOP.

Q: Do people at Marriott write more as they climb the corporate ladder?

R.C.: I can't speak for all of upper management, but my suspicion is that the higher levels do less writing and more reviewing and editing, which certainly requires a strong command of the skill of writing. One cannot edit without knowing how to write well. Senior managers need strong communication skills so they can do their reviewing and editing quickly, and so that they can judge good communication abilities in others, and know good communication when they see it.

Q: When you sit down to write business correspondence, what do you do? How do you write?

R.C.: I was a newspaper reporter right out of college. I went to the Newhouse School of Communications at Syracuse University. So I tend to follow a journalist's approach to writing and apply the "who, what, when, where, and why" thought process to my first paragraph. That method holds up very well for all kinds of writing. The journalistic style is often found in corporate environments because it speeds communication. The style requires that information be presented like an inverted pyramid: The most important facts are put at the beginning rather than at the end. That's crucial in a business environment because it speeds the decision-making process. When your idea is clearly presented in the opening of your memo or letter, the executives in the decision-making loop can act faster and your idea moves through the system faster. Putting the most important facts up front is more effective than building up to them, particularly in the fast-paced world of business.

Q: So because of your journalism background, you're good at outlining in your head?

R.C.: And on paper, too. Writing is not like math; it's not an automatic process like adding a column of numbers. Writing never gets automatic, no matter how much you've studied it and no matter how much you've done it. Writing is still always a choice of words, and you must spend time deciding how to put them into the right sequence to phrase your message. While it's not automatic, writing certainly becomes easier with practice and instruction.

Q: What do you do once you have a finished first draft?

R.C.: Edit. I've worked hard to become as good as I can at self-editing, but as you know, others are usually better at editing something you write. But I will go back and take words out that I've written, take sentences out. I try to be very critical as a self-editor. I'll also spend time rewriting. One of the problems I sometimes see when people edit their work is that they will change a word here and there and think they're done. What they're basically turning in is their first effort, their first draft, which may not communicate what they want to say in the clearest way possible. You have to spend more time playing with a first draft. You have to be very critical and constantly ask yourself, "Is this the right framework, the right way to say this?" That's a problem with some business writers; they do minimal editing and turn in their first draft.

Q: When you write something really important, do you give it to someone else to proofread?

R.C.: Yes. It's a standing SOP at Marriott that all external communications—which are one of the most important forms of communication that we do—get proofread by someone else. It doesn't matter what management level you are, if the public is going to read what you write, a proofreader must check it.

Q: Is proofreading their only job?

R.C.: No, that's not their sole job. It's an additional duty to their regular job, but we don't ask just anyone to be a proofreader. Each one is chosen for their expertise in proofreading and attention to detail, and most of them are in the communications department. They are specifically assigned to be proofreaders because they excel at it.

Q: Did good writing skills get you where you are today?

R.C.: In part, yes. But my relationship and interaction skills were just as important. It's a combination of those two, writing and relationships. To get ahead in any business environment, you need to have a solid foundation in your core area—finances, technology, sales, communications, etc. But that's kind of a given, a starting point in today's business world. After that, the ability to communicate in terms of writing, your verbal skills, and your personal skills will help you succeed the most. Without those talents, you are severely shortchanging yourself no matter how much you know about your core area.

Q: In your opinion, what shape is business writing in today?

R.C.: I think it needs improvement. I don't know if I would call it fair, but I certainly would not give it an excellent rating. The reason I say that is twofold. One, I think we have some of the same wordiness that's been around forever. Employees at corporations tend to overcommunicate, to be overly verbose. They mean well, but they seem to work too hard at writing and overdo it. But that's been a problem for generations and needs to be improved. My second reason is that I think some of today's technology is not conducive to good writing. I'm a fan of electronic communication and prefer receiving things electronically, but I also think e-mail encourages poor writing. It encourages speed and brevity of writing, which is good if you're a good writer. But when you have weak writers writing quickly then hitting the "send" button on their e-mail program without even a quick proofread of what they've written, that doesn't promote good writing skills.

Q: Especially if the e-mail is going to a customer, not just a colleague.

R.C.: Correct. I like the fact that e-mails encourage people to write succinctly. What I'm worried about is the outright ignorance of what good writing looks like.

Q: How well do schools prepare students for writing in the business world?

R.C.: Not very well. Writing is not being taught at the level it should be in primary and secondary schools. It's a big concern on the part of the major communications colleges. I know David Rubin, the dean of the

Newhouse School of Communications at Syracuse University, is always concerned about the writing skills of his incoming freshmen. These students come from excellent schools with a median grade point average of 3.7. They are the best of the best and still need to improve their writing skills. I think the problem is lower standards and a de-emphasis on the time spent on writing in the primary and secondary schools. Also, the students are more concerned about getting an A for the class than learning the skill. Students are asking their teachers, "What do I need to know, and what do I need to do, to get an A?" which is way different from the fundamental nature of a learning process.

Q: Is it fair to say that Marriott runs on writing?

R.C.: No. Marriott runs on effective communication, which includes writing, speaking, and relationships. It's a broader arrangement than just writing.

Q: What would you say to people who think they can't learn how to write well?

R.C.: It's important that every employee in today's business world does whatever it takes to have good writing skills. The notion that, one, I never learned to write, two, I don't care about it, and three, I don't need to write well, is a notion that's not going to serve anyone well in any job. I think to some degree, technology reinforces the notion that I really don't need to know how to write well. I know people feel intimidated by writing and feel it's something they can't learn, but the truth is they can learn it if they change their attitude and work at it. A big part of learning to write well is learning the frameworks or formats for the letters, memos, and other correspondence you write, and dropping your words into those frameworks. People have a sense that learning to write well is different from learning other business skills. It's not. Writing is a required skill for anyone who wants to do well in business. I'm not talking about writing the Great American Novel. Quite the contrary. I'm talking about the ability to simply communicate effectively through writing.

MOTOROLA
SHELAGH LESTER-SMITH, VICE PRESIDENT, DIRECTOR OF CORPORATE COMMUNICATIONS AND PUBLIC AFFAIRS

Shelagh Lester-Smith has worked in high-tech communications since 1980 in Western, Central, and Eastern Europe; in the Asia-Pacific region; and the Americas. Motorola, Inc. is a global leader in providing integrated communications solutions and embedded electronic solutions, including wireless automotive broadband. Sales in 2001 were $30 billion. More information on the company is available at www.motorola.com.

Q: How important are good writing skills in today's business world?

S.L-S.: This is a very personal point of view, but I was born and raised in England, and I grew up in an environment where good written English was considered to be very, very, important. I sometimes think I'm one of a dying breed, to be honest, and that has nothing to do with Motorola. Generally speaking, I don't think people set enough store by well-written business English. Motorola is no worse and is somewhat better than the average company when it comes to writing well, partly because we tend to hire highly educated people. But even highly educated people will make basic mistakes. Let's put it this way: Obviously, a large corporation is not set up to be a protector of the English language. And the fact that we work in the high-tech industry means that we are users of new language; we're always making up new words to describe new technologies. When I look at documents that come over my desk, I spend quite a lot of time editing them because I seldom think the English is good enough: too many acronyms and too much jargon.

Q: How much weight does Motorola give to good business-writing skills when it comes to reviews and raises?

S.L-S.: Writing is not singled out specifically. Now, obviously if some-one whose job is to write good English—for example, a speechwriter—habitually writes in poor English so that it interferes with his or her credibility, then I think it would be noticed and it would come up in a performance review. You expect people who are hired as writers at least to be able to set what they write aside and come back to it and check for errors. You also expect them to take and accept counsel from other people and have them look at their writing work with some objectivity. Finally, you expect them to use their computers' capabilities to help them get the spelling right, for example.

Q: What does your company do to evaluate and improve writing skills?

S.L-S.: We have a Silver Quill award in place for well-written articles. This encourages the good writers to test their skills and have their work published. We also have our own university, which offers a wide range of classes for employees in the interest of helping them be better at their job, to make them more competent and effective. Where a person needs to be a good writer, we would invest in developing that skill.

Q: Does Motorola have an established writing standard or style guide?

S.L-S.: Not a general style guide. Our style has emerged for items like the annual report, press releases, and so forth over time, because you tend to refer back to what has been done before. So a de facto style emerges. It's important that you make yourself clear and that you say things unequivocally and avoid ambiguity in the company's and your best interests. That's also part of our de facto style guide, but we don't have a physical, approved style guide per se. We do have our own guidelines for things like confidential and proprietary documents and for bids and tenders that have been developed over time.

Q: E-mail may be the most-used form of business writing today. What do you think of the medium?

S.L-S.: Let me express it this way. We are all assailed by an excess of e-mail today, which in itself generates a form of language and expres-sion that is a short form of writing. There's a sharp reaction, generally speaking, to the fact that we're all overwhelmed by e-mails because they're so easy to send. There's an informal cry, a groundswell almost, that's saying, why don't people just pick up the phone and talk to one another, instead of writing everything? Personally, I am of the opinion that if you work across three or four time zones, writing things and making them clear and succinct and understandable is actually very helpful, because it saves time and it allows people to be better communicators. They can take more time to form their thoughts than when they speak extemporaneously during, for example, a phone call—especially for those who speak more than one language.

Q: And it's hard to get people on the phone today, but you can always reach them by e-mail.

S.L-S.: Very true. As a matter of fact, I don't have voice mail on my phone. I gave it up because by the time I get someone's voice message it is probably out of date. But I'll answer e-mail instantly. I make e-mail a priority over everything else. So I think despite the fact that it may lead to people being more careless with the English language, as a means of communication e-mail is the best writing tool we have today.

Q: What business advantages do employees who write well give your company?

S.L-S.: Good expression will win out. You'll probably find most of the people who write well are in marketing. I'm going to generalize and say that your average engineer is probably not best with the written word. That's not to say some aren't masters of the English language, but it's not something that is required of them. The people who tend to be better written communicators are in advertising, marketing, maybe human resources and the law. Communicators certainly give Motorola an advantage because they have to communicate our brand and business messages with clarity for a range of audiences.

Q: Do people who write well get noticed more than those who don't?

S.L-S.: Not necessarily, but it's hard to generalize. I'll use myself as an example, as I have university-level English. I'm from that generation that cared about how we said things and wrote things and expressed ourselves in English, but I think that has only been a minor contributing factor to my progress during the past twenty years.

Q: What value does Motorola place on good writing and why?

S.L-S.: We certainly do value good written skills. And by that I mean we value thoughts and ideas that are clearly communicated. We know very well that some of the great writers of our time, as well as in times past, were poor spellers and weren't very good with grammar, but they knew how to convey ideas.

Q: Does Motorola run on writing? If you forbid all written communications, would the company run smoothly?

S.L-S.: No. Although there's a hue and cry for putting a stop to the flood of information and returning to making more phone calls, at the end of the day, writing is the single most useful tool we have. Also, for a company that's as diversified, complex, and global as Motorola, it's one of the most obvious ways we have to document things.

Q: Can poor writing cost Motorola time and money?

S.L-S.: Yes, it can in any organization. I've seen brochures in my career that have had to be redone because of poor writing and checking, because there is no centralized place to go and get things checked and approved. And one's external vendors can also make mistakes in writing copy. There has to be a clear process for writing, checking, and approving the written word.

Q: What writing process do you follow?

S.L-S.: First of all, I write down a half a dozen bullets of the main points I want to convey in my piece and then create the document. Typically I'll print out a copy so I can see it all at once and not piecemeal scrolling up on the screen. But not always, it depends on the importance of the message I'm composing. Then I'll leave it for an hour or two or longer, overnight if possible, before making edits. If I think it's something that's sensitive enough, I'll show it to others and see if they agree with what I'm saying and whether they think what I've said is clear. When I send memos I'm just as careful. My memos are often reports on meetings, calls to action, so I really want to be sure that people know what they are expected to do and when.

Q: Do you give what you write to a proofreader?

S.L-S.: Yes. And I do proofreading for a lot of other people, because I really do care about spelling and making sure we express ourselves elegantly in writing. I'm not so worried about internal communications but anything that goes outside clearly must be perfect. I'm involved with a lot of brochures, white papers, press releases, Web-based materials, and other documents seen by the public. All of that gets thoroughly proofread by someone else. You should never proofread your own writing.

Q: Nearly all successful people write well and speak well. Does that saying hold true for successful people at Motorola?

S.L-S.: I'm going to hedge and say yes and no. People who speak well are people who convey ideas with passion. They may not necessarily be able to write as well as they can speak, but that doesn't keep them from being successful or from being good communicators.

Q: Did good writing skills help you get where you are today?

S.L-S.: I think they did to a degree. I started my public relations career in an agency in Belgium. My boss there taught me everything I know about checks and balances—the process I just mentioned, about making sure you get other people to review what you've written and giving yourself time to think about what you've written before sharing it with others. Those principles hold true even now. But to answer your question, I don't think I was hired specifically because of my good writing skills. Good overall communications skills did help me move ahead, and writing is part of that skill set.

Q: In your opinion, what shape is business writing in today?

S.L-S.: I'm going to say "fair" for a number of reasons. I don't think schools teach people how to write with the same diligence with which we were taught. I'm part of a generation that was taught how to write. I also care about writing. I think language is a beautiful thing, that eloquence is important. But I don't think those values necessarily hold true today. Speed is one of the culprits. The speed with which everything has to get done these days is a factor that has caused a certain decline in writing standards. Another reason business writing is only in fair shape today is the willingness to experiment with language, especially in the U.S.A. Now one can argue—and I would—that it's right to experiment with language because it's a living thing that evolves. But when experimentation leads to using nouns like *impact* as verbs, where people write, "That report will impact my decision," that's regrettable. At the same time, people who spoke English in Dickens's day might have said the same things about the changes that were made to English in the nineteenth century. So I'm kind of caught between a rock and a hard place. I don't want the language to become static, but some of the changes devalue, and I think good writing skills should be valued, and the beauty and elegance of a language respected.

NEWS AMERICA MARKETING

PAUL CARLUCCI, CHAIRMAN AND CEO

News America Marketing's portfolio consists of *SmartSource Magazine*—the first branded, freestanding insert—various in-store advertising and promotional programs, merchandising services, and telephone promotions. These products and services allow marketers to deliver a branded message to more than 200 million consumers each month via a network of 750 newspapers and 33,000 supermarket, drug, and mass-merchandise locations across the country. News America Marketing, with $1 billion in annual revenues, is a division of The News Corporation Limited, one of the world's largest media companies with assets of $43 billion and annual revenues of $14 billion. Paul Carlucci, chairman and CEO of News America Marketing, is joined in this interview by Ian Moore, executive vice president for News America Corporation.

Q: Does News America have established writing standards?

P.C.: No, we don't have published writing standards. But our review process and other internal writing assignments, from memos to reports, do a good job establishing a norm of good writing. As people move up in the company, they do more writing, and if they have a writing weakness, that gets exposed pretty fast. However, I see a tremendous amount of writing from all levels within the corporation and it's quite good, above the norm.

Q: How do you define good writing?

P.C.: It's informative, simple, gets to the point, and the ideas are presented in an orderly fashion. I follow a simple rule: Don't make your writing complex. When we hire people and evaluate their communications skills, we ask, "Could she or he hold my interest and tell me something informative on an entry-level topic? Am I intrigued by the way people present themselves?" Part of our annual appraisal process includes being reviewed by other executives so we get a good consensus regarding how each executive is progressing. Writing skills are certainly a part of that review process, along with the executive's presentation and evaluation skills.

Q: What value does News America place on good writing?

P.C.: We place a high value on good writing because it's key to presenting our company in a proper, sophisticated fashion to our clients. Good writing correlates directly to financial reward for our company. It leads to career growth and financial reward for our employees, and so we clearly think it's important.

Q: Does News America run on writing?

P.C.: That's a tough question. Our success is based on many different factors, so I can't say we run solely on writing. However, having said that, e-mails are a much-used form of communication that everyone relies on, on a daily basis.

Q: I've heard different opinions. Do you think e-mails are an effective form of business correspondence?

P.C.: From a personal point of view, I think e-mail is incredibly overused. A good corporate culture is personal and friendly. But too much e-mail is very impersonal. Because it's a fast form of communication, people don't spend the time they should to work out their thoughts and ideas in their e-mails. Now, we do urge employees to use e-mail as an additional tool, but the downside is that they lose the face-to-face, personal contact with the person they're writing to. I also find that people are far more aggressive in e-mails than they are in conversation. Most people do not edit their e-mails, and you have to be an incredibly gifted writer to write e-mails, or anything for that matter, without editing. Also, some people are so flooded with e-mails that they don't have a chance to read them completely, so they act on them after only reading a few words or sentences. Finally, when you get into any type of legal action, the first thing they go after is e-mail. You have to be very careful about what you write to whom. So there are a lot of problems associated with the medium.

Q: Can poor writing cost your company time or money?

P.C.: Oh, sure. If you don't present your product or service just right and the competition does, then you just lost a sale. Poor writing and speaking skills can definitely cost a company money.

Q: What types of business correspondence do you write most often?

P.C.: First, I write as little as possible! My responsibilities are better served editing memos and reports. When I do write, I go back to the basic skills I learned in college. I write relatively quickly, reread it, and then send it out. As you gain experience in the business world, writing becomes easier and easier simply from writing the same type of format over and over.

Q: What are some of those college skills you recall?

P.C.: Just the basic composition skills: clearly saying what you have to say and making two or three different points. Make it as concise as possible and try to conclude by summarizing your main point. But rules aside, the main goal of all business writing is to clearly state your purpose, your main idea.

Q: Did good writing skills get you where you are today?

P.C.: Certainly. They played a definite role. And writing skills helped improve my presentation and verbal skills, too.

Q: In your opinion, what overall shape is business writing in today?

P.C.: Based on what I see in our company, I think it's in relatively very good shape.

Q: Do communication and leadership skills go hand in hand?

P.C.: Yes. High-level corporate executives are usually very articulate. They give good speeches and write well. Good communication skills are part of the overall executive package. Executives who excel at writing and speaking excel at logical thinking, which is part of the leadership package.

Q: Does News America use format templates for most of its writing projects?

P.C.: For some, but not all. A lot of our financial reports and sales proposals are very formatted. For example, there's a subhead for each week's sales and so forth. But letters do not have a strict format to follow. Typically, documents that are required to be written on a regular basis have templates.

Q: Do templates help speed the writing process?

P.C.: Without a doubt. Some writing projects that don't use templates not only take longer, but they may not be as accurate or consistent. Some information may be left out. Once we write, let's say, a certain type of proposal over and over and get a good feel for the type of information we want each one to have, we create a custom format or template for it.

Q: You said earlier that the writing you see at News America is very good overall. Is that true in all areas of the company?

P.C.: Let me have Ian Moore answer that question. He just walked into my office. Ian is executive vice president for News America Corporation and has a more global view of the situation.

Ian Moore: Because of the culture and the nature of our organization, face-to-face communication is extremely important, but our written skills are certainly just as important, particularly in terms of the increased use and misuse of e-mails nowadays. You'll find a lot of people with great verbal skills that may have difficulty putting together persuasive letters. They tend to just state facts, and it comes over very cold.

Q: Paul and I talked earlier about using templates to assist business writers and speed their writing. Is that one possible solution to the poor letter writing you see?

I.M.: Templates can be misused. Certain types of writing assignments can benefit from templates and others can't. For example, I see lots of resumes from people applying for jobs here. The people who use the resume and cover letter templates that come with their word processing software produce the worst documents in the world. Unfortunately, many outplacement people do not teach their clients how to individualize their resumes. It really is a big turnoff. I don't bother reading them. I get about twenty resumes a day and each one is worse than the last.

P.C.: It's a bad first impression. If you can't write a simple resume, how will you write on the job? We can't risk it.

Q: How much weight does your business give to good business-writing skills when it comes to annual reviews and pay raises?

P.C.: We have a very sophisticated annual review process that, in effect, evaluates the writing of the reviewer and the employee at the same time, because the person doing the review writes it out in prose. The reviews are more thorough and sophisticated if they're written instead of just bullet points or check boxes, although we have those in other parts of the process. Reviewers have to really think about the employee and what progress he or she has made. They start by writing a general overview or profile of the employee and then go into their accomplishments. Managers conclude with a summary that gives the employee some direction on where they need to improve. We actually teach review writing. It's an important part of our management process. As far as promotions and pay raises, the people being reviewed are judged in part on their writing and speaking skills, but it's not a major part unless they're hired as writers. Also, if the manager writing the review has good writing skills, that shows, and you can't help but consider that trait when it's time for the manager's review.

Q: What does News America do to evaluate and improve the communications skills of its employees?

P.C.: We recruit from colleges and only take graduates with 3.0 GPAs or higher, so that in a way guarantees we get people with good communications skills to begin with. During their first eighteen to thirty-six months on the job, we train them and develop their presentation skills, which are obviously very reliant on sound writing principles. You write a presentation before you give it. Good presentations require clear, logical thinking. How do you ask for an order? How do you present your case to a potential client? What are the needs of your audience and how do you touch on those in the presentation? All that has to be developed.

Q: Do you have a corporate university?

P.C.: We have an extensive training program, but we don't have a corporate university. The training includes writing. However, we find that most of the people coming out of school are relatively good writers. In fact, we're impressed and amazed sometimes at how well they come out of school now. Hiring employees who write well gives us a tremendous business advantage. Their presentations are more sophisticated, and successful presentations mean more business for the company. Also, good writing promotes personal growth, so we both win: The company benefits from employees with excellent writing skills, and certainly the individuals benefit, personally and financially.

PROCTER & GAMBLE
ED BURGHARD, MARKETING DIRECTOR, U.S. ACTONEL

Ed Burghard is one of three Harley Procter Marketers, a lifetime appointment based on exceptional business results achieved through marketing. The award is named after the son of William Procter, one of Procter & Gamble's founders, who first started national advertising at P&G in 1882. P&G is a recognized leader in the development, distribution, and marketing of superior fabric and home care, baby care, feminine care, family care, beauty care, health care, and food and beverage products. P&G markets over 250 brands to nearly five billion consumers in over 140 countries. Burghard oversees P&G's marketing of the Actonel brand, sold as medication for osteoporosis. Other P&G brands include Ivory, Tide, Crest, Pantene, Always, Pringles, Pampers, Olay, Folgers, Cover Girl, Downy, Dawn, Bounty, Charmin, Clairol Nice 'n Easy, and Herbal Essences. P&G employs nearly 106,000 people in more than eighty countries worldwide.

Q: How much weight does Procter & Gamble place on good writing skills when it comes to annual reviews and promotions?

E.B.: Ed Artzt, the CEO of Procter & Gamble from 1990–1995, talked about this subject to the Wharton Graduate Business School. He said, "Communication is a skill that quickly separates the winners from losers on most management ladders. At P&G we write to clarify thinking and to lead the organization." That clearly and emphatically defines the role writing plays within P&G. Our primary piece of correspondence is the memo. There are five key ways we use memos: 1) to initiate action, 2) confirm agreements, 3) inform, 4) summarize learning, and 5) reply to management questions.

Q: Is the memo sent electronically as an e-mail attachment?

E.B.: Not typically, because the use of attachments, which are often data intensive, would require electronic transmission of large files. We focus hard on developing the skill to author a traditional paper document. The preferred length of the memo is one page, but it can be longer and often includes attachments when required for effective communication. The concept behind the memo is more important than its length. The memo is really a tool to discipline our communication process. We always want the most important points communicated succinctly and quickly. To facilitate this, P&G memos have an established format based on a communication objective—for example, recommendation, learning summary, etc. Each format begins with what we call a strategy paragraph or executive summary. The idea is that a busy manager should only have to read the executive summary to understand the key points being communicated. The balance of the document should reinforce this opening paragraph. When I receive a memo, I should be able to quickly read the first paragraph and determine if I agree or disagree with the basic premise. If I have questions, then I read more of the memo, which should in turn answer them.

Q: Do you teach that format at Procter & Gamble?

E.B.: Yes, we have what I call a virtual university where standard courses are taught by internal company experts. A memo-writing course is part of the basic curriculum. We send new hires through the class to break the academic writing habits they may have and instill good business-writing habits. It is also important to note good writing skills are taught on the job by a person's management line.

Q: Does every new employee take the course?

E.B.: We allow individuals to choose which courses they want to take. Training course selection is tailored to the individual's skill development need. You can't point to any two P&G people and see the exact course selection. It's not like two math majors taking the same set of courses to obtain a degree.

Q: Do you teach more than one writing course?

E.B.: Yes, we offer both a Basic Writing Skills course and a more advanced Leading Management Thinking Through Writing class. The first course teaches the P&G process of writing and explains why the process makes sense. When people come out of the first course, you see a lot of standard formatted memos. That's good because it means they're practicing what they learned. The advanced course takes their skill to the next level. Once they understand the basics, we teach people how to tailor what they write to even more effectively deliver against their communication objective and target audience's specific needs. We teach the rules and then we teach people how to break the rules to optimize communication. That's how the basic and advanced courses fit together.

Q: Are the courses open to everyone in the organization?

E.B.: They are, but different groups within P&G have different writing needs. For example, we spend more time teaching writing to our marketing people because they write the bulk of the business recommendations, market research summaries, and so forth. They simply write more than, say, our field sales organization. Salespeople do more face-to-face verbal communication with customers than formal writing. They also use electronic tools to record brief, specific, sales-related information. Writing that information in a memo form doesn't make practical sense.

Q: What does Procter & Gamble do to evaluate employee writing skills?

E.B.: I'll use myself as a typical example. When I get a written document from one of the managers who report to me, besides evaluating the thinking reflected in the document—that is, whether the fundamental business proposition makes sense—I also review every document from a format and writing skills point of view. In the side margin of a memo I might jot a note that says, "At this point the reader would also be interested in knowing x, y, z," or "You should consider sharing supporting data here." That type of feedback helps make managers better writers; but it is a long-term, iterative process. Good writing simply doesn't happen overnight. The more experience you have writing memos, and the more detailed feedback you get on their content/format, the better writer you become.

Q: Does every document have to be perfect?

E.B.: No, that's counterproductive. I do not hold back a memo simply because it isn't perfect. Even if I provide format comments, I may still forward the document if the proposition is fundamentally strong and I believe the reader will both understand and be convinced by the rationale. However, the next time a similar document crosses my desk, I will expect my format feedback to be incorporated in it. But a few format problems will not stop a great idea from moving forward.

Q: What business advantage does an employee who writes well give your company?

E.B.: A big advantage. However, let me talk a bit about P&G's philosophy on writing. We don't view writing as the end goal; we view it as a means to an end. At P&G, effective memo writing reflects effective thinking and ideas, so the clearer an employee's thinking, the more successful P&G is going to be. When someone writes an idea on paper, flaws in the logic are easier to identify. Logic errors are harder to identify when an idea is presented verbally because so much is implicit in conversations. Writing is a more cost-effective medium because it allows identification and correction of problems before we spend money to implement an idea in the form of a P&G product or service. In that context, good, clear writing saves P&G untold amounts of money. It is good for the bottom line.

Q: What value does Procter & Gamble place on good writing?

E.B.: A very high value. For example, I tell my marketers they are paid for brilliant, business-building ideas, and brilliant ideas deserve outstanding packaging. The packaging for their ideas, in many cases, is a written document. The more succinct the document, the easier it is to read and understand, the easier it is to get through the management approval process. A lot of people in management have to read a document and reach alignment on an idea. The faster that happens the faster we can execute a brilliant, business-building idea in the marketplace. Time is money. Excellent communication—writing that is brief and not confusing in any way—means an idea has a much better chance of being implemented quickly. Simple, clear writing sharpens the underlying thinking behind ideas, improving the odds of success.

Q: Will you describe your writing process?

E.B.: First, I don't sit down to write unless I have a goal in mind. That sounds obvious, but I'm amazed at how many folks don't bother to take that step. A document can do a number of things—ask for approval, make a request, seek a recommendation, etc.—so I need to have my goal clear before I start. I begin by asking, "When the recipients finish reading my document, what do I want them to do? What action do I want them to take?" I have to think of the reader too, so I ask myself, "Is it reasonable to ask my reader to take that action? Are there other people I should get aligned to my document before I ask my reader to commit?" I can honestly say that when I'm done writing a memo, I know exactly what I want both my document and my reader to do.

The next step in my process, and I usually just scribble these thoughts out on a piece of paper, is to ask myself, "What information does the reader need to know to understand what I'm trying to communicate?" It's a very subtle but different question, mentally, than "What do I want to tell the reader?" I find that some businesspeople have a lot they want to say, but not all of it is worth reading, and I don't want to be one of those types of writers.

Q: What role do grammar, spelling, and punctuation play in your writing process?

E.B.: I've written long enough that I'm at a stage where I do a lot of editing in my head. I do, however, typically write an outline and approach each document as I would an advertisement. This technique is called storyboarding. I'm always thinking, "What's the headline, the key communication point that I want to get across? What are my subheads, the main supporting points?" And I make the answers to those questions the backbone of my outline. Then I write down two or three facts per subhead that will make my subheads convincing to my reader. I don't spend hours on this. I just scribble these points down, reread them, and ask myself, "What other data is required?" For instance, if I'm asking my reader for a decision, or an agreement on my recommendation, I'll make sure that I include the fundamental business data—financial data, perhaps, or background information—that the reader will need to make a yes or no decision. Finally, I just start writing. I always find once I've got an outline in front of me and I've identified the key data necessary, I'm in a better position to begin. I know where I'm going, what my key points are, and I telegraph those in the opening paragraph. For perspective, I don't wait until I have gathered every piece of supporting data before I start writing. I've found if you wait, you generally put yourself in a time bind and end up with a weak document because of a deadline. I jump in, and when I come to a point where I need more information, I'll put in a few X's and go back and fill in the blanks with the information after I have a complete rough draft.

Q: Successful people have two traits in common: They write well and speak well. Does this saying hold true at P&G?

E.B.: It certainly does. However, that's simply human dynamics. Business is an activity conducted by people. If you can't communicate with people, you can't accomplish great things.

Q: Does P&G recognize and reward good writing skills?

E.B.: We reward people for their results. To say good writing led to positive results, then yes, the person is ultimately getting rewarded for exhibiting that skill. On the reverse side, poor writing definitely gets noticed, too. Like sand in an engine, it slows everything down. A poor writer and a poor oral communicator could not be successful at Procter & Gamble. That's not to say that a few poorly written memos or weak presentations will land someone in the doghouse. We provide ongoing training to help them become better writers and presenters.

Q: Looking outside of P&G, what shape is business writing in today?

E.B.: I would say at best, it's fair. There are two key reasons why. First, I'd argue academia doesn't put the same emphasis on business writing as we do. In fact, it could be argued academic writing and business writing have two distinct purposes with very different goals. Professors want to see the student's thought process come through in the writing. Professors want proof their students have really internalized the subject matter and want to read how a student got from point A to point B. With business writing, there's an underlying assumption that the thought process is relatively robust. The purpose of business writing is not to double-check the writer's thought process. You don't care about every path a manager took to reach a conclusion. What you care about is the correctness of the final conclusion or idea. You do not get partial credit in the business world because your process was sound if your conclusion led to a market failure. To be sure, you want to read the reasons behind why the idea is a good one and what the business implications are in terms of resources and requirements; but compared to academic writing, business writing isn't as concerned about exposing the entire thought process.

My second reason for saying the shape of business writing is only fair is that all companies do not uniformly value written communication. You and I are talking about the topic as though businesspeople in all companies have to be very proficient writers in order to succeed. That's not the case. It varies depending on the company and the culture. Many organizations are a lot more comfortable with oral communication, and they don't use writing like we do at P&G. They may use writing to confirm meetings, summarize notes, and things like that, so the level of writing skills you need to be successful varies from company to company. I also think it's fair to say the larger the organization, the less face-to-face exposure you get with senior management and the more important writing becomes because it is your ambassador into those offices.

Q: Can poor writing cost your company time and money?

E.B.: From the standpoint that poor writing equals poor thinking, absolutely. If an idea is half-baked, the document doesn't get the level of scrutiny that it should, and we go to market and experience a failure, then you could strongly argue poor writing negatively affected the company bottom line.

UNITED PARCEL SERVICE, INC.
KEN STERNAD, VICE PRESIDENT OF PUBLIC AFFAIRS

United Parcel Service (UPS) is the world's largest express carrier and package-delivery company, serving more than 200 countries and territories around the world. Headquartered in Atlanta, Georgia, the company handles more than 3 billion packages every year and employs more than 370,000 people worldwide. A *Fortune* magazine survey named UPS the "World's Most Admired" mail and package-delivery company for the fourth consecutive year. UPS is located on the Web at www.ups.com.

Q: What role does writing play throughout UPS?

K.S.: In one sense, a big role. Our 80,000 drivers are our face to the public. They arrive in the morning and spend about fifteen minutes in the building and then they're out all day. They come back at night, spend another fifteen minutes and then they're gone. These people are not in a location where we can communicate with them throughout the course of the day. So every morning at every work location at UPS we hold what's called a prework communications meeting. It's three minutes of very valuable time. Because it's so short, internal communications sends out specific written messages with topics, outlines, and suggestions for how to spend that three minutes. Topics range from information about new services we're implementing to uniform requirements. That moment is so valuable, we make sure our internal communications people clearly write exactly what needs to be said. A little mistake in that memo and we could waste the time of 80,000+ people. We also use newsletters and the employee Web site to communicate, but that three minutes each day is key to getting out the latest information we want them to know. I fact, we estimate that little window of time costs UPS several million dollars in salaries and downtime alone. That's why writing is so very important to us compared to, I think, a lot of companies where your workers are present in the office all day.

Q: What is the connection between good writing skills and the image of your company?

K.S.: There's a direct connection in that we have a list of key messages that tell the world who we are, and if they are not clear, then obviously that affects our image. We spend a lot of time and effort making sure the messages are communicated correctly. That responsibility falls on a very small group of people in UPS, the internal and external communications folks who handle all of the public speaking, press releases, advertising, proposals, etc.

Q: What does your company do to evaluate and improve the writing skills of people who need help?

K.S.: Training is a very decentralized function at UPS. Throughout the company we run our regions and districts quite autonomously. Writing is not a major issue across the company, but in certain sectors that interface with the public, government officials, and potential clients, writing skills are evaluated and looked at carefully. When it comes to writing training, that's decided on a case-by-case basis.

Q: Do you have a corporate university?

K.S.: No. We spend in excess of $300 million a year on training, everything from leadership to safety, and we do it through a training program that includes online and in-person courses.

Q: How much weight does UPS give to good business-writing skills when it comes to promotions?

K.S.: In certain operations of the company, like internal communications, writing plays a significant role in annual reviews, but it's not something that is routinely a part of our company's review procedures for all employees. We're an operating company. We have a lot of front-line people. Writing is something that many people in management receive some training in—for example, in new supervisor orientations and management leadership schools—but for, let's say, our 80,000 drivers, it's not as important.

Q: What are some of the responsibilities of your communications department?

K.S.: We manage the correspondence and communications for our senior management team, the fifteen people who run UPS. We have an extensive public speaking program. Our senior executives do about 140 to 150 speeches a year, telling the UPS story. So we do a lot of speech writing. We also manage a large portion of our Web site, including a pressroom that has online press releases, press kits, and background information on the company. And of course there are the press releases themselves. We're a very diversified company with several business units. We're involved in finance and information services, so there's a lot of press activity. Finally, there's e-mail. The twenty-four professional communications people in my department alone receive close to 10,000 e-mails a week. That's a very potent and important way of communicating. With all the writing we do, I expect my team to receive ongoing training by attending writing workshops, executive communication workshops, speechwriting seminars, etc. They're required to do that during the course of the year.

Q: How do you hire your public relations people? Do you ask them to take a writing test?

K.S.: Some public relations departments include event managers and other nonwriting positions, but we expect every single one of the professionals on our team to be writers. They were either English or journalism majors in college, or have been professional writers for a long time. Many have significant journalism experience or have worked extensively in marketing and communications. So writing is mandatory for UPS public relations; it is our number-one skills requirement.

Q: What do you look for when you hire new people?

K.S.: We have a writing test, but put more weight on their experience and the writing they actually do for us. We spend a great deal of effort analyzing their press releases, speeches, and such. We really dig into them because you could come to an interview with a nice portfolio of articles and press releases that have been printed in newspapers, but chances are they've been edited by somebody else.

Q: What types of business writing do you do?

K.S.: I've been at UPS for twenty-five years. I started as a press release writer then moved up to primary speechwriter, but as head of public relations I play more of an editorial role. Nothing goes to our chairman or our senior management team that I haven't seen. I still write speeches for our chairman, handle some correspondence for the management team, and write internal proposals as well as my own e-mails, of course.

Q: As people move up in UPS, do they do more or less writing?

K.S.: Less. You move into more of a strategy, editorial, mentoring, and leadership role. You do less writing yourself, but the writing that you do is much more important. So while you actually do less writing, you still must have very good writing skills. You can't edit someone else's work if you don't know what you're doing.

Q: What advantage does an employee who writes well give your company?

K.S.: A tremendous advantage. I go back to the example of our 80,000 drivers. We have very little face time with those people. The communication we do have with them is written, so that has to be absolutely perfect. Our drivers represent UPS, and they have to be on message with the rest of the company. They need to know the direction we're going, the services we offer, our mission.

Q: How tough is it to get a company's message out to the public today?

K.S.: It's difficult and becoming more so because there is so much competition right now for the written word. Your target audience—share owners, customers, regulators, and other thought leaders and influencers—are bombarded with direct mail, e-mail, television, newspaper, and online ads. It's endless. There's such tremendous competition for their attention, and you're only going get so much of it, a small window. So you have to make the most of that time by making sure your message is not only right the first time, but interesting, appealing, and concise. That's a tall order. We emphasize the need for effective communication all the time. If you get four paragraphs or four minutes of speech time with a decision maker or potential client, the value of the written word at that moment is immeasurable. That's why we look at every word in a press release. Some companies throw platitudes in their releases, common, everyday statements about business that people don't pay much attention to. That's an incredibly wasted moment. We feel we don't have that luxury. Every word must count.

Q: Is it fair to say that UPS runs on writing?

K.S.: I think our company runs on personal communication, which includes writing and speaking. Spoken communication is enhanced and driven by writing, but interpersonal skills are the ones most used by employees on a day-to-day basis—whether it's a day-one employee sorting packages for us in Baltimore, or the drivers we see a few minutes every day, or the people answering the half a million calls that we get at our telephone centers each day. But again, the spoken word is influenced and enhanced by the written word, so it's a combination.

Q: Can poor writing cost your company time and or money?

K.S.: Absolutely. We compete against some highly professional companies, so our sales staff has to write excellent presentations tailored to specific, local audiences. Also, because we're in a regulated industry, there's a great risk and cost associated with presenting our image to the public. In addition, writing has a specific cost efficiency involved with it. Again, going back to that three minutes we have with our package sorters, drivers, and pilots each morning, if we can't communicate our latest initiatives, advice on safety, or information on how they need to do their job, that could potentially result in the loss of time or money. So, yes, I can think of many examples where a significant cost is associated with the written word.

Q: What's your personal writing process, for example, when you write a speech?

K.S.: First, I decide what we want to say about the company. I say "we" because I'm writing this, of course, for a senior executive. The first step is to be in control of the message. It's like Henry Kissinger's famous opening to many of his press conferences: "What questions do you have for my answers today?" The next step is to meet with the person who is giving the speech. I get as much personal input as I can, then go back and digest it. But the most critical aspect is the next one, which is choosing the key messages to put in the speech. As a company, we spend an inordinate amount of time determining and writing out the key messages for our organization. What is our core set of eight or ten messages that explain to people what we do? We're financially sound, a technological leader, an employer of choice, open to diversity, etc. So before we start, we outline the speech and match it to our core messages. We don't accept an opportunity to communicate or start the process of putting together that piece of communication without linking it to our core values or messages. After that, it's a matter of writing the speech, which is the process of fine-tuning and lots of rewriting.

Q: Would you say that good writing skills helped you get where you are today?

K.S.: Without question. From very early on in my career, everything I did was all about writing.

Q: Do communication and leadership skills go hand in hand?

K.S.: They are absolutely linked. Speaking, writing, and leadership are inseparable. Leaders have more opportunities to present ideas and proposals to other decision makers, so they must be good at writing and speaking on the fly. But even for them, time is at a premium, so they can't waste it with vague speeches or letters. You have to get right to the point. I can't put enough value on that. I see that every day.

Q: What in your opinion is the overall shape of business writing today?

K.S.: I think it's fair. I think it's a lot less well done than it was ten or certainly twenty years ago. There's not as much discipline, and there are a lot of people in communications who aren't communicators. They're creative, they're good at running programs, they're good at manning an event, but they're not writers or speakers. That's why we demand that the number-one skill you have when you work for us is writing, and specifically journalistic writing, because it's so important. So I would say business writing today is fair, but not getting better.

Q: What's your advice to beginning business writers?

K.S.: My primary advice would be to make sure that your writing is being seen or screened by somebody whose skills you respect. But backing up, the first thing you need is training and to take writing seriously. If you don't understand the value of good writing, your writing will suffer. It's that simple. You need to take the time to train yourself or be trained so you can do it well. For example, I'm surprised at the things that get through to me or the chairman. People with a proposal or who are trying to make an impression of some kind have blown it with the very first piece of correspondence they send. Terrible writing forms an immediate and indelible bad impression. People think their idea is all that counts, not how they present it. They couldn't be more wrong. When you're competing for a few moments of the chairman's time, a very small and valuable window of opportunity, a rambling four-page proposal that could easily have been written in one page if the person simply took the time, will end your chances in a heartbeat. Poor writing says a lot about you, and certainly enough to sink a proposal on first impressions alone.

APPENDIX A:
ONLINE WRITING RESOURCES GUIDE

The following list of Web sites will put a wealth of writing information at your fingertips. At the time of publication, each site was up and running; however, as you know, things change fast on the Internet. If any of these sites are down, please search www.google.com to find the new address for the site or a related one.

Tip: If you have trouble getting on to a Web site that has a long address, try logging in to just the domain portion of the address and then navigating around the home page looking for the specific page you need. For example: If you have trouble visiting www.eeicom.com/eye/eyeindex.html, just log in to the home page www.eeicom.com. It should have a table of contents with click-on icons that will get you to the eyeindex.

1. http://www.bartleby.com/

Click on this site's Reference menu and you'll find hot links to *The Elements of Style*, online dictionaries, encyclopedias, grammar guides, Bartlett's Familiar Quotations, and much more.

2. http://www.computeruser.com/resources/dictionary/dictionary.html?

High-tech online dictionary from *Computer User* magazine.

3. http://andromeda.rutgers.edu/~jlynch/Writing//links.html

Rutgers-Newark State University of New Jersey's resource center for writers. One of the most comprehensive writing resource sites on the Web.

4. http://dictionary.reference.com/others/

A range of references from foreign language, rhyming, and pronouncing dictionaries to acronym, legal, and slang dictionaries.

5. http://www.m-w.com/

Merriam-Webster's Web site includes links to its dictionary, Word of the Day, Word Games, and other helpful features. You can also download a free toolbar that attaches to your Internet Explorer browser toolbar, so you can look up words in the Merriam-Webster dictionary or thesaurus no matter where you are on the Web.

6. http://www.uottawa.ca/academic/arts/writcent/
hypergrammar/punct.html

Everything you want to know about punctuation, produced by the Writing Center at the University of Ottawa.

7. http://www.uottawa.ca/academic/arts/writcent/
hypergrammar/

Everything you want to know about grammar, produced by the Writing Center at the University of Ottawa.

8. http://www.britannica.com/

Encyclopedia Britannica search engine.

9. http://lcweb.loc.gov/homepage/lchp.html

The Library of Congress Web site is a good place to start any personal, work-related, or academic research project. Includes hot links to many other helpful sites.

10. http://www.mhra.org.uk/

Modern Humanities Research Association (MHRA) is another good research site with connections to Cambridge University.

11. http://lcweb.loc.gov/copyright/

U.S. Copyright Office. Comprehensive information on copyright issues, right from the horse's mouth.

12. http://www.eeicommunications.com/eye/eyeindex.html

The Editorial Eye. A potpourri of reference Web sites, all with hot links. A bonanza for anyone in communications.

13. http://www.yourdictionary.com/

More than 280 online foreign language dictionaries from French and German to Frisian and Gaelic.

14. http://www.wfi.fr/volterre/dictionnaires.html

An eclectic mix of online dictionaries, from translation and medical dictionaries to science and technology.

15. http://www.ualr.edu/~cmbarger/resources.htm

Complete list of resources for legal writers.

NOTES

Chapter 1

1. Anthony Burgess, *Shakespeare* (Chicago: Elephant Paperbacks, 1994), pp. 14–15.
2. Elizabeth Longford, *Wellington: The Years of the Sword* (New York: Konecky & Konecky, 1969), p. 454.

Chapter 2

1. Stephen Krashen, *Writing—Research, Theory, and Applications* (Torrance, Calif.: Laredo Publishing, 1984), p. 12.
2. Krashen, p. 12.
3. Krashen, p. 15.
4. Linda Flower, "Revising Writer-Based Prose," *Journal of Basic Writing* Vol. 3 (1981), p. 62.
5. Karen Gocsik, "Process Pedagogy: A Brief Explanation," Dartmouth College Web site (available at: http://www.dartmouth.edu/~compose/faculty/pedagogies/process.html), 1997.
6. Flower, p. 67.
7. Michael Rose, "Rigid Rules, Inflexible Plans, and the Stifling of Language: A Cognitivist Analysis of Writer's Block," *College Composition and Communication* Vol. 31, 4 (1980), pp. 394–395.
8. Rose, pp. 391, 397, 398.
9. Rose, p. 389.
10. Ibid.

11. Rose, p. 393.
12. Rose, p. 392.

Chapter 4

1. Stephen Krashen, *Writing—Research, Theory, and Applications* (Torrance, Calif.: Laredo Publishing, 1984), p. 14.
2. Linda Flower, "Revising Writer-Based Prose," *Journal of Basic Writing* Vol. 3 (1981), pp. 63–64.

Chapter 5

1. William F. Irmscher, *The Holt Guide to English,* Second Edition (New York: Holt, Reinhart, and Winston, 1972), p. 224.
2. Michael Rose, "Rigid Rules, Inflexible Plans, and the Stifling of Language: A Cognitivist Analysis of Writer's Block," *College Composition and Communication* Vol. 31, 4 (1980), pp. 398.
3. James Boswell, *The Life of Samuel Johnson* (New York: Everyman's Library, 1978), p. 5.
4. *The Chicago Manual of Style,* Fourteenth Edition (Chicago: The University of Chicago Press, 1993), p. 165.
5. Pogo Earth Day 1971 cartoon, Walt Kelly (available at http://www.nauticom.net/www/chuckm/whmte.htm).
6. Professor Gio Valiante, "Can Professors Influence the Writing Confidence of College Students? The Power of Feedback on the Writing Self-Efficacy Beliefs of College Students," p. 1 (available at http://www.rollins.edu/effectiveteaching/scholarteachlinks_examples_valiante.doc).
7. Valiante, p. 2.
8. William Strunk, Jr. and E. B. White, *The Elements of Style,* Third Edition (Boston: Allyn & Bacon, 1979), p. xii.
9. Strunk and White, p. xv.

Chapter 6

1. *The Rhetoric and the Poetics of Aristotle,* introduction by Edward P. J. Corbett, *Rhetoric* translated by W. Rhys Roberts, *Poetics* translated by Ingram Bywater (New York: The Modern Library, 1984), p. vii.

Chapter 7

1. The information on Lincoln and the "Gettysburg Address" is available at http://www.loc.gov/exhibits/gadd/gainvi.html.
2. "Business Briefs," *Salt Lake Tribune* (May 27, 2002). Reprinted from *The Record* (Bergen County, New Jersey).

3. Floyd Norris, "Erroneous Order for Big Sales Briefly Stirs Up the Big Board," *The New York Times* (October 3, 2002).

Chapter 8

1. Stephen Krashen, *Writing—Research, Theory, and Applications* (Torrance, Calif.: Laredo Publishing, 1984), p. 9.

BIBLIOGRAPHY

Burgess, Anthony. *Shakespeare*. Chicago: Elephant Paperbacks, 1994.

Flower, Linda. "Revising Writer-Based Prose." *Journal of Basic Writing* Vol. 3 (1981), pp. 62–74.

Irmscher, William F. *The Holt Guide to English*, Second Edition. New York: Holt, Reinhart, and Winston, 1972.

Krashen, Stephen. *Writing—Research, Theory, and Applications*. Torrance, CA: Laredo Publishing, 1984.

Longford, Elizabeth. *Wellington: The Years of the Sword*. New York: Konecky & Konecky, 1969.

Rose, Michael. "Rigid Rules, Inflexible Plans, and the Stifling of Language: A Cognitivist Analysis of Writer's Block." *College Composition and Communication* Vol. 31, 4 (1980), pp. 389–400. Copyright 2002 by the National Council of the Teachers of English.

Strunk, Jr., William, and E. B. White. *The Elements of Style*, Third Edition. Boston: Allyn & Bacon, 1979.

INDEX

ABOUT THE AUTHOR

Kevin Ryan is president of The Executive Writer, a writing, training, and consulting company that provides one-on-one and group tutorials and seminars. Clients include Lucent Technologies, Procter & Gamble, and Novell. Kevin's freelance work has appeared in the *Los Angeles Times*, *Chicago Tribune*, *PC Magazine*, *Business Communication Quarterly*, the *Iowa Review*, and other national publications. Kevin holds a Ph.D. in creative writing and literature from the University of Utah and an M.A. and B.A. in English from U.C.L.A. In addition, he has taught writing on the college level for more than eight years. Kevin's business background and academic experience make The Executive Writer program one of the most effective in the business-writing field.

You can learn more about Kevin by visiting his Web site at http://www.executivewriter.com. He can be contacted at 801-553-0906 or kevin@executivewriter.com.